Canoe Country Wilderness

Canoe Country Wilderness

A GUIDE'S CANOE TRAILS THROUGH THE BWCA AND QUETICO

William N. Rom, M.D.

VOYAGEUR PRESS

Printed in the United States of America
95   96   97   98   99   6   5   4   3   2

Library of Congress Cataloging-in-Publication data available upon request.

ISBN 0-89658-065-2

Published by Voyageur Press, Inc.
123 North Second Street, P.O. Box 338, Stillwater, MN 55082 U.S.A.
612-430-2210, fax 612-430-2211

To my parents,
who introduced me to the canoe country
where I learned
the permanent and intrinsic values of wilderness

Contents

Foreword

MY TIES TO the Rom family go back more than a quarter century to the early 1960s, when I lived in Grand Rapids, Minnesota, and Bill Rom, Sr., and I were working in the Izaak Walton League to secure better protection for the canoe country wilderness. Bill and Barb Rom then ran Canoe Country Outfitters in Ely. Bill Jr., the author of this book (whom everyone called "Rommie"), and his brothers and sisters worked summers as guides for the family business.

The Roms introduced countless thousands of canoeists to the glories of the Quetico-Superior wilderness. It was a task for which Bill Sr. and his young family were uniquely fitted. Bill Sr. was born and raised in Ely, studied at the Ely Junior College under famed author, teacher, and naturalist Sigurd Olson, and obtained a degree in wildlife from the University of Minnesota. Bill, Barb, and their children roamed the lakes, rivers, and portages of the canoe country from their earliest days together. Bill Sr. is also a bush pilot who has canoed and fished in the Far North for decades. This, then, is the family background from which Bill Jr. came.

Over the years my wife, Fran, and I had come to know the Rom family quite well, but our first opportunity to really know Bill Jr. came on a short fall canoe trip in the late sixties. Bill Jr. guided Clayton and Grace Rudd, of the Minnesota Natural History Society, on a trip north from the Echo Trail down the Little Indian Sioux River. Fran and I came along as friends of both the Rudds and the Roms. This was in the years when I was working on the fire history of the virgin forests of the BWCAW, and we had an endless supply of natural history topics to discuss around our campfire on Little Loon Lake. It was there that we also discovered Rommie's talents as a wilderness cook.

I next met Bill Jr. in his natural setting one winter day on Lake of the Clouds, east of Knife Lake. I was helping Dr. Herbert Wright, of the University of Minnesota's Limnological Research Center, and Albert Swain, then a doctoral student in ecology, to obtain cores from the bottom muds of the lake for charcoal and pollen studies (which became the subject of Al Swain's dissertation). While we were working on the cores, a lone showshoer approached from the North. It was Rommie, who had come in to try his luck for trout and to see what we were up to.

Our paths crossed again in 1977 and 1978 when I was in Washington helping the Friends of the Boundary Waters Wilderness and several national environmental organizations work toward passage of the Boundary Waters Wilderness Act by the U.S. Congress. Bill Jr., who was then in medical research in New York, came down to Washington to help us lobby key members of Congress. We were far from the wilderness we loved, but it was memories of those bracing days on the Little Indian Sioux, and of the starlit winter nights in the Knife Lake–Saganaga country, that helped us persevere until Public Law 95-495 became reality.

In the pages ahead, Bill Jr. will be your guide through the canoe trails of the Boundary Waters, the Quetico, and the Far North. He knows the North both from the perspective of a native son and from that of the many urban voyageurs he has introduced to its charms. Enjoy the journey!

M. L. (Bud) Heinselman
Founder, Friends of the Boundary Waters Canoe Area Wilderness

Canoe Country Wilderness

CHAPTER ONE
The Canoeing Wilderness

AT THE END of the road to the North in Minnesota, near the edge of the great Laurentian Shield country of wild lakes, rivers, pine forests, and high rock cliffs, lies a small community. Ely, Minnesota, is home to canoe guides and canoe outfitters. It's the jumping-off place for the famous Quetico-Superior canoeing wilderness.

In 1946, at the age of two, I had my first glimpse of the vast canoe country as I peered out of the ears of my Duluth packsack. (The ends to the top of a Duluth packsack are called ears.) My voyageurs were Jerry Patterson, Hollis Latourelle, and Gus Walske, three of Ely's foremost early guides and raconteurs. Those were the early days of Canoe Country Outfitters, which was begun by my father to bring the wilderness experience to everyone. Wilderness, he firmly believed, was the tonic that could set just about anything straight.

Bill Rom, Sr., opened Canoe Country Outfitters (CCO) in 1946, initially to guide young boys and girls on ten-day excursions into the canoe country wilderness. After two summers of guiding, babysitting, and suffering daily frustrations, he realized that the future of his canoeing business would be to offer his guiding knowledge in completely outfitting groups and families for the wilderness experience.

CCO, located on the main street of Ely, grew and profited during the 1950s; in Minneapolis and throughout the American Midwest, we attended sports shows and advertised the family vacation of canoeing. A GI loan of $2500 helped build the outfitting warehouse, and the first two years' savings were invested in the new aluminum canoe. Many seasoned guides, with their fealty to the weighty canvas-covered wooden canoe, frowned on the aluminum model. But it could withstand the scrapes and bumps on the rocks that neophyte canoeists often inflict. That durability, with the lighter weight and lower cost, led to my father's popularizing the aluminum canoe for an inexpensive family vacation.

Canoe, paddles, yoke, food (in cardboard boxes in Duluth packs), tent, sleeping bags, pots and utensils, matches, toilet paper, axe, ponchos, fire grate, and even a reflector oven were provided for $4.50 per person per day (pre-inflation!). The food was expertly packed by Bernie at phone number 40 and dropped off at the CCO warehouse each day. Matt supervised the packing of the camping gear and ran his domain with a stern fervor. Further up front in the warehouse were the routers and off-duty guides, who met each party, found out their interests, desires, strengths, available time, and experience, and planned a canoe route into the wilderness. An overall map was brought out, a canoe route chosen, and the route outlined, with fishing holes, portages, campsites, marauding bears, and special points of interest (such as Indian pictographs on shoreline cliffs) marked in grease pen on waterproof paper. The routers had to learn not only the canoe routes, but how to write upside down as they faced the customers over the map! The log-front store was a beehive of activity from early May to late September. The tourists arrived, left on their journeys, and often brought back a veritable ton of wet tents to be dried, sleeping bags to be washed, and black pots to be shined in the back of the warehouse by the low man on the outfitting totem pole — the so-called potlicker.

Above the store was the office and nerve center of CCO. My father diligently and swiftly responded to every inquiry about a canoe venture into the wilderness. Each letter received a personalized response. The large scout groups received special consideration and a reduced per-person fare. My mother assiduously typed all of the letters — typical of the American small family business. My father, who longed to be on the canoe trails rather than writing to customers about them, enjoyed his two- or three-day escapes with the family.

Canoe Country Outfitters grew to thirty seasonal employees, four hundred canoes, four hundred sleeping bags, three hundred tents, and a thousand Duluth packs. *Argosy* magazine featured an article on my father as the "Canoe King of Ely."

Engulfing Ely is the Superior National Forest, with three large roadless-area canoe sections within the forest. One million acres, or one-third of the entire Superior National Forest, is protected as the

Canoe Country Outfiitters, Ely, Minnesota.

A midday break on Brent Lake. Credit: Roger Rom

My father, Bill Rom, Sr., when he was owner-operator of Canoe Country Outfitters.

Boundary Waters Canoe Area Wilderness. However, three roads encroach on the wilderness: the Echo Trail, a road established in 1927 over the protests of the Izaak Walton League, divides the Little Indian Sioux area; the Fernberg Road, originally a logging trail, provides access to Moose Lake and Lake One; and the Gunflint Trail leads to Big Saganaga Lake.

The original three canoe country Roadless Areas were renamed the Boundary Waters Canoe Area in 1958 by the United States Forest Service, without wilderness classification. Logging roads at the southern fringe and along the Gunflint and Echo Trails began to make inroads on the area's remaining virgin timber and wilderness. The Forest Service managed the area for "multiple use," including wilderness canoeing and logging. The conflict between those two diametrically opposed uses would eventually be solved by full wilderness protection.

The Superior National Forest was established in 1909 as one of the final conservation achievements of President Theodore Roosevelt, forming the largest national forest in the country. A good deal of the boundary waters had been logged by the last of the timber barons. Large sawmills kept the village of Winton roaring. A railway went to Gun and Horse Lakes to bring back logs from the north; the Four-Mile portage provided access to Basswood Lake and its timber; sluiceways for moving logs extended up to Knife Lake so the lumberjacks could get as far as Kekekabic; logging relics extended into Ensign, Ima, and Fraser Lakes. A tripod system with telephone wires may still be found deep in the forest, paralleling the ridges south of Moose and Newfound Lakes toward Ensign and Prairie portage on the east end of Basswood Lake. Yet a good part of the interior remained untouched, fortunately, approximately a half million acres of virgin forest being spared the axe. Besides the interior of the canoe country, vast tracts of white and Norway pines south of Lac La Croix escaped logging. These still-virgin forests form the heart of the present-day canoe country.

Since the 1920s, the remaining beauty of this lake country has captured the imagination of a few dedicated wilderness zealots, who have fought off three major schemes that would have wrecked the canoe country wilderness. The first scheme, albeit well-meaning on the surface, was to build a series of dams on the border lakes to create huge reservoirs to feed projected hydroelectric power developments.

This grandiose plan by E. W. Backus faltered because of the far-sighted opposition of a few individuals such as Ernest Oberholtzer and Sig Olson, and because there was no real market for this power. A small storage dam on Gabbro Lake within the canoe country and a power plant on Garden Lake outside of the Boundary Waters Canoe Area were built by the Minnesota Power and Light Company, flooding the backwaters of Gabbro and Bald Eagle Lakes and providing an ominous reminder of what the precious border lakes chain could look like today.

Next came a commercial fervor to build roads. One, the Echo Trail, crossed several great rivers to the north, under the guise of being needed for fire protection. The Gunflint Trail to the east traversed deep into the wilderness to the shores of Big Saganaga Lake on the border. A logging road to Moose Lake and Lake One twenty miles east of Ely was upgraded and extended to Snowbank Lake. Fortunately, the plan to connect the Gunflint to the Fernberg, cutting the main body of the canoe country in two, was never realized. Roads in other parts of the Superior were also stopped by vocal opposition. But the Quetico Provincial Park in Ontario, adjoining the Minnesota canoe country, is now facing a road crisis of its own. Roads are edging toward Beaverhouse, Namakan, and McKenzie Lakes to the north and Saganagons and Big Saganaga from Northern Light Lake on the east.

Lastly came airplanes. Seaplanes landed at will at private landholdings, resorts, and any good fishing lake deep in the wilderness after World War II. The Quetico-Superior Council and the Friends of the Wilderness led a bitter struggle to obtain an executive order to create an airspace reservation over the Roadless Areas. Finally, in late 1949, President Truman signed an airspace reservation order prohibiting aircraft from flying below 4,000 feet above sea level over the Roadless Areas. The resorters and bush pilots fought back. The executive order was challenged in court. Appeals followed. In 1951, the executive order was upheld by the United States Supreme Court. From then until the late 1950s, major changes in the canoe country came as a result of its steadily increasing popularity and the purchase by the federal government of resorts within the canoe country. About this time, just before my fourteenth birthday, I guided my first canoe trip into the Quetico-Superior, the start of seven intensive years of cruising and exploring every part of this huge wilderness.

CHAPTER TWO

Moose Lake to the High Country around Knife Lake

MOST CANOE TRIPS from Ely began at Moose Lake near the end of the Fernberg Trail. The Fernberg was a narrow, winding, chuckhole-laden road. A fine layer of dust covered the leaves of the bushes and birches for a dozen feet off the tread. Along this thoroughfare our open-air GMC truck hauled two canoes, a trailer with six more, and a ton or two of gear. The journey to Moose Lake was twenty miles and took almost an hour. This bumpy ride was analogous to the hike to the base of a mountain where the climb would really begin.

In the summers of 1958 and 1959, the familiar road began to change. The U.S. Forest Service was rebuilding the road into a su-perhighway! In my young exuberance, I protested to the supervisor of the forest that we were making the wild country too accessible. Why not just pave the winding road and keep down the dust? Why spend thousands for a whole new road with nary a curve or hill when it really wasn't needed? I complained about the Cadillacs and trailers — all to no avail. The U.S. Forest Service officials in Duluth listened kindly but said that the new road spelled progress — and they were determined to have their way.

My dad's outfitting company had a large canoe landing on Moose Lake that became a major jumping-off spot for canoe trips, as it was a natural gateway to the Canadian Quetico and several major routes on the U.S. side. I remember one scout group that got off to a disap-pointing start there. Three of their burly members loaded their ca-noe with their center man sitting atop the center yoke rather than on the bottom of the canoe. All three eagerly grabbed their paddles and stroked together on the right side of the canoe against a stiff left broadside breeze. Before one could blink an eye, the canoe flipped and all three were in the cold water. Over the years, many such neo-

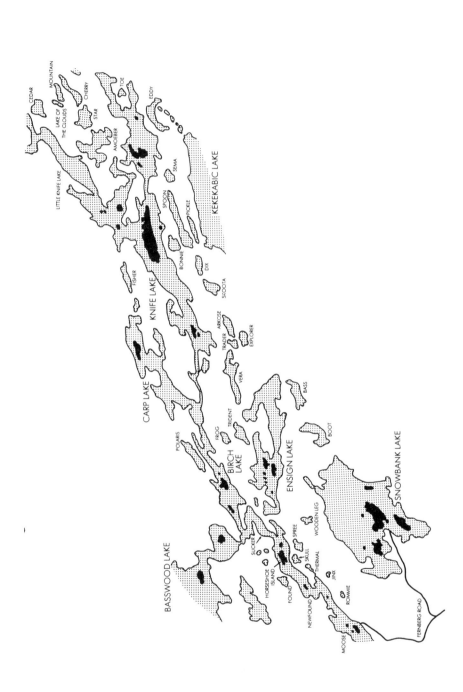

CEDAR
MOUNTAIN
LAKE OF THE CLOUDS
CHERRY
TOE
EDDY
STAR
LITTLE KNIFE LAKE
AMOEBER
SEMA
SPOON
PICKLE
KEKEKABIC LAKE
BONNIE
DIX
FISHER
SCOOTA
KNIFE LAKE
CARP LAKE
ARKOSE
TRADER
EXPLORER
VERA
BASS
TRIDENT
FROG
BIRCH LAKE
BOOT
POLARIS
ENSIGN LAKE
SNOWBANK LAKE
SPREE
WOODEN LEG
SUCKER
BASSWOOD LAKE
SKULL
HORSESHOE ISLAND
THERMAL
FOUND
JINX
NEWFOUND
ROMMIE
MOOSE
FERNBERG ROAD

phytes departed our landing, only to return from their canoe trips with assurance and skill in handling the canoe. They quickly learned to paddle on the opposite sides of the canoe, to keep their arms straight to feather their paddles against the wind, and to maintain a steady rhythm. A few J-strokes at the stern would keep the canoe on course.

The western half of Moose Lake is outside of the Boundary Waters Canoe Area and is the terminus of the Moose Lake road off the Fernberg Trail. A high hill with several cliffs overlooks several commercial canoe landings and provides a lovely view from the south shore. During the off-season this view is most breathtaking — in the late fall when the leaves have fallen and the quiet waters await silently the coming of winter and freeze-up, or in the early spring when the hot sun beats on the receding ice and the forest has a reddish-purple tinge in the crowns of the birches due to the still-dormant buds.

Moose is the headwaters of a series of lakes leading to Basswood Lake and beyond. The canoe country drains into Basswood from long chains of lakes to the east and north. Basswood is like a centerpiece — a large collecting basin. Actually, the drainage divides further east at Big Saganaga Lake, with waters rushing north around the top of the Quetico and eventually ending at Lac La Croix. The other fork from Saganaga leads to the Knife River on the Basswood, Crooked Lake, and Curtain Falls, and thence on the Lac La Croix, forming Hunter's Island, the heart of the Quetico.

The Moose chain leads to Basswood via Newfound and Sucker Lakes, joining the flowage from the Knife River above Prairie Portage Falls. This chain of lakes is several feet above its original watermark, due to an old logging-days dam (recently restored) at Prairie Portage Falls. The dam was built to back up water to drive logs from the Knife Lake area into Basswood and, eventually, to the old sawmill town of Winton. The Moose chain receives heavy canoe and boat traffic today, with overlapping canoe parties departing and returning.

A little more than halfway down Moose Lake and a half mile to the south lies a small lake named Rommie Lake. The lake has several beaver lodges but shows no sign of civilization and has no trail leading to it. It is surrounded by many felled aspens, reflecting the lifestyle of the lake's denizens. The lake has often been a destination hike for me, but is easy to miss. The intervening ridges from Moose are mostly second-growth aspens and birches, and the swamps are full of large cedars. I've often thought of planting stream trout in this lake, as in others off the Moose chain. This lake was named after my boyhood nickname when I shot my first deer near its shores at age thirteen.

On the forest ridges beyond Rommie Lake extending to Jinx Lake is an old telephone line stretched out atop a series of tripod poles. Most of the wire is gone but occasional stretches are intact. Jinx Lake has a small outlet that trickles down a hillside to Moose. Along these pools I once followed the trail of a large timber wolf, its footprints being very fresh — probably made only a few moments before. I crossed back over to Jinx Lake, where the bays were all covered with newly formed ice. The stately spruces and glacial ledges with a light covering of fresh snow created an inspiring sight, one I studied in awe, knowing that I shared it with a lonely timber wolf.

Onward along the southern ridge of Moose Lake one comes to Thermal Lake and eventually to a high piney ridge and plateau south of Skull Lake. The edge of the long ridge abruptly ends at Spree Lake and a swampy area just off Newfound Lake. The ridges south of Skull and Spree Lakes were some of my favorites, as deer abound there and I spent many joyful hours exploring the forest in search of them. From the high ridge overlooking Skull, one can see most of Newfound and Horseshoe Island with the deep indentation that gave it its name. Especially here, one captures the music of Sigurd Olson's *Singing Wilderness*. I frequently climbed this ridge during the summer, while paddling by on canoe trips, to revel in the scenery. Between Spree and Newfound is another high hill topped by a small fireplace, perhaps built by a group of intrepid campers willing to make the descent and ascent for water from Newfound in exchange for the magnificent view of the Moose chain.

On the north side of Newfound lies another series of ridges with large muskegs reaching to Manomin and Basswood Lakes. The ridges skirt around small Found Lake. One fall I glanced through the trees atop the ridge and noticed five otters crossing the lake. Half of the lake was frozen. The otters dove in and out of the water until they reached the edge of the ice, where they had a veritable carnival. They were barking and diving, returning to the ice and diving in again. The otter is a fairly common resident of the canoe country, and seeing one so joyful in its pursuits reminds a person that this wilderness is really theirs, man being a mere intruder.

Prairie Portage is a rendezvous for the modern-day voyageur just as in the days of old. The Canadian customs station, a white, undistinguished clapboard building, is on the Basswood side, and the log cabin and porch office of the ranger station and the Prairie Portage Lodge are on the American side. The lodge is a remnant of the resort development era. I often visited the lodge to see the Indian Chosa family and thought of the original Ojibways who once inhabited this region. The Chosas would always have a treat for me. In present days a jeep portage hauls day-fishermen's boats to Basswood, but new laws give boat hauling a short life, another step toward preserving the wilderness character of this area.

Many interesting Canadians have manned these outlying posts over the years, including the Hendrickson brothers, old Oscar Frederickson, Rod Salchert, Gerry Payne, and Mike O'Brien of this present day. I could tell that one thing was common among them — they were an integral part of the great north country. The last time I returned across Prairie Portage, I looked up from under the canoe and recognized the customs official from fifteen years earlier! His affection for the canoe country had become ingrained; probably he will never leave. He smiled as I told how I had caught three trout in fifteen minutes in an unnamed lake a few miles back and added that my partner was carrying them in a pack on his back. (Although not much for paddling, my partner was a pleasant companion. He was an Alaskan malamute named Talkeetna, whose story is told later in this book.)

Though Prairie Portage Falls was altered by the logging dam, it provided a pleasant and welcome sight after the long and often rough paddle across mighty Basswood. Fishing for smallmouth bass is notably excellent at the base of the falls, and walleye or northern pike may occasionally be caught there. However, when I was guiding two notable Minnesota football coaches, Murray Warmath and Norm van Brocklin, to Basswood, all we caught to show for a full day's fishing was a four-pound bass.

One enviable guiding venture on the Moose chain involved eighteen high school girls. They were Campfire Girls, all a year older than I and all attractive — and eager to learn about the outdoors! We visited with the customs agent, and camped on Birch Lake after a

Canoe landing on Moose Lake, where many canoeing adventures began.
Credit: Roger Rom

long day's paddle. I spent most of my time arranging two fireplaces and cooking breakfasts and dinners. Outdoor cooking is a combination of art and science, but cooking for almost twenty people was a considerable challenge. The knack of successful outdoor cooking is to have a good fireplace and plenty of dry firewood on hand to maintain a constant, hot fire. I always cleaned out the bottom of the fireplace first and then erected a fire grate over the rocks. (The Boundary Waters campsites now are equipped with a permanent steel grate, as well as a box biffy back in the woods.) Dead branches from the base of spruce trees make excellent kindling when broken and placed over dried birch bark gathered from fallen dead trees. Beaver wood from the tops of beaver houses and dams makes excellent firewood; I would cut these with a small saw held vertically between my legs, moving the log instead of the saw. Then, I'd split the larger pieces with an axe.

Food in the wilderness now includes a wide variety, the advances in freeze-dried foods being substantial, but it is the produce of the land that is really special on canoe trips. "Kala Mojaka" is my favorite. This is a Finnish fish stew made as follows: Clean and fillet one or two northern pike and cut the fillets into one-inch cubes. Boil small pieces of potato, diced onions, whole allspice, and salt and pepper until the potatoes are almost done. Add the fish ten minutes before removal from the fire. Lastly, pour condensed or powdered milk over the stew and cook long enough just to heat the milk. A heartier meal one will never find! Fresh fish is also good deep fried, particularly walleye and lake trout. I moisten the seasoned fillets in an egg batter, then roll them in a flour-cornmeal mixture and place them in a frying pan with a quarter inch of hot grease. A special treat is trout smothered in butter, cheese, seasoning, and onion, wrapped well in tin foil and placed in the coals.

A reflector oven affords additional treats in the wilderness. On each trip I baked brownies, gingerbread, and pies, to the delight of my crew. For successful oven use, the fire must be kept hot and the oven must be perfectly balanced and close to the fire. The dessert must be started before the rest of the meal, since baking in the woods always takes a good deal of time. Making pies was quite a challenge, and I'd roll the pie dough on the bottom of the canoe, using a jar or anything round, and then spread it in a pie tin. Dried fruit mix is good, but fresh blueberries make the most delicious pie. A generous supply of sugar and butter are the secret to making good pies. One may lay a criss-cross of dough on the top or cover it with a full piece of dough.

Another treat is corn or blueberry fritters. A Crisco can is convenient to heat the grease in. When the grease is hot, the fritters (flour, baking powder, 2 eggs, milk, oil) are added. Whole kernel corn or blueberries add a delightful flavor. The fritter needs to be turned over just once. When they're done, I roll them in sugar or serve them with maple syrup for a delightful and unique sweet. I made several items from this repertoire for the Campfire Girls, who assisted me by picking blueberries, gathering firewood, and washing dishes.

We ventured on a side trip to Knife Lake and back; the return was memorable in that we all ran several small rapids on the Knife River. A small rapids below Seed Lake can be run, and all of the girls — except one — negotiated it perfectly. The least experienced girl turned broadside and took in half a canoeful of water.

The Knife River canoe route is perhaps the most popular in the canoe country. There are five easy portages to traverse — the first on the right from Birch to Carp Lake around a rapids, and four on the Knife

River around additional rapids. The first river portage leads to a quiet pond, and the second around two small rapids into Seed Lake, a widening of the river. Seed Lake is a shallow walleye lake, and I've used a campsite on the east shore often for a lunch stop. There is another river portage on the right, followed by the last and longest one, called Big Knife Portage. Big Knife is the remnant of a logging trail, and large deadheads (logs that have become waterlogged, with one end sinking to the bottom and the other rising to the surface, creating a hazard to the canoeist) and relics of the old logging days may be seen in the river.

Knife River was a main travel route in the voyageur days. The Basswood River and Gunflint River had previously given up treasures of pots, rifles, and other relics lost when a voyageur's canoe overturned in the rapids. One hot summer day, two friends and I carried scuba gear up the Knife River to search the pools below the various rapids for relics, but found nothing except — to our surprise — a logger's peavey, used to move logs. It had a three-inch flower of deep red rust on the end that added to the beauty of the find. Had a logger dropped it, or had he fallen in during a log drive?

On reaching Knife Lake after five portages and a long paddle, one is always ready for a respite. To the tired canoeist's delight, just a mile down the lake is the most tasty homemade root beer in America, made by reclusive Dorothy Molter, who has been serving root beer to canoeists for over thirty years. She inherited three islands with several cabins from Bill Berglund, a logger of the old days who stayed on because he loved Knife Lake.

Dorothy cuts her own ice during the winter, stores it in a sawdust-insulated ice house during the summer, and serves it with her famous root beer. She is full of tales about the various canoeists and wild animals that are her companions during the long winter months. Her fence is made of countless broken paddle blades. For many years she hauled her supplies up the Knife River by canoe until the snowmobile came onto the scene during the 1960s, allowing her to stock heavily in the winter months in preparation for the following summer. I remember stopping in at her house in the 1960s, one blustery early May Saturday following breakup. She already had hot soup brewing, and offered a friendly, robust smile and an ear for our adventures at a distant trout lake. She had an accurate geography of the Midwest, since her visitors were people from Oshkosh to Peoria, as well as Knife Lake's beavers and red squirrels.

Knife Lake is a long, crystal-clear, deep trout lake forming the border between the United States and Canada. It is surrounded by high hills and rocky bluffs; and since its American shores were logged near the turn of the century, the southern shore is dominated by aspens and birch. The northern Canadian shore is still graced by tall Norway and white pines, a virgin pine forest.

The snowmobile radically changed the winter scene at Knife Lake during the late 1960s and early 1970s, giving rise to a major new controversy. Tourists from the outside seldom visited the canoe country during the winter, but the snowmobile brought unrestricted and easy weekend access to the local fishermen. In the matter of an hour, they roared to a favorite lake trout fishing hole on Ima, Thomas, or Knife Lake. The snow machine made a mockery of the sweat and portaging required to get about by canoe during the summer months. The tranquility of the wilderness was threatened. What the canoe country was to man — escape from mechanization, respite, and reconciliation within oneself — was certain to disappear. The locals seemingly weren't concerned — their blind desire was a fast trip and good fishing, regardless of the cost to the wilderness state of the area. The snowmobile became a cause célèbre for local residents, and snowmobilers became the folk heroes of the rural north. Dorothy Molter received some of her supplies by snowmobile, and her cabins often became a popular way station. After a bitterly fought two-year battle, the BWCA became the official Boundary Waters Canoe Area Wilderness. A compromise had finally been reached, restricting the snowmobile.

The south arm of the "V" of Knife Lake has many campsites and is popular with large scout groups. I found a series of lovely campsites on several small islands about midway along the north shore of the south arm. From these campsites, I had a favorite portage across the peninsula to the north arm into a deep bay full of smallmouth bass. The bay was shallow with a sandy bottom and was perfect for the light green smallmouth bass. Casting a Rapala lure or tossing a night crawler in on a harness was sure to get a rise. The bass were generally between one and two pounds, with an occasional one going up to three or four pounds.

The bass bay is sheltered and usually still, so one may observe beaver swimming or occasionally see a deer come down to the shoreline in the dwindling light. One evening we watched the sun disappear and a bright orange moon simultaneously rise over the tree tops. The sights and sounds of nature overruled the experience of fishing, but that sportful tug on the end of the line was always fun.

Back in the channel toward our camp, I once encountered a pair of otters swimming straight toward my canoe. They stopped with their backs arched, peered at me curiously with their beady eyes, and apparently marveled at me more than I at them. An echo or two between the shoreline cliffs caught their attention before they dove and disappeared.

In late 1961, I guided two families that included seven girls. On our second night, we camped on an island past Birch Point on the south arm of Knife. After pitching the tents, I hiked back in the woods to gather firewood. I came across a convenient dry log with no branches, so sat down on the smooth surface to take advantage of this natural biffy (before the days of USFS latrines). As soon as I had my pants down, I was swarmed upon by a profusion of angry wasps, causing me to dash embarrassingly to the lake and into the water to cool off.

Beyond the south arm, there are several lakes and side trips that are always enjoyable. It's the side lakes off main canoe routes that are the most fascinating, offering untrammeled solitude and excellent fishing. Over a long, flat portage is Sema Lake, an example of one of these off-route gems. I fished the middle of the lake, where rumor had it lake trout abounded, but had no luck. Back to Knife again, I ventured further east to Toe Lake and caught numerous northern pike, releasing all except for two for supper and Finnish Kala Mojaka.

The most interesting lakes around Knife lie to the north, however. I've portaged many times to Cherry Lake via Hanson. Cherry has a high cliff along the north shore, narrows, and a pretty campsite about midway down the lake. Walleyes abound in the deep water below the cliff. Cherry Lake is shaped like a dumbbell; perhaps it resembles two cherries on the map. North of Cherry, I followed a worn and hilly trail to glimpse a lake some call Mountain Lake and others, Lunar Lake. To the west of Cherry, I'd paddle and portage through Star and Amoeber Lakes back to Little Knife and to the south arm to complete a full day's circle. To the east of Hanson is a series of small lakes leading to Fish and Nawakwa Lakes. I explored this route one day but couldn't understand how Fish Lake got its name, because I didn't get a single bite, though I fished the entire shoreline.

Traveling north up Little Knife Lake (the north arm), one comes to a small brook and lift-over into Ottertrack Lake. Ottertrack is also called Cypress because the many leaning cedars along the shore remind some of southern cypresses. The shores are surrounded by high hills, giving it a canyonlike effect. On the south shore lived another recluse, Benny Ambrose, who passed away during the 1982–83 winter. He lived much like Dorothy Molter; both were given the opportunity to live the remainder of their lives at their wilderness retreats, after which their properties return to the U.S. government, to be allowed to revert back to wilderness.

South of Ottertrack is a portage up a steep hill to Cedar Lake, which sits atop the high hills of Ottertrack. It is another picturesque clear-water lake. I drifted lazily across the lake with a daredevil spoon deep in the cold water. A strike! For what seemed like an eternity I fought a five-pound trout, with more than 100 yards of line reaching into the depths. The trout swam in wide arcs, back and forth. Finally the fish tired, and I pulled in a cold, shiny beauty. Back on my island campsite on Knife, I wrapped the trout in foil and baked it amidst the coals for a dinner to finish a perfect day.

Beyond Cedar Lake is a lake of mystery called Lake of the Clouds. It's a long, narrow lake that I've longed to visit by canoe. Do fish haunt its waters? Is it a hidden trout lake? One winter day I scrambled up the steep portage to Cedar and walked across the ice to search for the portage into Lake of the Clouds. With only four inches of snow on top of the ice, the going was good. I found a break in the trees and headed south to what appeared to be the portage. Four inches of windblown snow on the ice became two feet of powder in the forest. I found myself churning through it, sometimes crawling on all fours, and at last broke out and looked on Lake of the Clouds. Was I surprised to see a half dozen people out on the ice! I hiked across the lake only to find old friend Bud Heinselman and a group of university researchers taking core samples of the lake bottom. They had flown into Mountain Lake courtesy of the USFS and hiked in from there. We all joked about the oddity of ever seeing anyone so deep in the wilderness! I dropped a line with a frozen smelt on it into the lake through one of their bore holes. No luck, but their boring into the bottom evidently disturbed the sediment and drove the fish away.

Thus are my joyful reminiscences of the historical border lake country of Knife Lake; and now further into the wilderness.

CHAPTER THREE

Ogishkemuncie and Gabimichigami

THE CANOE COUNTRY was once the home of the Ojibway, or Chippewa, Indian, preceding the incursion of the white man. There are a few Ojibways left near the canoe country, most of them living in reservations or assimilated into the white man's way of life. Scattered here and there on high cliffs lining the shores of many canoe country lakes are Indian pictographs, some painted by the Ojibway tribe and some older ones by the Sioux. Ogishkemuncie and Gabimichigami are Ojibway names; the latter means "Cross Lake," so named because here the duck flights merge during the migration to the south.

Ogishkemuncie is a long lake scattered with islands and peninsulas, reached by a few easy portages beyond Eddy Lake off the south arm of Knife. Portages take one past Jean, or Jenny, Lake and Annie Lake. There are fighting bass and walleyes in Ogish. From Ogishkemuncie there are three portages to Mueller, Agamok, and Gabimichigami. The Kekekabic Trail from Lake One to Gunflint Lake passes north of Agamok. A high ridge of beautiful birches parallels Agamok on into Gabi.

Gabimichigami is another treasure of the canoe country, being an interior lake with clear water and fighting trout. For beauty it has few equals. My first visit to Gabimichigami was in early May, when the buds of the birches were in their purple freshness. We caught the late sunset and early sunrise with the morning mists rising from the water. It was cold and the trout were near the surface. We could see them in the clear, shallow water, but as they weren't "feeding," we caught only a few. The first of the loons had already come this far north and charmed us with their plaintive cries far into the night.

From Gabimichigami there are two short portages through Rattle

GUNFLINT TRAIL ROAD

SEAGULL LAKE

ALPINE LAKE

JAP LAKE

TUSCARORA

OWL

GILLIS

CROOKED

MORA

FRENCH

JASPER

PETER

POWELL

HOWARD

W. FERN

FERN

VIRGIN

ELM

HOLT

OGISHKEMUNCIE LAKE

AGAMOK

MUELLER

GABIMICHIGAMI

RATTLE

LITTLE SAGANAGA LAKE

HORSEFISH

ELTON

KNIFE LAKE

EDDY

JEAN

ANNIE

BEAR LAKE

PAN

KIVANIVA

RAVEN LAKE

VAN

ROE

SAGAS

JUG

ADAMS LAKE

BOULDER LAKE

MALBERG

ELBOW

KAWISHIWI RIVER

FISHER

BOW

AMBER

Lake south into Little Saganaga Lake. Little Sag has good walleye fishing and is loaded with islands. The remains of four old cabins are on the west shore, and I found an old gramophone in one in 1963, with records and all! I explored several of the islands and hiked over to Elm Lake to the east, a pretty little lake sitting off by itself.

There are numerous little lakes to the east of Little Sag, and at Tuscarora Lake one meets the canoe traffic from the Gunflint Trail. One route that appealed to me as being less traveled was from Gabimichigami to the Chub River and up to Jap Lake. I left Little Sag with two partners and headed through Gabi to another clear-water trout lake—Peter Lake. From there we visited Virgin, West Fern, Powell, and French Lakes. We pitched camp and set out to explore the Chub River. Then we passed Fay and Glee Lakes, and after numerous streams, beaver dams, and unnamed ponds, finally arrived at Jap Lake. This beautiful lake had crystal-clear water surrounded by symmetrical hills, with a rocky shoreline covered with hardy pines. The whole lake had the appearance of a Japanese garden, undoubtedly the origin of its name. We trolled for trout without luck and noted two campsites on the lake. That night we tried our fishing luck on French Lake as the northern lights bounced around the sky. There is a hiking trail from Seagull Lake into Jap Lake, where, reportedly, rainbow trout have been planted.

Next, we ventured from French Lake into Gillis, another trout lake, and through the dark waters of Crooked, Harry, and Mora Lakes back to Little Sag. All of these lakes looked like good walleye lakes, but we didn't take the time to test them.

The route from Little Sag to Fraser is long and rugged, with a half-dozen intervening small lakes. Fortunately, a portage crew (including my father) spent 67 days on Ledge Lake years ago and cut out excellent portage trails. We tried a new route to Gabi by portaging into the small lake off the western shore and taking the river into Gabi. It wasn't easy! We made Gabi, portaged into Leo Lake, then two unnamed lakes, then Horsefish, followed by half-mile portages into an unnamed lake, Vee Lake, and Ledge Lake. From Ledge there are two long portages into Roe Lake and Sagas (or Peterson) Lake, and then on to Fraser over a third, shorter portage.

In this low country of small lakes, one stands out in my mind, Bear Lake (Indian name Muckwa). One takes the same route to Ledge and Vee Lakes but heads southeast across two portages into Hoe

Lake, from which there is a 100-rod portage into Bear. With a couple of high school classmates, I chose to camp on the point opposite the second island we passed. We tried Bear for lake trout, which it is noted for, but didn't have any luck, so we lifted over three beaver dams into Elton Lake — and didn't catch anything there either. We went back to our campsite on Bear, climbed a high hill, and engaged in the old pastime of rolling big boulders into the water. Viewing Bear Lake from this vantage point really struck me with its beauty. The light green birches of mid-May and dark jack pines surrounded its shores. I hated ever to leave there. That evening, I went trout fishing alone. I caught a small trout, but it dropped back into the lake as I lifted it into the canoe. We had a bonfire that evening to keep warm; and that night I left a line with a smelt on it in the water. A two-pound lake trout was on the other end by morning.

We broke camp and made three portages via two beaver ponds into Pan Lake. Pan is well-known for its walleye fishing, so we tried it, but to no avail. We pulled over several beaver dams and portaged into Kivaniva Lake and on into the South Kawishiwi River on our way home.

CHAPTER FOUR

Kekekabic and Ima Lake Country

SOUTH OF KNIFE LAKE lies the limit of the loggers' early penetration to Kekekabic Lake. Here tall pines can again be found. Two major routes lead to Kekekabic from the north, one from the south arm of Knife Lake, past a small waterfall, and via Eddy Lake. Eddy is known to have all species of fish and, seemingly, none that ever bite. I hurry along the small ponds that double back westward from Eddy's eastern end. It's usually more portaging work than one desires, but Kekekabic is worth it. The other route is from Knife via Pickle, Spoon, and Bonnie through vigorous second-growth forest.

Kekekabic is ringed by high hills, has few islands, and is a broad expanse of water in contrast to the small lakes one paddles through enroute. One day I caught Kekekabic and the canoe country in a rare mood. It was a day of total silence. No waves. No ripples. No clouds. We sat in the middle of the lake and marveled at the merging of sky and lake into one continuous blue. The sun beat down on us in a frenzy, reflecting off the becalmed lake.

Kekekabic is also trout water. Kekekabic's trout, which are known to rise in the early evening, are hard to find, since the lake is so large; I've preferred to paddle on to smaller lakes where the trout can be more easily found. One is Kek Lake off the south shore, where trout can be found in the center of the lake, like Sema to the north.

The U.S. Forest Service built a ranger cabin on the south shore of Kekekabic in the 1930s. Atop a high hill about a half mile further south, they erected a fire lookout tower. I've visited the cabin several times and once hiked the trail to the lookout tower. I climbed the hill and ladder up the tower to a perch for a panoramic view of the hills to the north. I could see the intervening ridges and blue sparkling

waters of the narrow lakes all the way to Knife and beyond. Recently, the tower and cabin, remaining vestiges of man's intrusion, have been removed.

During 1939, my father spent a summer manning that lookout tower to earn money to help defray the expenses of his college education in wildlife management. He had the joys of a summer alone in the wilderness. To pass the time, he set dozens of mousetraps in the forest, became expert on the many kinds of small mammals that inhabit the forest, and wrote an essay on the nine different species he caught, including the rare northern woodland jumping mouse. He earned a degree in wildlife management at the University of Minnesota, but found no jobs available when he returned to Minnesota after five years in the Navy in the Pacific theater. So he and his bride, Barb, pursued a career in the out-of-doors by beginning Canoe Country Outfitters.

Another canoe route from the Moose chain that leads to either Knife or Kekekabic passes through Ensign Lake. Ensign is a long lake with deep bays, and at one time was heavily logged. A vigorous second-growth forest has regenerated, with a few Norway and white pines poking through along the ridges. This canoe route begins at Newfound Lake with a portage to the north of a small rapids into Little Iron Lake, also called Splash Lake. Before the canoe country was declared a wilderness, this portage was the scene of considerable controversy, for the far side was cached with numerous fishing boats. Resort patrons on the west end of Moose Lake would motor up to the portage, carry their motor across, and motor down Ensign. The motorboat battles of the canoe country principally involved lakes such as Ensign that were large, had good fishing, and were only a single portage away. Unfortunately, that included almost half of the wilderness canoe country, since so many large lakes were near roadheads. Motors have since been banned from most of the Boundary Waters Canoe Area Wilderness, including Ensign Lake.

Across Little Iron Lake is a shallow channel with a small rapids flowing from Ensign. Ensign Lake has over a dozen good campsites and has excellent walleye fishing. Walleyes may be found in many places, but a few secrets help to find them. They travel in schools, whereas northerns are usually loners. Walleyes pursue minnows and northerns pursue walleyes, the northern being the barracuda of the north country. The walleye frequents deep pools below rapids and occasionally feeds above rapids; they prefer rocky shorelines, reefs, areas around rocks in the middle of lakes, islands, points, drop-offs, and rocky ledges. There often is good walleye fishing above the rapids into Little Iron, along the rocky shore before the portage into Trident, and along the southern shore of the bay as one leaves the Vera Lake portage.

The half-mile portage from Ensign into Vera is dreaded for its mudholes, with the black, sloshy swamp mud typical of the canoe country. Occasionally, someone dropped a log or two in the muddy spots, only adding to the challenge of balancing a canoe and pack on one's back while walking the slippery logs. Vera Lake has a portage leading to a small bay of Knife that leads to the lake proper through a narrow rocky channel.

Due east of Vera Lake is a series of small lakes; one, Arkose, has a reputation for fighting lake trout. Most maps label Arkose Lake as Missionary Lake, and a small pond to the north as Arkose Lake. But that's only where the confusion begins! One weekend, a couple of canoe outfitter friends and I decided to try our luck trout fishing in Arkose. We came to the end of Vera and found the portage into the small lake shown as Trader on various maps. We crossed the lake and searched the far shoreline for a trail. We found several beaver trails into the woods but nothing that resembled a portage. We finally decided to follow a well-traveled game trail up a hill, where it became indistinct and bushy. We saw a clearing through the trees to our left and some water. The new lake seemed to veer to our left, which was strange, but we loaded our canoe and paddled around the point. To our amazement (and embarrassment) we were right back in Trader Lake. We had portaged across a peninsula! We went back to our drawing boards (and our compass this time) and followed a game trail eastward instead of north and finally came to Arkose Lake. On its north shore at the far end we found a sloping rock, an ideal campsite. From there, in our canoe we explored every nook and cranny of the lake in search of the elusive lake trout.

At the far end of Ensign Lake to the southeast is a canoe route to Ima Lake. A short portage leads into Bass Lake (also called Ashigan Lake), a long, flat portage into Gibson Lake, and two short portages via Cattyman Lake into Jordan Lake. This series of lakes shows extensive scars of logging, including some huge stumps still to be seen on the shoreline of Jordan Lake. There are several faded Indian pictographs along the ledges on the eastern shore of Jordan just before the portage into Ima.

At Cattyman Lake, a southern route to Ima from Snowbank converges. This route was developed to ease the canoeing pressure from Moose and Ensign Lakes. The U.S. Forest Service built a public landing on Snowbank Lake, opening up a picturesque and wild route into Ima via Disappointment Lake. My father and I were among the first to explore this route. Snowbank Lake is a deep lake-trout lake, and Disappointment is good for walleyes. To the northeast of Disappointment is a 300-foot-high hill, Disappointment Mountain. At the end of Disappointment Lake is a portage into Ahsub Lake, ringed by dark jack pines, followed by a short portage with a muddy landing into Jitterbug Lake (a swampy duck haven), followed by another portage into Adventure Lake and a liftover into Cattyman Lake.

Ima Lake has a flat northern shore, but its eastern side is ringed by rock cliffs. From the rock cliffs, one can look across the shimmering waters to the slopes of Disappointment Mountain. In the late fall, when the aspens and birches have turned bright yellow, few lakes can match this view. Ima has many campsites and is noted for its early spring trout fishing. Two interesting side trips are to Alworth and Sedative Lakes. Alworth Lake has fat walleyes as well as frequent snags, since this lake has a very rocky bottom. Fred McReady, an Ely schoolteacher and guide, and I built a new campsite atop a hill between Alworth and Ima. From this vantage point, we could see both lakes. We were guiding two large families and needed a large site after all of the well-trodden ones were taken — an example of the wilderness canoeing pressures of the 1960s.

One evening I paddled several children into Alworth. We heard a loud splash by a beaver as he warned his family of our intrusion. As I paddled a few more strokes, he surfaced and splashed his tail again. We passed several beaver houses of piled sticks and mud along the shoreline. It seemed as if we could hear a beaver panting as we passed one; perhaps our swimmer friend had finally surfaced inside.

A second side route leads from Ima into Sedative Lake to the northeast. There are two short portages and a paddle along a stream to a long lake with water as black as tar. The shoreline has many flat rocky ledges for campsites. The two families' five children and I trolled with Daredevil spoons and discovered that the lake was full of hungry northerns. They would strike and swim with powerful strokes in long, straight lines, frenzied to free themselves. We caught twelve and kept only enough for a Kala Mojaka that evening. As we feasted late on our Finnish fish soup, we viewed a faint white aurora borealis to the north, announcing too soon the coming of autumn.

From Ima there are four short portages to Thomas and Fraser Lakes. The first lake out of Ima, called Hatchet Lake because of its shape, has several campsites, and good walleye fishing in the narrows of the hatchet. There are three more good portages along the stream flowing from Thomas Lake. Both Thomas and Fraser Lakes have many campsites and good fishing for walleyes and lake trout. A large island on Fraser has several log cabins, including a large hall, and a small sawmill nearby. These were built in 1945, but have been recently purchased by the U.S. Forest Service in their wilderness restoration program.

I especially enjoy two walleye lakes near Fraser; both are only a portage away and form a small circle route. One is Sagas, which has campsites on its east shore and on a high, rocky ledge to the south. The east campsite offers a sunset view of gorgeous pink, orange, purple, and gray clouds as the sun dips beneath the horizon. Between Sagas and Fraser lies a small triangular lake where in years past I was always able to catch a few walleyes for dinner; but fishing pressure in recent years has depleted the supply.

During the summer of 1979, I visited Fraser, Sagas, and Roe Lakes again and was surprised to see that a forest fire had raged through the region. The north bay of Fraser displayed hundreds of trees with stark, blackened trunks; and white rocks were everywhere. The thin topsoil, rich in humus and needles, had burned. The fire must have been fanned by strong winds, since so many trees were still standing. I looked for jack pine seedlings but found none. The jack pine releases its seeds after a fire, and thus is usually the first tree to repopulate a burn. There are many stands of jack pine of even age in the canoe country, evidence of nature's own reforestation following a fire.

A short canoe route connects Fraser to Kekekabic Lake to the north. A short liftover leads into Gerund Lake, followed by a hilly portage to Ahmakose Lake. This small clearwater jewel, which has trout in the center, is now surrounded by a blackened forest. Next is Wisini Lake. Wisini has cliffs along the eastern shore (Cliffs of

Wisini) and a curious "Tripod Rock" near a point on the southern end of the lake. Tripod Rock is a one-meter rock deposited by the glaciers atop three smaller rocks, forming a perfect tripod.

We named our pet timberwolf Wisini after this lake. We got her when she was only ten days old. She was a loving and friendly animal, but she never lost her true wolf characteristics. She dug deep pits about her little house, so that all one could see were her ears sticking above the surface. Her beady green eyes would follow a person's every move. She was docile if I took a forceful stance, but was shy and suspicious as wolves are wont to be.

Beyond Wisini is Strup Lake; both of these lakes have dark water and contain largemouth bass. The largemouths differ from their smallmouth cousins in that they are native to the canoe country, have vertical dark markings on their sides, and fight with a vengeance. They leap out of the water and dance on their tails along the surface — all of the time trying to spit out the hook. Bass fishing is best done from a canoe, casting with a surface lure toward the shore. The Jitterbug, Hula Popper, and Rapala all work well. I have fished Strup many times and have always been excited by the action I inevitably experience.

From Strup Lake to Kekekabic, the portage crosses the Kekekabic fire trail. This trail connects the end of the Fernberg with the end of the Gunflint roads and is a three-day hike.

Most of the portages in this area have docks built by the portage crews of the Civilian Conservation Corps during the 1930s Depression. The CCC boys also built many of the portages. Some of the portages are marked by U.S. Forest Service signs indicating the next lake and the length of the portage. These signs are becoming less common as time slips by, as they are not being replaced. Even portage signs are an intrusion on the wilderness experience.

On one of half a dozen journeys through Wisini and Strup Lake, I set the canoe down perfectly atop a log from the old dock, where an unseen sharp nail was sticking up. As I stepped into the canoe to load a pack, the nail punctured the aluminum and started a small geyser. Fortunately, I was able to fashion a wooden plug that lasted for the remainder of the journey.

One mid-October I took a jaunt amidst flaming yellow and red colors of the autumn leaves to the Wisini Lake country. It was very cold, with a freezing rain that turned to sleet and snow. Two of us paddled to the far end of Wisini to explore a stream, portaged twice, and finally bushwhacked a half mile through the forest to Baker (or Bakekana) Lake, another dark-water lake with a rocky bottom. We suspected it had largemouth bass, and we hoped we were the first people to visit this lake. I explored the shoreline and found some remnants of a campfire, however, dashing our hopes. It appeared as if some beaver trapper years earlier had camped there. We hurried back and braved more wind, cold, and snow before reaching Snowbank Lake.

CHAPTER FIVE

Raven Lake

EVERYONE HAS A favorite treasure, dream, or love. Mine is a lake —
Raven — secluded and not easy to paddle and portage to. God seemed
to have made it just far enough away and just about perfect. Raven
has been discovered, raped, rediscovered, and burned, and now perhaps has reached a new status of balance with the natural forces of
nature — sans man. It lies just off the Thomas-Fraser series of lakes.
There is the portage into Sagas, a short one into Roe, and two portages up a meandering stream into Raven. The first is short and
muddy. The stream can be paddled, but it traverses swampland
where the color of the water resembles root beer. After several dozen
turns in the narrow stream, near a large rock one can, if very obser-
vant, detect the faint trail that leads on to Raven.

In 1958, my father, my brother, and I decided to explore the distant reaches beyond Fraser and to visit Raven. We portaged into
Sagas and into Roe. The day was windless and silent. As we paddled
across Roe Lake, we passed a bay of lilies with a marshy shoreline.
A beautiful giant moose was feeding on the lily pad roots. We drifted
and watched him as he curiously observed us and finally sauntered
off into the forest of black spruce and tamarack.

We found the stream coming from Raven and cut through the
woods to a large swamp where the stream once again was visible. We
paddled onward over logs, around an occasional rock, and over more
logs. The logs were the trunks of black spruce that had grown to
maturity and finally crashed into their graveyard of the tiny stream.
We had to get out of the canoe countless times and pull over. It was
hot, sweaty, and tiring. We finally reached a point where the stream
was no longer navigable. My dad searched ahead into the forest for
a trail but found none. He saw a glimpse of lake through the forest,

so knew he was on the right track. We followed closely when he returned for the canoe and crashed through the forest along a trail outlined by a few blazes that my dad had made. We finally reached a flat rock ledge at the edge of the lake, with a few birches and perfect lichen-covered rocks for seats. We saw the outlet for the small stream that had been our channel, and scourge, through the swamp.

Raven had crystal-clear water that was obviously spring-fed, since there was no inlet. It reflected the blue sky perfectly. We ate lunch on our flat rock ledge as we rigged our fishing lines. We paddled out into the lake to a 20-foot rock sticking up only 200 yards from shore. We were dive-bombed by a pair of sea gulls, and their screeching anger intensified as we neared the rock. We were entertained by their flight as they rose to new heights, only to turn and buzz us within a few feet. What could trigger such an ill reception? As we rounded the rock, my dad spotted a downy baby bird paddling like mad across the water — it was a young sea gull! We spotted another, and another. The rock was well whitewashed with sea gull excrement and on top was a nest of twigs, needles, and mud. We drifted slowly lakeward and watched as the sea gulls returned to their roost and gathered up their young brood.

Our shiny Daredevil spoons dropped into the clear depths of the lake as we slowly drifted across. It was a peaceful day, the wind picking up so that we had a nice breeze. On the north shore we spotted another flat ledge that could be used as a potential campsite. We all got caught up in watching the forest and the puffs of white cumulus drifting overhead when, suddenly, both my dad and I felt a tugging fury on our lines. We reeled in and gleefully landed two beautiful ice-cold lake trout. By the time they came up to the surface from the depths, they were nearly exhausted. As soon as we took the hooks out of their mouths, we were surprised at how quickly they recovered and darted off. We caught three more, and then paddled over to the nearby rock ledge to explore. We had a beautiful view of the lake, but time was passing, so we returned to our portage. My dad cut out more of a trail, but it proved difficult to follow. Ten-year-old Larry managed to get lost returning over the portage, only to be found in tears.

Two springs later I again returned to Raven. My dad wanted to try early May lake trout fishing and brought another guide, Don Beland, along with us. We took the Snowbank route, but were almost thwarted by huge ice flows. Snowbanks lined the shorelines. We pushed our way through to the south and were able to make the portage to Parent Lake. Fortunately, the smaller lakes to Ima were free of ice, so we continued onward to Fraser and Sagas. We passed Roe and took the two long portages into Ledge Lake. From there we turned northward and portaged into a pond that led into Van Lake. We had made good time, but it was now late. We found a likely campsite spot on the north shore. The branches of the trees had been cut off by an axe, especially near the shoreline, surprising us that there would be any evidence of man in a lake as remote as Van. We surmised that in the late 1940s, prior to the air ban, seaplanes had flown in to Van for its excellent fishing. That buoyed our spirits, and we gave Van a real try. We fished for trout and walleyes but had nary a strike — not even a hungry northern! However, Van Lake had dark, although clear, water rather than the clear, cold water of a spring-fed trout lake, so we gave up, crawled into our sleeping bags, and went to sleep.

In the morning we found a blazed trail from Van to a pond where we bushwhacked through the forest to Raven. There were no leaves on the trees, nor any bushes, making the portaging relatively easy. The forest was budding, giving the birches and aspens a special inviting look. It was bitterly cold, and Raven was still partially frozen. We had to chop and break ice to reach open water. We unpacked our fishing gear and prepared to give early May trout fishing a try. At that time of year, trout are in shallow water and relatively easy to catch — even by casting instead of the deep trolling necessary later in the season. The trout were crazy with hunger; we got strike after strike and quickly had ten trout. That was our limit, so we quit fishing and concentrated our efforts on the long return to Fraser, Ima, and Snowbank.

Later that summer I again returned to Raven. But the route appeared different — there were markings along the trail from Roe into the stream, and the logs were gone! They had been sawed so that now there could be free passage. What could this portend? The going was too easy. The wildness, the wilderness was disappearing. The final portage was now a well-marked trail! I flipped on the canoe and portaged to our old rock ledge. As I reached the lake, I was shocked. A huge group was camped there. They had chopped down all the birches and had made a large table, with a smaller table nearby.

Author and father with our limit of lake trout on a spring canoe trip to Raven Lake.

They had built a large fireplace, and junk was everywhere. I was furious. What wanton destruction! Building a fancy campsite might be fine on a canoe route, but at a remote, beautiful, unspoiled lake off the beaten path, such amenities were despicable. I paddled off in disgust, restraining my feelings as the damage had been done.

At the sea gull rock I couldn't believe my eyes. Where the nest had perched for years past, there was now a freshly cut balsam cross with all of the canoe parties' names, addresses, and comments carved into it. A huge rock pile held it in place. Could there be religious significance to this shameful act? I couldn't believe it — this sacrilege was too much. I leaped out of the canoe and began throwing the rocks into the lake. An armada of canoes bore down on me, and angry words were exchanged. I told the ringleader, a burly character with a long beard, that he was hell-bent on destroying the wilderness, that his destructive cross was contrary to the teachings of religions, and that he was destroying a natural sea gull nesting site. I sped off following this exchange, but could hardly contain myself. My memories of virgin Raven Lake had been violated.

The notes in my canoeing journal of July 23, 1961, are revealing: "Took river ⅓ mile — someone has sawed out all the log obstructions. Next portage was ⅜ mile and rough into Raven, but now is cut out wide. A man by the name of Nolan and 8 others destroyed Raven. Large cleared tent sites, tables, and fireplaces were erected, and a 15-foot cross was placed on sea gull rock with initials carved. I next to lost my temper with such a guy who thinks he can do anything he wants to destroy the wilderness."

It was two years before I returned to Raven again. The fishing was not as good as before, and my feelings were still strong. Over fifteen years later, I finally returned to see what had happened. My wife and I noted that the north shore of Fraser leading into Sagas had been burned by a forest fire. The trees were blackened, yet still standing. It must have been a rapidly spreading, very hot fire. The portage into Sagas was intact, but the northern shore of Sagas was also burned. We portaged into Roe Lake, and the north shore was burned here too. We took the portage into the stream and again paddled onward. The last portage was as difficult to find as the first time I had traversed it, and the trail appeared seldom traveled.

I lifted the canoe from my shoulders and glanced around the flat rock ledge. The table was gone, the fireplace was gone, and the tent sites had been reclaimed by the forest! The west shore had been touched by the fire, but the rest of the lake remained untouched. Sea gull rock even appeared clean. There was no evidence of a pole or pile of rocks, but the sea gulls had chosen not to return.

I wetted my line and sank my Daredevil spoon. It wasn't long before I had a strike and landed a beautiful four-pound lake trout. It was a hot, sunny day with a brisk breeze; the trout would not have kept, so I returned it to the lake and watched it disappear below the ripples. The wildness of Raven had returned.

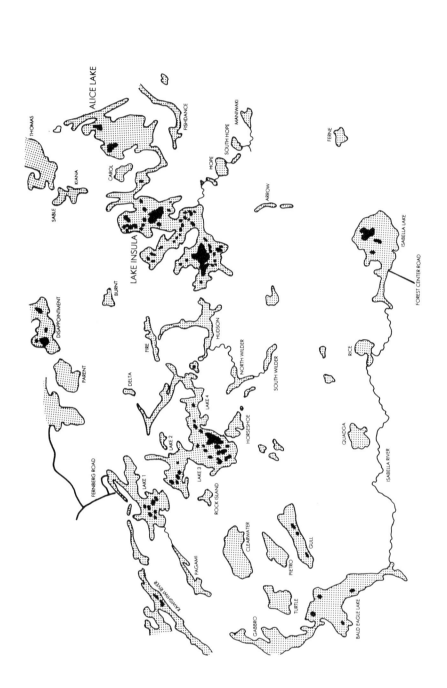

ALICE LAKE

THOMAS

FISHDANCE

SOUTH HOPE

MANIWAKI

HOPE

KIANA

SABLE

CAROL

FERNE

ISABELLA LAKE

ARROW

LAKE INSULA

BURNT

FOREST CENTER ROAD

DISAPPOINTMENT

PARENT

FIRE

HUDSON

DELTA

NORTH WILDER

RICE

SOUTH WILDER

LAKE 4

FERNBERG ROAD

LAKE 2

HORSESHOE

QUADGA

LAKE 3

LAKE 1

ROCK ISLAND

ISABELLA RIVER

PAGAMI

CLEARWATER

KAWISHIWI RIVER

PIETRO

GULL

TURTLE

GABBRO

BALD EAGLE LAKE

CHAPTER SIX

The Kawishiwi River and Insula Lake Region

AT THE END of the Fernberg Trail is a series of lakes called Lakes 1, 2, 3, and 4. The topography of the canoe country is different there: the land is flat, jack pine is the predominant tree, and the water is dark and ideal for walleyes. The Kawishiwi (pronounced "Kashway," meaning "endless waters" in Ojibway) River begins in the lake country around Adams and Pan Lakes and divides immediately; one arm (North Kawishiwi) flows through Alice, Insula, Hudson, and Lakes 1, 2, 3, and 4, converging with the south arm (South Kawishiwi) at Farm and Garden Lakes. The South Kawishiwi follows Koma, Polly, Isabella, Bald Eagle, Gabbro, Birch, and White Iron Lakes. An old logging dam on the north side of Lake 2 maintains the present water level of the North Kawishiwi.

In several tall dead trees along the south shore of Lake 2, I've frequently spotted bald eagles, with their white heads and white tails. From Lake 3 one can take a short route to Horseshoe Lake and North Wilder, then go to South Wilder for walleyes or down a wide, meandering river into Hudson Lake. My father and I canoed this route many years ago and stayed at a campsite opposite the river entrance on Hudson Lake. That evening, we fished with nightcrawlers at the river mouth and had an exciting time catching over a dozen fat, beautiful bluegills. From Hudson there is a pullover and two short portages downriver and back into Lake 4. Another interesting route from Hudson is to paddle north into Fire Lake and back to Lake 4, escaping the two river portages.

One weekend our entire family went to Lake 4 and paddled up the long, narrow northern arm. We found a nice campsite in time for dinner, only to find that I had forgotten to pack the plates. Somehow we managed to eat off pot lids, dish-ups (shallow aluminum bowls), and the pots themselves. The next day, we paddled westward to a short portage, then made a sharp right turn to an arm leading to another portage and into Delta Lake. This small lake is reputable among local walleye fishermen, but all we caught were small northerns.

From Hudson Lake there is a hilly, 90-rod portage into Insula Lake, known for its myriad islands and bays. It's a nightmare to traverse — there are tales of canoeists confused for days trying to find their way across. Insula, a good walleye lake, is a favorite haunt of locals; it has many campsites and is renowned for colorful sunsets.

Southeast of Insula is an interesting side route to Maniwaki. There are three portages into Hope Lake, followed by Middle Hope, South Hope, and finally a half-mile portage into Maniwaki. This portage is bisected by a logging road of high-quality gravel, a remnant of the logging of the 1950s. I followed the road to some tar paper logging shacks. During the 1950s, the U.S. Forest Service built a road and railroad spur to a town called Forest Center, just south of Isabella Lake. They built a road across the Isabella River and spent almost two decades clear-cutting jack pine for pulpwood. The country from Gull Lake to Insula and across Maniwaki to the South Kawishiwi was logged. From the air, this part of the canoe country still looks desolate. There are few canoe routes through this region, which is perhaps why heavy logging became so prevalent.

Returning to Insula, I found a school of walleyes in the bay where the Hope River entered Insula. We feasted on walleye fillets that night.

From Insula there is a short portage into Alice, a large, open lake with several fine sandy beaches, a rarity in the canoe country. At age eight, I caught a five-pound northern there; it was the largest fish I had ever seen up to that time. I remember petting it proudly on a stringer alongside the canoe. We put it in a small rock enclosure along the shoreline overnight, and the next morning I found it belly up with a huge hole pecked out of it by a hungry sea gull. I sadly buried it in the sand at our beach campsite.

Two routes lead north to Thomas Lake, one from Alice via Cacabic Lake and the other from Insula via Kiana Lake. Both have long, well-marked portages. The North Kawishiwi River skirts across the south end of Alice, where walleyes are almost always feeding. Up the river beyond Alice, over two portages, is Fishdance

Lake, which is really a long bay off the Kawishiwi River. Indian pictographs — a canoe, a moose, and several other paintings — are on the cliffs a half mile down Fishdance Lake along the western shore. That the pictographs persist through the centuries speaks well of the durability of the paint. Its composition remains a mystery, but it probably included ground hematite, fish oils, and perhaps berries.

Fishdance Lake was of prominence to me because I learned more about the politics of wilderness from the logging conducted near it. In 1930, the Shipstead-Nolan Act was enacted to help preserve the wild character of the lake country by providing that along all canoeing lakes, streams, and portages a 400-foot strip be free from the ravages of logging. I had heard of extensive logging near Fishdance, so prepared to hike into the forest to investigate. With me was noted environmentalist Dr. Clayton Rudd, editor and publisher of *Naturalist* magazine. He was a dentist by profession, but a stalwart wilderness advocate by choice.

One article in *Naturalist* highlighted the need to protect the wilderness from violations of the Shipstead-Nolan Act. Long, narrow Finn Lake off the Gunflint Trail had a gravel road constructed across the end of the lake in direct violation of the law. We were now interested in exploring Fishdance Lake to see how close the loggers had come to the deep interior of the canoe country. The birches atop the ridged looked isolated and dried out — as if the forest about them had been stripped away. I wondered if the loggers had cut to the hilltops, leaving only sparse, small birches in their wake. We hiked inward, and the 400-foot strip preserved by the Shipstead-Nolan Act was intact. But within another 100 feet or so, we emerged from the forest primeval into a land of stumps. It was a shock for me to see how they had cut over this once lovely wild forest. Logging roads were prevalent. Surprisingly, the only place that we found any tree-planting was where large jack pines had been planted along the tracks made when logs were skidded through the forest to gravel logging roads. We hiked a half mile to Assawan Lake, due east of Fishdance, and saw stumps the entire way, leading right down to the shoreline. We photographed the stumps with disgust and anger. We asked ourselves why a few temporary jobs and a few bucks for a distant corporate landlord could be worth the desecration of a wilderness. Assawan Lake was a cutover mess, but Assawan was not on any major canoe route. It was merely one of many small lakes back in the bush that are what wilderness is all about. As we trudged along, I noted a set of huge moose antlers, chewed, perhaps by a porcupine. The walking was wet and boggy, with the bogs filled with ladyslippers — the moccasin flower, or ladyslipper, is the Minnesota state flower. They are very rare and delicate, and a beautiful purple-pink color. At least the loggers did not cut down the flowers!

Further up the North Kawishiwi is another series of destination lakes that connect canoe routes coming east from Fraser and west from Little Saganaga. From here, one has a couple of easy portages into Elbow Lake. Elbow is good fishing for walleyes and northerns. I once guided a die-hard fisherman through the waters of this lake. He was a master at discovering where the "houkie," or northern pike, could be hiding. He hooked one in Elbow that easily weighed 20 pounds; but alas, when he got the fish near shore, it flipped and snapped the lightweight monofilament line and darted straight out for deeper water.

West in a bay is a trail to Fisher Lake. Once I fished there for lake trout but caught none; I then tried casting toward shore and caught several largemouth bass. On the far end, I found a campsite that had all the tree branches cut up to a height of ten feet. This lake had been frequented by the fly-in bush pilots over two decades earlier. They probably cut the tree branches up high to clear the wings of their seaplanes.

A short portage east from Elbow is Adams Lake. My father cut the first portage to Adams in 1937. Adams is a beautiful lake with at least three lovely campsites. It is a walleye lake, but I've never camped there. At least there is one lake to go back to and explore!

A series of beaver dams and a short portage brings one northward from Adams to Boulder Lake. Boulder's one large island holds a heron rookery. Heron rookeries create large areas of whitish excrement, lots of noise, a bit of smell, and are generally foul. Boulder is full of northerns, and my professional fisherman partner caught several over five pounds. We portaged one day over the muskeg into tiny Jug Lake and caught an eleven pounder. Jug, a shallow (6 to 10 feet) mud-bottomed lake, was home to two beaver families and undoubtedly harbored several large northerns, as I had heard stories of others catching monsters there too. Just after we caught the eleven pounder, another one equally as large leaped out of the water and landed with a big splash.

Canoeing on Alice Lake. Credit: Roger Rom

The Gabbro and Bald Eagle series of lakes are best reached from the Spruce Road and other recent logging roads. On one trip, I headed west from the Lake 1 landing and paddled and portaged down the Kawishiwi River to Gabbro Lake. This is a long way to get there, but the canoe route has short portages and fewer people. Gabbro Lake was flooded by a logging dam years ago, killing the shoreline forest. The water level receded many years later, leaving ugly, dead trees, stumps, and rocks along the shore. A small pullover at the end of the lake takes one into Bald Eagle Lake, which is much more attractive. Walleye fishing with nightcrawlers is successful throughout this area, and both lakes have large northerns.

There is a long portage into Gull Lake, which is secluded and also has good fishing. The island on the right as one enters has a good campsite. Just before the island is a reef, which is a good walleye hole — though the last time I was there, I caught more rocks than fish and broke the fiberglass rod trying to free my hook and sinker. Farther north, shallow Pietro and Turtle Lakes are full of northern pike. However, Clearwater Lake is wild and beautiful and is stocked with rainbow trout. I've explored the stream from there back to Lake 1 but found it unnavigable for a canoe. The Isabella and Snake Rivers enter at the south end of Bald Eagle. The Snake River is jet black and

43

has several portages leading to a logging road access. The U.S. Forest Service has blocked the logging road with huge boulders at the boundary of the wilderness, so visitors must leave their vehicles and portage a half mile to the Snake River.

The country south and west of Gabbro and Bald Eagle was heavily logged during the 1950s. Once, I hiked south of Gabbro to find a small lake called Nickel Lake. The country around there has a nickel-copper outcropping. The metallic ores are dark, heavy, and rather shiny (probably from the mica). I have also found outcrops of amphibole minerals, which are asbestiform and could create a fiber-exposure hazard in the mining and milling process. Mining, and potentially smelting, near a wilderness could create environmental conflicts. Of special concern would be sulfur dioxide, which not only is toxic to vegetation but is probably the main cause of acid rain, a major threat to the canoe country lakes today.

There are three other interesting canoe routes in the southern part of the U.S. canoe country. One is the Farm Lake access to the North Kawishiwi River, making a loop through Clear Lake. Another is at the Sawbill Landing farther east of Insula. I paddled once from Sawbill to Alton, Grace, Phoebe, and Lake Polly. I saw few canoeists, but the number of portages explained why. The third route is Brule Lake, east of Sawbill Lake. The Brule Lake country has high hills and is very attractive. My wife and I recently paddled our young daughter across Brule to the series of long lakes and the half-mile portage into Davis Lake. Here we found a secluded campsite on the northwest shore, with a sloping flat rock. On our return, we saw on a small island on Brule a concrete sculpture of a woman, an artistic intrusion in the wilderness that would best be removed.

CHAPTER SEVEN

Basswood—The Heart of the Canoe Country

IN THE CENTER of the canoe country lies a 40-mile-long lake shaped like a giant Z—Basswood Lake. Basswood is the heart of the canoe country, with countless canoeists passing over its waters to the many routes of the Quetico and to the Basswood River–Crooked Lake country to the west. It is also a destination lake for many day fishermen and for base campers who wish to explore the many bays and side lakes around Basswood. The history of Basswood dates back to the Ojibway and the voyageurs, followed by loggers and resorters, and concludes with wilderness canoeists. Basswood is probably from the Ojibway word *Bassemenani*, meaning "Dried Blueberry Lake."

Jackfish Bay on the west end was the site of a recent Indian village and cemetery. In the 1950s, I visited the Ojibway graves, which were covered with huts resembling little open-slat houses with pitched roofs. The foundations of several buildings still exist, evidence of recent Indian life. Another Indian burial ground is reported to be on a small island north of Washington Island, opposite Ottawa Island. One can still envision the voyageurs singing their chansons and dipping their flashing red paddles as they swept across the waters of Basswood on their way to and from the far Northwest. Following their July rendezvous at Grand Portage, the voyageurs returned along this canoe route through Saganaga to Knife, Basswood, and Lac La Croix. The Hudson's Bay Company and other fur companies had posts on Ottawa Island and near Bayley Bay to conduct business with the Indians, trading for the Indians' furs, wild rice, blueberries, gum, and bark for birchbark canoes.

Basswood Lake is divided between Canada and the United States, with Bayley, Merriam, North, and Ranger Bays deep on the Canadian side, and Jackfish, Pipestone, Back, Hoist, and Wind Bays on

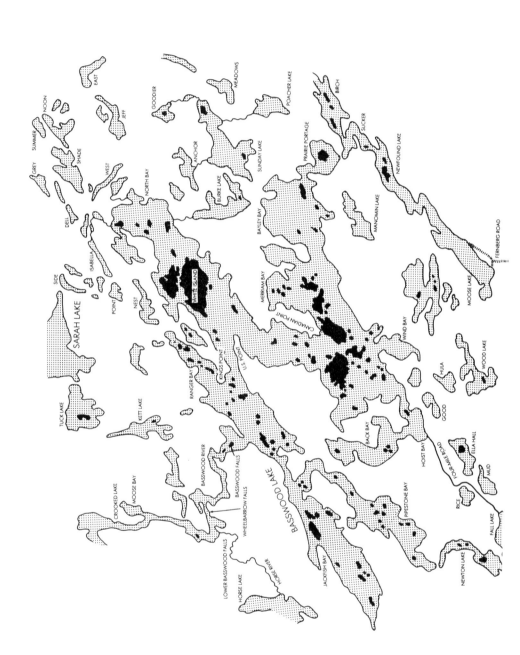

the American side. The Canadian shores still have many tall white and Norway pines; the American side has been logged, but a vigorous second-growth forest has returned. During the early years of the twentieth century, the timber barons roamed the canoe country and clear-cut the tall pines to provide lumber for a growing America. Unfortunately, the forest was never replanted. A railroad spur for hauling logs linked Basswood to Fall Lake; the spur later became known as the Four-Mile Portage, serving the resorts on Basswood.

Following the logging period and World War II came an era when many private landholdings on the lake were developed for a variety of purposes — resorts, houseboats, private cabins, and a private wilderness research center. Speedy launches steamed down Fall Lake to the Four-Mile Portage with tourists to be loaded aboard buses for the ride to Hoist Bay. A fancy gift shop to serve the tourists was built at the end of the Four-Mile. Basswood had speedboats, cruisers, and a brisk houseboat trade on waters once plied only by the voyageur's birchbark canoe. Leftover "ducks," or amphibious vehicles, became popular. Giant resorts such as Basswood Lodge had a brisk business. Resorts were built at Pipestone Falls, at several points along Pipestone Bay, at Prairie Portage Falls, and at a half-dozen other points on Basswood. After numerous battles to protect the wilderness after the air ban, the resorts were gradually purchased by the United States government under the Thye-Blatnik Act. The Forest Service has completed the task of removing resorts, lodges, and cabins. The lake has now returned to a near-pristine state with the cruisers, ducks, houseboats, and commercial enterprises gone.

One of the more popular routes to Basswood is from Fall Lake to Pipestone Bay. There is a portage along on old road from Fall Lake past an old logging dam into Newton Lake. From Newton there is a portage on the east shore past Pipestone Falls. Both Pipestone and Jackfish Bays are noted for their walleye, northern pike, lake trout, and smallmouth bass fishing. Portages lead from Pipestone directly into Back and Jackfish Bays, eliminating a long paddle.

The east end of Basswood, with its Canadian customs and ranger stations, is the leading entry point to Basswood, aptly named Inlet Bay. Next comes Basswood's vast expanse of Bayley Bay, the most treacherous on the lake because of its long westerly exposure. Two popular portages from Bayley Bay lead to Sunday and Burke Lakes to the north. These two lakes are joined by Singing Brook, a short waterway with a beautiful campsite on the north side. Unfortunately, this campsite is also popular for bears; one guide, Gus Walske, even reported seeing a grizzly bear there—probably a figment of his excited imagination, as it tore his camp up while he sat helplessly by in his canoe. The north portage from Bayley Bay to Sunday ends near the largest white pine I've seen in the Quetico-Superior. The portage from Bayley Bay to Burke is noted for its fine sand beach.

On one trip we found a group of names and writings scratched into the lichen on a cliff just around the corner from Singing Brook. My partner and I spent a full afternoon scraping all of the names off the lichen—bare rock being more in keeping with the surroundings than a busy "newspaper." Sadly, it's little crimes such as this that often result in capture, conviction, and news, whereas the destruction of the wilderness by resorts, logging, and other massive developments that scar forever proceeds unimpeded.

Sunday Lake has many excellent campsites for a base camp from which one can explore many interesting side routes. To the north there is a portage to Anchor Lake, the trail going via a beaver pond. The largemouth bass fishing makes the effort to get there worthwhile. On the south shore of Anchor, named because of its shape, there is an excellent campsite. To the northeast of Sunday are three short portages into Goodier Lake, a small, pretty lake where my mother caught her first lake trout. South of Sunday is Poacher Lake, reached by two portages along a small river. There is also a trail to Poacher from Inlet Bay of Basswood, but it is over a mile and seldom used except in winter by poachers, from which the lake supposedly got its name. Poacher has clear, cold water, with excellent trout fishing.

North of Burke Lake are two short portages leading into the North Bay of Basswood. The Burke Lake route to North Bay is a shortcut, saving hours of paddling around Canadian Point. Just west of Bayley Bay is Merriam Bay, which is sheltered and secluded. A heron rookery is on the north end of one of the islands. A second Canadian customs and ranger station has been located for many years on Ottawa Island just out of Merriam Bay, and another ranger cabin was located on King's Point near Ranger Bay. Wind Bay on the American side is known for its giant northerns, and Back Bay for its smallmouth bass and wild rice beds.

North Bay of Basswood is almost a landlocked lake in itself. There are many excellent campsites here, my favorite being on Cigar Island and near the entering streams on the extreme north and east ends. There are numerous reefs, rocks, and small islands in North Bay, all good spots for walleyes. To the north is secluded Hidden Bay, with several channels that are also excellent walleye holes.

There are a number of routes for side trips from North Bay. One of my favorites, to Sultry Lake, follows a stream to South Lake, then over a short portage to West Lake. Many beaver houses, covered with peeled saplings, lie along this route. One evening, while I cast for bass in the twilight shadows, I noticed a fat beaver emerge and wallow up onto the top of its house, unaware of my presence. Its tiny forepaws carried a load of mud, which it quietly patted into place. Then the beaver slipped into the water and propelled itself silently past us by its webbed rear feet.

From West Lake, one portages into a pond a short paddle from Shade Lake. Shade Lake has good lake trout fishing and clear Indian paintings on a cliff on the northeast corner of the lake. Beyond Shade is Noon Lake, noted for its largemouth bass. There are several campsites along its north shore. Across from Noon is a poorly marked trail leading to a small, narrow lake inhabited by a ferocious, fighting breed of bass that dances across the waters. I've hiked into a round-shaped lake south of there, but never caught any fish. Onward from Noon are Summer and Sultry Lakes. Sultry has excellent walleye fishing, and I once caught and released twenty-five!

From the north end of North Bay, a popular canoe route leads to Sarah Lake, and there is an interesting side trip to Grey Lake en route. A good stream with several beaver dams leads to Lily Pad Lake, where the stream continues on to Isabella. The route to Grey diverges just before one swings west to Isabella on this stream. There are two portages into Dell, then another into a long, deep lake, followed by two more via a beaver pond into Grey. Grey Lake has high cliffs along the western shore and is home to the native largemouth bass.

To the west are several more interesting side trips from Basswood. One can go to Nest Lake, where I caught several lake trout, or to a small lake in the center of Kings Point, where there are perch and northerns. An island in the center of this lake has been completely burned. A rock fireplace marks an old campsite, suggesting careless campers as the cause of the fire. From the end of Ranger Bay, there is a route via an unnamed lake to another famed largemouth bass lake, McNaught Lake. Once, while fishing there, I saw several canoes coming south on a river from Tuck Lake, a very tough route, with many portages, beaver dams, and meandering streams, although it looks easy on the map.

The international border follows the center of Basswood River, the outlet from Basswood Lake. Basswood River, with spectacular waterfalls and roaring rapids along a five-mile course, empties into Crooked Lake. There are five portages along the route. Basswood fishermen often frequent the area above Basswood Falls, fishing for walleyes. The Horse Portage is a mile-long trail on the left of Basswood Falls, bypassing several rapids as well as the falls. The loud roar of the 10-foot falls can be heard for miles. One can shorten the long Horse Portage by portaging around the falls, entering the water below, shooting a small rapids to a quiet bay, and following the Horse Portage the rest of the way. Horse Portage passes through high rock ledges, with a lot of ferns and thick patches of blueberries alongside the trail. A short paddle from Horse Portage, there is another small rapids with a good portage on the southern shore. This unnamed rapids is tempting to shoot, but the full force of the river passes down a narrow channel, creating high rooster tails of white water at the base. The rapids also tempted the voyageurs of yesteryear, who considered the gamble, pointed their canoes into the current, and often met with misfortune. The National Geographic Society sponsored a scuba expedition to this river and recovered numerous eighteenth-century artifacts below this rapids.

A mile farther downstream is Wheelbarrow Falls, which is really two sets of rapids, both of which are too dangerous and rocky to shoot. Even though the rapids are full of pitfalls, attempts have been made. One of my trips to Wheelbarrow Falls was strictly to portage a block and tackle to retrieve what remained of an aluminum canoe wrapped around a rock. The best portage is along the north shore on the Canadian side.

The prettiest falls along the Basswood River are reserved for the last — Lower Basswood Falls — almost twice as high as Basswood Falls and separated in the center by a small island. The portage is along the north shore and ends along a rock ledge. A small cabin hidden on the American side was built by the U.S. Forest Service for overnight use before the advent of the seaplane. Lower Basswood Falls is the end of the historic Basswood River and the beginning of the long, narrow, twisting Crooked Lake.

CHAPTER EIGHT

McIntyre Lake Country

BEYOND BASSWOOD LAKE's North Bay stretches a series of small lakes leading to two intricate canoe areas. One is the Kahshahpiwi route, and the other is highlighted by McIntyre and Brent Lakes. To enter this area, one must venture to the north end of North Bay and paddle up a small stream to Lily Pad Lake, pulling over a half-dozen beaver dams en route. Lily Pad Lake has many pond lilies and water lilies, often in full bloom following the sunrise. The route to Isabella Lake bisects beyond Lily Pad. One route, via an unnamed lake, requires two portages; the other, up a river that is navigable only in the spring and early summer, has one rocky, muddy portage. Isabella has several campsites suitable for itinerant canoeists. From Isabella there are two routes to Side Lake, both via two unnamed lakes. There are two campsites on the small lake on the northern route, and there are many bluegills and a few small lake trout in this lake.

Side Lake, another lake-trout lake, has two campsites on the western shore that are popular respites. I stopped at one of these camps one night but had little sleep. In the tent, I had just finished writing the day's log in my journal when I heard suspicious noises about camp. I listened intently. I had turned the canoe upside down over the food packs and placed pots, pans, and other paraphernalia on top to awaken me if a black bear were to visit. When I heard a scraping on the ground, I realized a packsack was being dragged from under the canoe. Instantly, I yelled, "Bear!" I heard several pots crash and rapid movement in the bushes. I put on my pants, grabbed my flashlight, and searched about, still yelling "Bear." One packsack had been pulled out silently, without tripping my alarm system of pans atop the canoe, and dragged about 20 feet from the canoe. This was an accomplished burglar! There were five or six loaves of bread scattered about the ground, but my yelling scared the bear away and nothing was lost. Wisely, I never close the straps on the packsacks at night, because a bear will tear the pack apart to get at the contents, or drag the full pack out of sight.

There are two short portages downhill through a beaver pond to Sarah Lake. Sarah is noted for its beautiful sand beaches and has a log ranger cabin on one of its islands. At the end of a long bay on the eastern shore is a small, unnamed lake with largemouth bass. Usually, I just passed through Sarah enroute to McIntyre Lake. The portage to McIntyre, known as the wall portage or goat portage, is short but practically straight up. There are large rocks as steps, but balancing a pack and canoe up this face is not a joy.

McIntyre is one of my favorite lakes because of excellent fishing and campsites. One especially good site, on a northern island among the Norway pines, provides a spectacular view to the south. My favorite is a well-hidden spot on a small point that has many comforts, including a log table, a fireplace, and a sloping flat rock for pulling up the canoe.

Near this campsite is a narrow bay that for some reason contains schools of young walleyes. I've named it "Grocery Store Bay," since it always provides us with walleyes for dinner. Toward the north end of the lake is a deep channel, a hole between the first two islands, that is excellent for large walleyes. I've named these narrows "Super Market Narrows," since usually 8- to 10-pound walleyes are caught there. Toward the west side of McIntyre is another deep bay that is excellent for largemouth bass. To complete the fisherman's paradise, McIntyre is also an excellent lake-trout lake. The trout are more difficult to find, living deep in the middle of the lake close to the west shore. Jeep Latourelle was the guide who first introduced me to the fishing secrets of McIntyre. He would maneuver the canoe perfectly over the lake-trout reef far below us. I would troll with practically all of my line out with my favorite spoon, the Jarvinen. This Finnish spoon is three inches long and seldom misses a trout on each pass. Fishing for lake trout in deep holes reminds me of snagging a large log, because they are so deep during midsummer that they are almost lifeless by the time they are pulled up to the surface. Reeling in several hundred feet of line with 20 pounds of trout is exhausting for me, too.

While in high school, I visited McIntyre with a schoolmate. We camped at the site near Grocery Store Bay, since the campsite on the large island was taken by a large group of attractive Girl Scouts. We sat around our campfire and plotted devious tricks as nightfall descended. When it was completely black and the loons had retired, we quietly paddled over to the back side of the girls' island, docked the canoe, and readied it for a speedy escape. We walked through the dark forest to their tents and quietly crawled the last few feet. We heard their evening conversations as we slithered forward and quickly cut their tentropes. Frantic screaming pierced the night as we turned and ran, and total confusion prevailed as the startled girls tried to make their way out of the collapsed tents.

Several lakes near McIntyre are worthy of exploration. Near the northeast end is a short portage into Paulette Lake. Paulette has dark waters with many lily pads, a perfect home for largemouth bass. Deer Lake to the south is a lift-over to more excellent walleye fishing. To the north over two short portages is walleye- and trout-laden Brent Lake, which is long, narrow, and twisting. Immediately along the left shore is a rocky ledge that is another of my favorite campsites. There is a deep lake-trout hole in the middle of the widest part of the lake, but the trout are not the size of McIntyre's. At the far west end of Brent are two small islands that mark excellent walleye holes. One is near the Darky River, and it seems that every time one paddles around it, a walleye strikes. The other island is opposite this one, toward the eastern shore a mile or so away. There are two small largemouth bass lakes near the portage into Conmee. The northern one is larger and has better fishing, but the northerns seem to be crowding out the bass. The southern lake supports fewer bass, but they run larger in size.

On one journey to Brent, I decided to visit William Lake to the northwest. The portage was very difficult to find because few people had ever visited it. When I discovered the path, it resembled a faint game trail. William is surrounded by a scrawny jack pine forest, with many dead trees along its shore. I trolled my trusty Daredevil along the shoreline with two other fishermen, rounded the first point, and had an immediate strike. At the same time, one of my partners caught a 2-pound walleye and a 10-pound northern on his one flatfish lure! We caught and released several dozen fish by lunch and stopped at the one campsite with a huge fireplace for a fish fry. After lunch we paddled to the northern shore to try that side of the lake. My partner's flatfish was immediately struck by a king-sized fighter. When the fish came near, it seemed like the whole bottom of the lake was coming up. It was a gigantic northern pike! It darted in a straight line under the canoe and out into deeper water — the tug of war continued for 45 minutes. I was certain that the fish would not fit into the canoe, so we landed on shore to continue the battle. Here I might be able to pull the fish up on the beach. I thought for sure that the monster had to weigh 40 to 50 pounds. He had a dark green top, yellow-green sides, and two lures in his mouth. One was a red-eyed spoon from a previous struggle, and the other was our favorite orange flatfish. The fish's eyes glowered with anger as I waded into the water and prepared for a fight. Suddenly he was close, and I grabbed him by the gills. A mighty lurch lifted him out of the water and out of my grasp. He came down with a huge splash; I grabbed my paddle to stun him by clobbering his head, but splintered the paddle into three pieces. The giant darted for the deep, breaking the 30-pound test line as it dashed away. We were all heartbroken that it got away, but also somewhat relieved, since the giant really belonged to the wilds of William Lake.

Another time I headed north from Brent through a small lake to Conmee. Conmee had been badly burned, with much of the lake showing fire scars and new growth. Along the islands there once had been a favorite campsite, but it had been vandalized, with the table destroyed, fireplace dismantled, and several of the large trees cut down, crisscrossing the site. This is an unusual occurrence in the canoe country.

Conmee is another walleye and northern lake, with one of the best holes I know, at the mouth of the river coming in from the high country around Delahey. From Conmee there are two routes to Suzanette Lake, another walleye lake. There are two portages from Suzanette through a small lake and bypassing a small rapids into Burt Lake.

Burt Lake is another one of the jewels in the vast McIntyre country. Several large islands with climax stands of white pine are scattered around the lake. The islands have a towering canopy of white and red pine, with a few white spruce, balsam fir, and birch forming an understory, and an occasional cedar hugging the shoreline. There are several ideal campsites, strategically located to capture beautiful sunsets and the northern lights. Near the north end of one of the smaller islands we discovered a walleye hole that kept our frying pan full with fresh walleye fillets.

Just east of Burt is one of the two or three lakes in the Quetico-Superior that have become well known for no other reason than a required degree of madness being necessary to want to go there. I was determined to make my way to this one, Gamble Mater, a lake isolated enough to be in the middle of nowhere. On one trip I found a blazed trail going east from Burt, so I portaged a canoe about a third of a mile into a small, unnamed, muddy lake. From there, I found no blazes, trails, fireplaces, or other markings of humans. I bushwhacked for more than an hour through the virgin forest and eventually, exhausted, peered through the forest at Gamble Mater. I hiked down the shoreline and marveled at the fact that few if any people had ever portaged to this remote spot. I returned to camp tired, but joyful to have made it to one of the most remote lakes in the Quetico-Superior.

A short portage from the south of Burt leads to Marj Lake, another clear water lake holding lake trout. Marj is also a short side trip from Kahshahpiwi, except that the portage from Kahshahpiwi goes uphill, then passes through wet swamps and muskeg. There are three more portages via Joyce on into Marj. Marj Lake was a breath of fresh air after all those portages, and my first journey there was rewarded with several beautiful trout.

Another route to the McIntyre Lake country is via the Basswood River to Robinson Lake, which is connected to McIntyre by three smaller lakes. A mile below Lower Basswood Falls is a high overhanging cliff with excellent Indian pictographs. This rock cliff has historical significance; the early voyageurs remarked about it. David Thompson, in the 1700s, told how the rock was named "Arrows Stick in the Rock." A Sioux war party was searching for their enemies, the Ojibway, who had eluded them. When they reached this place, they expressed their anger by shooting their arrows into a crack in the rock. Reddish Indian pictographs of a pelican, a canoe, and several animals are painted on the smooth rock below the overhangs.

Beyond the Indian pictographs is shallow Moose Bay of Crooked Lake, with its reeds and sandy bottom. Deer and moose often frequent the shores of Moose Bay, and I once counted a group of five deer around one island. A log sluiceway is at the end of the bay, and a portage on the right of it brings one into the Tuck River, where paddling upstream takes one the remainder of the way into Robinson Lake. Bass are often seen in Tuck's clear waters.

Loggers cut over Crooked and Robinson Lakes after the turn of the century, as the unnatural sluiceway unfortunately reminded us. However, a vigorous second growth surrounds these lakes, hiding the effects of logging.

Robinson is a long, curved lake that is a favorite base camp spot. I found a nice campsite about a fifth of a mile from an old log ranger cabin that still stands on the western shore. The lake has several sand beaches, which is remarkable since they are so uncommon in the rocky Laurentian Shield lake country. I spotted an Arctic three-toed woodpecker and a downy woodpecker near our campsite. Fishing has never been overwhelming in Robinson, but there are scrappy bass and trout, and a few walleye holes.

I base-camped at one time on Robinson with a family that included several young children. I took two of the youngsters with me, placing them in the bow while we explored for walleye and trout holes. As we paddled down the blue-tinted waters, we saw a large moving black object ahead of us — a large black bear swimming across the lake. He panicked on seeing our canoe, and swam at a frenetic pace for shore. We followed behind him at a safe distance and were most excited when he emerged, shook, and scrambled up a hill without ever looking back.

From Robinson, another of my favorite sidetrips is north to Ted Lake. The route leads up a small river, over three beaver dams, and to a portage about 35 rods long on the left. Next it crosses a pond, which is really a swamp flooded by an ambitious beaver family. The next portage is enough to challenge an expert, with much mud and large windfalls to crawl over. Another unnamed lake and a 40-rod portage end at Ted. Leaving the lake on my first journey to this lake, I watched several brown wrens near a small stream. They were such small, delicate birds.

Ted Lake is another jewel in the canoe country. To the right is a high cliff offering spectacular views of the lake, expressing its sheer solitude. Along the west shore are a dozen or so rock-ribbed islands lush with blueberry bushes. On my first journey I found no camp-sites, and before setting up a rudimentary camp on a flat ledge, I trolled with nightcrawlers among the islands, catching several walleyes.

Author portaging with canoe and pack.

I longed to return to Ted Lake, and several years later, in 1964, an opportunity arose. I guided twenty-two Explorer Scouts from Phoenix, Arizona, whose goal was to build a base camp spot on the eastern shore. I remembered a small rocky point near a bay that had looked ideal on my initial trip. Guiding twenty-two scouts was an exercise in organization, but their leader woke them at the crack of dawn with his "Daylight in the swamps!"

On our first morning at Ted, we felled a huge dead Norway pine to build a table. I cleared an area near our fireplace, cut the pine into sections, and drifted them to our developing campsite. Two 7-foot sections formed a table base; next came two 15-foot lengths for seats, two more 7-foot sections for the upper base, and finally fifteen lengths of smaller jack pine poles for a tabletop. Surprisingly, it ended up practically level. Everyone was proud of the work of craftsmanship. We then explored the lake — I found two Indian paintings on the cliff at the south end. The scouts caught no end of fish, including a 16-pound northern.

We side-tripped east to the lake next door, which is long and narrow, resembling a fishhook. Fishhook Lake just happened to be full of lake trout ranging from 2 to 8 pounds, and we had a grand time catching and releasing them. We took another side trip westward to

Milt Lake and portaged into the north end of Big Newt Lake. This was a dark-water lake, so largemouth bass should be there. We tried casting, and sure enough, the first cast caught a 2- to 3-pounder that leaped out of the water and spat the lure high into the air. We caught several more king-sized bass, including one giant that weighed 6 pounds. I hiked into Little Newt Lake alone and caught a bass from the shoreline. We were finally exhausted so portaged back into Milt and drifted across the lake toward Ted, trolling deeply for trout. My bowman laid into a fighting 4-pounder that added a pleasant climax to a very enjoyable side trip.

Another route to Ted Lake enters from the northwest from Hurn Lake, which is a deep, clear, tantalizing blue. All of these lakes seem to be loaded with trout — except Ted, where I've surprisingly never caught any. From Hurn there is a rocky portage into Elk. North from Elk Lake is a route to Cone and a long, hilly portage from Cone to the west end of Brent. There is an old trapper's cabin on the north shore of Cone. One evening I fished for trout there and lost several, including one that followed my lure to the canoe and jumped out of the water in the evening dusk. Three more short portages lead from Elk into Gardner Bay of Crooked Lake. I usually take a short-cut portage from Gardner Bay's south end back into Crooked, eliminating a long paddle. From this point, it is only a short distance to Bart Lake and two portages to Robinson.

Fifteen years later, I took my wife to Ted Lake to see if the campsite was still there. It was untouched, neat and clean. I climbed the cliff at the south end to view the beauty of the wilderness. We then portaged into Fishhook Lake, observed a family of loons, and caught a fat trout. We left via Milt and Hurn in beautiful sunlight and calm of the day, happy to have seen Ted again.

CHAPTER NINE

Agnes, Kahshahpiwi, That Man, This Man, No Man, and Other Man Lakes

AGNES LAKE IS the central Quetico's dominant lake, 20 miles long and narrow, with high pine-clad hills lining the shore. Agnes often offers the epitome of the Canadian sunset, with ebony black horizons silhouetted against a stark, glowing sky. I once paddled Agnes in a full moon, with loon echoes rebounding back and forth across the hillsides. The moonlight glistened across the water, and in the distance I could see several loons flapping their wings and chasing one another. They would practically stand atop the water while they pranced about and bellowed out their yodel. I wondered what ritual they were practicing — or were they merely exulting in the pure joy of the wilderness?

The southern half of Agnes is surrounded by high rocky ridges. These hills dwarf a canoe as it slowly meanders northward. The views of the lake from atop the ridges are my favorite. About two-thirds of the way up the lake to the north are a pair of islands with a high cliff and a few Indian pictographs. One of the islands is rumored to have the remnants of an Indian birch-bark canoe.

There are several routes to Agnes, the most popular being via Sunday Lake. There are two long portages from Sunday to Meadows Lake and Agnes. The first is about two-thirds of a mile and, depending on one's load, may require several rests. I usually would carry a double load about 200 yards, then go back for the next load, so that I'd reach Meadows in about five stages rather than one. The next portage is a half mile, but it is downhill into Agnes. It is always a relief to flip off the canoe and pack, to relish the cold water of Agnes after these two portages.

Louisa Falls is just a short paddle away. The falls crash 60 feet into a pool that makes a natural bathtub, then career another 60 feet to

Agnes. There is a sand beach for swimming at the base of the falls, and several good campsites nearby.

Another route to Agnes is via North Bay to South and West Lakes, over two portages to Jeff Lake, and over another to East Lake. Both East and Jeff Lakes have trout, but East is prettier and has only a lift-over to Agnes.

Halfway down Agnes there is a side route to Silence Lake, which is another of my favorite lakes. There is a beautiful campsite on Silence on a long point facing the lake proper, about a third of the way down the lake. There are two rocky reefs in the main part of the lake, and both are feeding grounds for walleyes. After setting up camp and cooking dinner, I've often paddled out to the rocks to lure a few walleyes up from the depths. To the north of Silence are several canoe routes, but they are difficult because the lakes are small and portages long. After the third pond north of Silence, the routes diverge, with the main one leading to Trant Lake and Kahshahpiwi to the west. The route to Woodside has at least six small intervening lakes, each pair connected by a rough, rocky, muddy, and usually obscure portage trail. The last two portages into Woodside have no trails at all, so it is necessary to barge through the woods. Woodside is a lovely lake with a rocky shoreline, clear water, and hungry walleyes. I caught three in a few minutes, released them, and headed on to Reid Lake and down a rocky half-mile trail back into Agnes.

After the third lake and a pond north of Silence on this latter route is a small waterfall along a stream coming from a distant lake. The map labeled the lake above the falls Ptolemy, but I renamed it God-forsaken. I once hiked up over the waterfall to a dried-up beaver pond and jumped from rock to rock around the mud; I then skirted two more beaver ponds, pushed through a thicket of brush and cedars, and emerged at the shore of Ptolemy. I wondered if anyone had ever been there before. The sun was shimmering across the waves. I cast several times, but no fish seemed interested.

Two more portages beyond the Ptolemy cutoff lead to Trant Lake; Trant, Hurlburt, and Williams Lakes form a direct canoe route from Kahshahpiwi to Agnes. Trant is a small lake with excellent large-mouth bass fishing. There are several Indian pictographs, including a fine one of a moose, on a cliff near the south end of the lake. Williams was also visited by the artistic American natives, and more Indian pictographs can be found there. A couple of portages down the

Hurlburt Creek lead one to Keewatin Lake, between Agnes and Kawnipi, which also has Indian paintings.

Kahshahpiwi is another long narrow lake, perhaps the result of an earthquake or a deep glacier gouge, since the cleft forms a series of lakes heading in a perfectly straight line to the northeast. It lies between the Agnes and McIntyre country. Two portages from Side Lake lead north to Kahshahpiwi, passing the Sarah and McIntyre cutoff. Another route from North Bay of Basswood and Isabella leads through Grey and Yum Yum Lakes. This is the route of the famous Yum Yum portage, which is longer, hillier, muddier, rockier, and seemingly more infested with mosquitoes than any other. After one journey, canoeists are known to avoid this route like the plague.

Kahshahpiwi is a beautiful lake ringed by high hills. The Ontario Department of Lands and Forests built a fire lookout tower on the southern end in the mid-1960s. Kahshahpiwi is the beginning of a route that veers northeast in a straight line through Keefer, Sark, and Cairn Lakes. All of these are beautiful lakes without many visitors. My favorite is Cairn; from Sark there is a series of lakes via Cutty, Metacryst, and Heronshaw back to Cairn. I've canoed from Metacryst into Baird, Keats, and then Kawnipi. A more exciting route is to follow this series of lakes deep into the center of the Quetico to Veron and Delahey.

Veron and Delahey have always intrigued me, since they are large lakes but are at the very end of a canoe route and very difficult to get to. One early morning, I left from my campsite on Keats back up the hill to Baird and paddled through a pleasant route to Cub, Eag, and Camel, lined with tall pines and excellent campsites. The river to Veron was navigable but had almost ten portages. Veron had an even-growth stand of jack pine and aspens, and I could hardly wait to try the fishing. As soon as my line was out, I had a strike by a large fish, but it got away. We canoed on into Delahey, took a quick look, and then headed back to Keats all in the same day. We took thirty-four portages, which when added to all that paddling made for a very long but exciting day.

East of Agnes and starting at Louisa Falls is a parallel canoe route to Kawnipi, highlighted by Louisa and McEwen Lakes. Louisa has clear water, lake trout, and a feminine ambience. Not only does the lake have a lady's name, but tall trees, rocky shore, and shimmering waters add a graceful friendliness to its lure. One of the smaller islands has a lovely campsite with a log table built decades ago with huge Norway pine logs. I've tried the small lake to the north for trout twice but have been skunked both times. A decade ago I took the route to McEwen, and the portages were barely extant at the time. My journal notes that we spent three or four hours lost, arriving at McEwen after dark. There were three portages into Fauquier, which was followed by Dumas, Rod, Edge, and Turn Lakes. As I recollect, we wound up in a lake northeast of Turn, thinking we were already in McEwen. We compounded that mistake by going the wrong way back to and down Glacier Lake. It was an interesting paddle anyway. We paddled in the dim evening light, hitting the rising ciscos with our paddles. We finally got into the McEwen River leaving Glacier and speedily traveled in the right direction. We rounded a bend in the river in the dim light and practically piled into what appeared to be a tree with several branches. Suddenly a giant bull moose emerged from the water, not ten feet from us and not very happy about our intrusion. With bulging eyes and a loud bellow, it quickly moved off into the muskeg and tamarack cover along the river. Exhausted, but relieved to reach McEwen, we pitched camp in the dark and savored some quickly prepared macaroni and cheese before crawling into our sleeping bags for the night.

Between the Louisa-McEwen route and the Knife-Cypress border lakes is another popular canoe route referred to as the Man Chain. There are four lakes lying along a northeastern line — That Man, No Man, This Man, and Other Man. That Man and This Man are known for their trout fishing, while Other Man is a walleye lake. The route goes through Carp Lake, which is poorly named — it has clear water and good fishing, but no carp. Over a hill into Sheridan Lake, a half-mile portage takes one to That Man Lake. The river into No Man is passable, and there is a well-marked portage into This Man.

There are several private mineral holdings on the Man Chain, and evidence of a prospecting expedition of the 1950s can be found. An old cabin once existed on This Man, but is now burned down; and there is evidence of some logging on That Man. This Man has excellent trout fishing along the north shore, deep off several reefs, and in Cheatan Bay.

Exploring new and hidden lakes off the beaten path was always especially exciting for me. I once whetted my curiosity by bushwhacking into the strangely shaped lake south of Cheatan called whacking into the strangely shaped lake south of Cheatan called Ferol Lake. This small lake churned with lake trout, but they were all small, between 1 and 2 pounds. I next satiated my curiosity by exploring northward to Bock Lake, near This Man. I crashed through the woods to a small, shallow, unnamed lake, crossed to the other shore, hiked up a high rocky ridge, and spotted Bock Lake through the trees. I carried the canoe up the ledge, but the far side was too steep to carry it down, so I lowered it gently down onto a moss runway and pushed and pulled it safely along. I blazed a trail through a cedar swamp and returned to carry the canoe. Bock Lake was small, but I thought it should have trout. We tried our luck and found ourselves in another trout frenzy. They were all small but fighters. There were three of us in the canoe, and one time we all caught a fighting lake trout at the same time. The fun was dispelled when we had to return over the rugged portage marked only by broken branches.

Several more unnamed lakes to the northwest of This Man looked wild and interesting on the map. We named the largest lake Rom Lake and sent the name to several map companies. Their next issues all carried the names, and I began to wonder how all of the lakes had actually been named. Perhaps they were named at a map company's Christmas party?

Those lakes to the northwest beckoned. What did they look like? Were there any portages or campsites there? What kinds of fish were in the lakes? I ventured northward from This Man along a stream to a narrow lake we named Rog Lake after my youngest brother. From there, I explored westward to find Rom Lake. It took at least two hikes, but on the second I spotted the lake. I blazed a trail and portaged in the canoe. It was a pretty lake with white pines and clear water, but it seemed a bit shallow. We tried fishing and caught nothing.

From This Man there is a short portage into Other Man, where there are many good campsites. I guided ten Boy Scouts there once, and on our first evening we caught two dozen walleyes in the deep channels among the lake's many islands. A series of lakes and easy portages goes from Other Man through Bit, Bell, and Fran Lakes on to Slate Lake. We camped on the portage between Slate and Saganagons Lakes and listened to the distant roar of Silver Falls emptying Saganaga into Saganagons. Beyond Slate Lake is a lake called Blackstone, named after Chief Blackstone, a famous Ojibway of the Kawnipi region. There were no marked canoe routes or portages to this lake, but it reportedly had good lake-trout fishing.

One early morning I explored with my hardy scouts to the west end of Slate, but found no evidence of a trail or portage. We paddled back to our camp, portaged into Saganagons, paddled around a corner, and decided to explore a river that came from the eastern end of Blackstone. The river was navigable for our canoes, but we had several portages along poorly blazed trails and scores of beaver dams to pull over along the way. We reached Blackstone by lunch, for a much deserved respite. We tried our luck fishing but were disappointed. We noticed on the map the possibility of a different route back to Slate Lake, so tried this more direct route through two unnamed lakes, searching for the shore along which we had searched for a trail early in the morning. There were no portages into either of these lakes, and the bushwhack was a real challenge. I blazed a trail to the top of the highest ridge, climbed a pine, and actually could see the hills along the shores of Knife miles away; but more important, I spotted the far shore and a small reflection of Slate Lake. I finished cutting and blazing the trail so that we could pull our three canoes through. We finally crashed through the forest and, spent and exhausted, reached Slate Lake. We caught our breath while drifting and paddling back, and one of the scouts still had the energy to fish, surprising us with a 5-pound northern pike.

Just south of the Man Chain lies Emerald Lake. Emerald is another deep, clear trout lake. At the far end of Emerald is a portage through a cedar swamp into Plough Lake. This cedar swamp is the home of giant cedars, frequently exceeding 25 feet in circumference. These giants are the oldest living things in the Quetico-Superior.

North of Agnes lies the huge lake known as Kawnipi. Three arms from Agnes lead to Kawnipi. The most popular east channel of the Agnes River has four portages through Bird and Anubis Lakes. The western route has only three portages via Keewatin Lake. The middle route, the western channel of the Agnes River, has four rough portages to Murdock Lake.

Across Murdock Lake is a small channel with a swift current, pouring into Kawnipi. Years ago, Gus Walske introduced me to a campsite at this spot. He loved the flat rocks there, but refused to build a log table or add amenities that might attract others. He assembled a fireplace and used nearby rocks to store his cooking uten-sils. The fishing in the currents around the campsite was superb. One evening while I was cooking and stirring a stew, I cast my lure into the swift current, hooking a walleye and reeling it in without missing a stir.

CHAPTER TEN
Kahnipiminanikok

AT THE END of the long journey down Agnes and the Agnes River lies the broad expanse of Kawnipi Lake—known as Kahnipiminanikok to the Ojibway. Kawnipi was inhabited not too long ago by the native Americans. Evidence of their camps can still be found on such locations as the east end of Kawa Bay. During a lunch break many years ago, I noticed something vaguely out of place leaning against a tree behind me. I walked across the rocky spit for a closer inspection. There was a handmade toboggan against the tree. It was only about five feet long, made of spruce saplings smooth on the bottom and bent upward at the end. The toboggan, which probably was used for winter hauling across the ice, reminded me of the Ojibway who were part of Kawnipi in years past. The remnants of Chief Blackstone's cabin still stand at the mouth of the Wawiag River in Kawa Bay; highbush cranberries, which were part of the Indian existence, are there too.

Kawnipi is a series of deep bays beginning below Kennebas Falls on the east, expanding into Kawa Bay (which receives the Wawiag River), indenting southward to McVicar Bay and Agnes, then reaching toward the northeast and McKenzie Bay, and finally veering northwest over a series of waterfalls that lead to Russell Lake. Kawnipi has many well-developed camping spots with fireplaces and tent sites. Walleye and northern fishing is excellent practically everywhere. However, the water is uninvitingly dark, and the lake doesn't have the rocky cliffs of Agnes. I liked to use Kawnipi as a base camp to explore its many deep bays, adjacent lakes, and new canoe routes.

On one canoe trip to Kawnipi I camped on the north end of an island a short way past a swift current in a narrows toward the end

CACHE LAKE

LINDSAY

McKENZIE LAKE

FERGUSON LAKE

CACHE RIVER

MONTGOMERY

STURGEON LAKE

ALICE LAKE

CHATTERTON FALLS

SPLITROCK FALLS

CHATTERTON

RUSSELL LAKE

McDOUGALL

CUB

EAG

SHELLEY

SNAKE FALLS

KEATS

BAIRD

HERONSHAW

KELSO ISLAND

ROSE ISLAND

KAWNIPI

LEMAY

MACKENZIE BAY

KANA BAY

WAWIAG RIVER

MACK LAKE

CULLEN

MUNRO

OSSIAN

KENNY LAKE

KENNABAS FALLS

CANYON FALLS

KOKO

LITTLE

WET

JOUAT

SAGANAGONS LAKE

McEWEN LAKE

LAKE

McVICAR BAY

MURDOCH

ANUBIS

BIRD

EAST AGNES RIVER

WEST AGNES RIVER

AGNES LAKE

WILLIAMS

KEEWATIN

CARN LAKE

CUTTY

SARK

HURLBURT

KEEFER

WOODSIDE

TRANT

REID

of McKenzie Bay. The fishing was good and atmosphere enjoyable. One morning while I was cooking delicious blueberry flapjacks, I was concentrating on the secret of pancake cooking, a steady hot fire. Occasionally, the frying pan gets too hot and needs to be taken off the fire to cool. When I grasped the handle that morning, it was extremely hot. I quickly dropped the pan onto a pointed rock, flipping the scalding grease into my face, causing a second-degree burn on my chin. My beard seemed to protect my skin, but I was in misery all morning.

Beyond McKenzie Bay to the northeast lies McKenzie Lake. McKenzie is another huge body of water like Kawnipi and is excellent for walleye and northern pike fishing. About a third of the way down the lake are more Indian paintings, including excellent ones of two canoes. The large island to the east has the remains of an old ranger cabin. To the north about a mile from Lindsay Lake is another single white clapboard cabin, home for the fire lookout attendant for the tower about a mile back into the forest. I stopped there one day and hiked into the woods to visit the attendant. I jogged over the rocks and along the trail, and after about fifteen minutes came upon the tower with its octagon-shaped hut on top. I climbed the ladder and knocked on the small trap door at its end. A surprised and shocked lookout tower man let me in. He hadn't seen a human being in several weeks so was loquacious, but somewhat inhibited as well. He chatted about his work, how he plotted fires, and what radio stations were best at night. It was a pleasure to meet a woodsman to whom McKenzie was home.

Beyond the white cabin is a small bay with a lift-over into Lindsay Lake. Lindsay is just a small pond but is the beginning of a two-mile portage into Cache Lake. Cache Lake is about as remote as can be, for there is another two-mile portage out of the lake heading northward. Out of curiosity I hiked the portage to see what Cache had hidden away. The real spectacle, however, was the forest the trail traversed.

One of the parties that I had guided had read reports of an old timber cruiser who had explored the forest north of McKenzie. We began our two-mile hike through a garden of Indian paintbrush flowers. As we entered the woods, we were humbled. Giant aspens towered into the sky, their trunks two to three feet in diameter. Huge white and Norway pines surrounded us, growing perfectly straight as they reached upward. A few smaller balsam firs and spruces filled the understory. We found such a climax forest to inspire a special reverence in us. At last we came to the shores of Cache Lake. We caught our breath, rested, enjoyed the view, and reveled in the impressive forest we had just witnessed.

Many years later, sad news from Canada reached me. A gravel road had been cut from the northeast and a bridge had been built across the Baptism and Trousers Lakes canoe routes. The loggers had come. From Trousers the northern two-mile portage led to Cache Lake. The loggers were clearcutting an entire climax forest — the whole northeastern Quetico. They cut south to Cache and to the northern shores of McKenzie. The virgin forest was gone. In a few short months the result of eons — a virgin wilderness — had been destroyed. I couldn't comprehend why they had to log within the confines of the Quetico when ample timber was available elsewhere. I was sick. I never had the courage or forbearance to return.

West of McKenzie, a river winds through miles of muskeg without a portage to isolated Ferguson Lake. Northern fishing was excellent here, but drifting across the lake's deeper waters didn't produce a trout.

We returned from McKenzie to Kawnipi via a half-mile portage on the west end near a river connecting it to Kawnipi. The river was interesting with a pretty waterfall, but had more portages requiring considerably more time. The portage ends on the Kawnipi side on a wide sand beach.

I have explored three interesting lakes north of Kawnipi. One, Lemay Lake, is at the end of Lemay Creek. The lake's shape is similar to a horseshoe. Fishing for walleyes and northerns was excellent. Another is Montgomery Lake, a short portage off Kawnipi, which is another good walleye lake. Old guide and mentor Gus Walske always talked about a superb bass lake along these western reaches of Kawnipi but never dropped any hints as to which lake it was. I found one lake on the map, west of Kawnipi, that was narrow and a mile long that could have been it.

I tried hiking in to this lake, but after several beaver ponds, I decided that it was too far and not worth the bushwhack with a heavy canoe. Thus, Gus Walske's bass hole in the haunts of Kawnipi remains undiscovered.

Northeast of Kawnipi is another famous lake, called Mack Lake.

More tall tales have been spun about fishing in this lake than any other. Walleyes are supposed to be over 10 pounds and are to be caught by the bushel, and northerns just don't come under 30 pounds. Mack had to be my destination. I talked two friends into making the trip, and we decided to experiment by trying to navigate the stream from Kenny Lake. This route traverses many cross-country miles to distant Munro Lake, one portage south of Mack. My notes from June 18, 1960, tell the story: "Pretty bad day. Wind from the south. Never take creek out of Kenny Lake again. It was the roughest ever. Two long, three-fourths mile portages and around six or seven shorter ones that were just blazed trails. For 400 yards in a hailstorm we pulled up rapids, over beaver dams, logs, etc. Rough as dickens. The rest of the creek was quite easy going except for logs. Saw lots of ducks and beaver. Arrived at Mack at 9 P.M. in driving rain." A rainbow appeared in the declining daylight as we finally skimmed our canoe into Mack Lake. During the next three days we caught seventy-five fish, including many 10-pounders, but no real giants. We camped at a narrow isthmus on a long point jutting into the lake. A large scout troop arrived on our last evening. We permitted them to camp at our site in exchange for dinner and breakfast, thus saving ourselves some cooking. They built a long birch table that evening, proving that the scouts could produce a marvel of wilderness engineering. They even had a two-log bench to sit on instead of the usual one-log one.

Over the next few years Mack's reputation as a fishing paradise led to its eventual decline. Canoe parties chartered bush seaplanes out of Ely to fly to Clay Lake, outside of the Quetico Park and only a couple hours' paddle to Mack. The Canadians built a fly-in resort on Powell Lake just above Clay, so the traffic increased even more. Wilderness sport fishing just can't bear such pressure, and I suspect the Mack Lake I discovered in 1960 isn't the same anymore.

The canoe route from Saganagons to Kawnipi follows the beautiful Saganagons River. There are treacherous rapids and crashing waterfalls along this route. Fortunately, I saw this route before 1961, the year a forest fire turned this area into a black ruin. The charred forest accompanies the first portion of this route, and evidence of the fire can be seen as far south as the stream I had followed into Blackstone Lake. I found fire hoses left behind along the beaver dams into Blackstone.

On both sides of the border, large seaplanes are used to fight fires in the canoe country. They taxi on lakes close to the fire, suck up large volumes of water into fuselage tanks, and fly back to the fire with their water bombs. It has been determined that fire control may upset the natural cycle of the forest, since fires are part of nature's way to rejuvenate the forest. Old, dead trees are cleaned out, and the cones of jack pines are stimulated by the heat of the fire to release their seeds; they are often the first species to return after a fire. However, with increased visitation by man, many of the current fires are also caused by humans; perhaps not all of them should be allowed to burn out of control. Also, shorelines and lakes scarred by fire are not attractive to those searching for wilderness beauty. Forest researchers are now considering fire as a part of wilderness management, which adds fuel to the wisdom of leaving wilderness entirely alone.

There are three portages around rapids on the Saganagons River to an unnamed lake. I've often portaged over an island on the second rapids, but it is tricky since the rapids break on both sides at the base of the island. It's safer to take the trails on the mainland. From the unnamed lake I've taken side trips over to Wet Lake and down into Joliat and north into Ossian Lake. On the river into Ossian, I once flipped the canoe off after a portage, only to see a bull moose staring at me and a cow moose swimming to the other shore. Next down the Saganagons comes Little Falls, followed by a long portage around Koko Falls. The portage around Canyon Falls is the most spectacular of all, with beautiful cascading water funneled through a narrow sluiceway. The water is also swift and dangerous below the portage. From Kenny Lake there is a smaller waterfall, 10-foot Kennebas Falls, that leads directly into Kawnipi Lake.

This is an exciting and spectacular canoe route, but its future remains uncertain because Saganagons Lake and nearby Saganaga lie on the edge of the Quetico and a road has reached Northern Light Lake nearby. In addition, seaplanes may land at Saganaga to drop off canoe parties. Private resorts could be developed on superb canoeing lakes adjacent to the Quetico. Logging is unrestricted. Saganagons and Big Sag always seemed too distant to ever be threatened by roads, but the road breaching the wilderness at Northern Light Lake is skirting the lake, leaving the southeastern portion of the Quetico vulnerable. Expansion of the Quetico to include Saganagons and Saganaga Lakes and to protect both from roads and logging not only is desirable, but is essential, bare-bones wilderness protection.

Between Saganagons and Saganaga within Quetico is one of the more spectacular waterfalls, Silver Falls. The waters of Cache Bay and mighty Big Sag come crashing over a 20-foot drop. The water takes on a glistening sheen before breaking up into bubbles and foam. A one-third mile portage skirts the falls and rapids along the eastern shore. Until recently, the surface grave of an Indian girl who drowned in Silver Falls was on the island above the falls, but the island has been burned by careless campers, consuming the coffin as well.

To the west of Kawnipi, river country continues with rapids and waterfalls into Sturgeon Lake, which dominates the Hunter's Island canoe route on the north. There are two liftovers around rapids into Shelley Lake, followed by Have-a-Smoke Portage around Snake Falls into Keats Lake. There is an excellent campsite on a point opposite these falls. Splitrock Falls drops 11 feet into Chatterton Lake. From Chatterton, as well as from Keats, there are trails into McDougall Lake. McDougall's water is clear; although I've fished for trout, all that I've caught were northerns. Chatterton's northern end has many tall red Norway pines. From there, one can take a side trip to Alice Lake, which is also good northern fishing. I've explored the stream that is quite wide near the far end, where you can take a short portage back into Shelley Lake for a complete circle via Alice. From Chatterton, there is another large falls (Chatterton Falls, 33 feet) and rapids leading into Russell Lake. Russell has excellent fishing for walleyes and northerns and has several fine campsites.

From Russell Lake one floats down the current into Sturgeon Narrows and into the main part of Sturgeon Lake. Sturgeon is huge, with a low horizon, and is not known for great fishing. It was once part of the Kaministiquia voyageurs' canoe route to the Canadian West from Fort William–Port Arthur, also known as the Dawson Trail. Pioneers rode steamships on Sturgeon en route to settle the great Canadian West. From Sturgeon, a major river leads on to Lac La Croix—the Maligne River. There are three portages along the Maligne around rapids, followed by Flat Rapids, which can be floated, taking one into Tanner Lake.

Tanner Lake was named after a white man who was captured and

Between waterfalls on the Kawnipi River toward Saganagons Lake.

Rocky outcrop on McKenzie Lake north of Kawnipi Lake. Credit: Roger Rom

Silver Falls at Cache Bay on Saganaga Lake. Credit: Roger Rom

raised by the Indians in the canoe country in the early part of the 19th century. This lake is where John Tanner was shot and wounded by a disappointed Indian relative when he heard John Tanner was leaving his Indian wife and taking his children east to school. A route to the south from Tanner can be taken to the Darky River, but it passes over a long, muddy portage. Another canoe route is up the Pooh Bah Creek to Pooh Bah Lake. I curiously paddled upstream to see what Pooh Bah Lake looked like. The creek was once a logging route, and three rotting log sluiceways must be crossed along the way. The river was low and muddy because the water had receded to its natural level after the dams had failed. There are two long portages and a two-mile paddle before one can see the main body of Pooh Bah. Since the loggers had been there, the lake was shorn of timber, but isolation and quietude still prevailed. The route continues from Pooh Bah south to Conmee Lake with three very long portages. Just the thought of that route made me shudder, so I returned to Tanner Lake and the shelter of an old ranger cabin, where I spent the night.

From Tanner down the Maligne is a short portage followed by a long paddle to Twin Falls, which leads into Lac La Croix. Just before Twin Falls is a dried-up river route south to Minn Lake. This route may have been easily traversed in the old logging days, but now it is a hellish mess of rocks and portages through a series of small ponds. Below Twin Falls one is in Lac La Croix, "Lake of the Cross."

North of Sturgeon are several interesting canoe routes. This area was heavily logged years ago, and logging relics can still be found in many places. The forest over much of this country has recovered, but some lakes, such as Quetico Lake, have only small second-growth trees.

On one journey, I paddled across Lac La Croix to the Namakan River. An Indian village stands on the northern shore (Neguaguon Lake Indian Reservation). The Indians are trappers, fishermen, and guides. Bob Handberg's Lac La Croix Resort is only a few miles to the west, just outside of the Quetico, and is a source of employment for them. Guests are flown in to his resort from Crane Lake or cross a series of lakes and truck portages to his lodge.

Once on the mighty Namakan, we portaged around Snake Falls, shot two rapids, and portaged around Ivy Falls to Three-mile Lake. Next we paddled into the Quetico River and carried over another long portage and headed upstream to Beaverhouse Lake. We pulled up the next two rapids, wading in the water up to our waists, and had three more portages into Beaverhouse.

Beaverhouse is another beauty, with high hills and clear water, but alas, small trees. An active ranger cabin was on the southeast shore, with a beautiful sand beach. Handberg and other fly-in camps enter the Quetico by airplane here to fish in Quetico and Jean Lakes. A road has recently been cut from the Atikokan to Fort Frances highway south toward Beaverhouse. Unfortunately, this will destroy another wild lake and provide easy access to a part of the Quetico that can already be reached from Nym or Pickerel Lakes. Another reason for the road may be to lead to the Indian village on Lac La Croix, which would certainly destroy the wildness of that lake, as well as the business of the two fly-in Canadian fishing camps there. The road currently leads a dozen miles southward, stopping only a quarter of a mile north of Beaverhouse.

From Beaverhouse there is a short portage around a logging chute into Quetico Lake. Quetico is huge, but the shoreline is not attractive and campsites are scarce. The route I followed led to the McAlpine Creek and a portage into Kasakokwag Lake. I paddled into another creek and a short portage around a logging sluiceway to McAlpine Lake. There were many stumps along the shoreline there. From McAlpine there was a three-fourths mile portage into Batchewaung Bay of Pickerel Lake, followed by Maria and, finally, Jesse Lakes. At Jesse I found an old logging camp, complete with saws, cabin foundations, and all types of relics. I portaged into Elizabeth, Walter, and Lonely Lakes, finally leaving the evidence of logging behind. My partners, Tom "Ropie" Mackie and John Schwegel, and I camped on a rocky point near the north end of Lonely Lake, where the walleye fishing was excellent. Enjoying the beauty of the sun-glistened ripples across the lake's expanse, we lounged around on sloping rocks interspersed with knobby jack pines growing from crevices.

From Lonely we explored two unnamed lakes to the east, but found no decent fishing holes. Draper Lake caught my fancy next, so I talked my two partners into a tough bushwhack into this lake. We followed the stream and portaged the canoe over rocks and windfalls that should never have been passable. Finally we came upon the clear water of Draper. We soon caught a 10-pound northern, but lost it right next to the canoe. John was so excited that he cast again, throwing his rod and reel right into the lake! We could see his fishing gear on the bottom through the clear water, and fortunately, with a little trolling, we were able to snag the gear. We portaged back into Walter, where we caught four fat walleyes, and then paddled back to Lonely for dinner.

From the far end of Lonely there is a mile-long portage into Yeh Lake and a short portage from there to Jean Lake. From Lonely there is also a standard route south into Sturgeon Lake. We chose the wilder passage into Jean, which is another large lake-trout lake. We were paddling over to Conk Lake when we spotted my dad's seaplane flying over. He owned unmistakable orange floats, the only ones in this area. Seaplanes may fly at any altitude over Ontario's Quetico Provincial Park but are restricted from landing in the park unless it is an emergency. He tossed out a cookie can that landed nearby. Inside was a note asking me to paddle back to Beaverhouse, where he could land. He had a couple of outdoor magazine writers with him who wanted to take a ten-day canoe trip. Advertising the family canoe trip was part of his business as a canoe outfitter. We paddled quickly to Conk Lake, portaged back into Quetico, and had a long afternoon paddle back to Beaverhouse. John and Tom, two of Ely's Finnish descendants, paddled on back through the central part of the Quetico back to Moose Lake landing.

Another route around the Quetico Lake country is further south, highlighted by Your and Badwater Lakes. I had another bright idea for a shortcut to explore this country. Late one summer, I paddled back to Lac La Croix and crossed to the northeastern shore. I entered a shallow bay with a lot a reeds and paddled up the Wildgoose Creek. There were several portages, beaver dams, and countless log obstacles through this swampy country en route to Orion Lake. Evidence of trapping was everywhere. Several beaver dams were cluttered with old traps, no fresh saplings floated in front of the beaver houses, no fresh mud was atop the houses, and many of the beaver dams were in disrepair — all evidence that the beaver had disappeared. The Wildgoose is in the Indian reservation, and the Indians did the trapping. From Orion Lake we continued on to Wildgoose Lake. This was the end of the line, and I couldn't find the portage into Your Lake. I took out my axe, blazed and cut a half-mile trail through the forest, found a nice campsite on Your Lake, and caught several walleyes for my reward. I then ventured via Fair Lake to fish Badwater Lake; then from Your, I portaged south into Snow, Little Pine, Trail, and March Lakes back to Sturgeon. I stopped in Bentpine Lake for a look around, and there was considerable logging evidence. There were several logging dams en route back to Sturgeon, and logging remnants were ubiquitous. The land fortunately was on its way back to recovery from the logging scars.

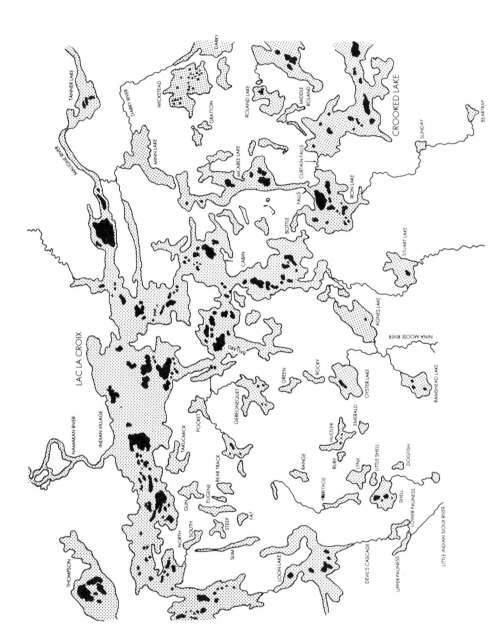

TANNER LAKE

MALIGNE RIVER

DARKY RIVER

WICKSTEAD

DARKY

GRATTON

ROLAND LAKE

MIDDLE ROLAND

CROOKED LAKE

MINN LAKE

McAREE LAKE

CURTAIN FALLS

SUNDAY

BEARTRAP

FALLS

IRON LAKE

BOTTLE

CABIN

STUART LAKE

LAC LA CROIX

BALLARD

AGNES LAKE

NINA·MOOSE RIVER

NAMAKAN RIVER

INDIAN VILLAGE

GEBEONEQUET

GREEN

ROCKY

OYSTER LAKE

RAMSHEAD LAKE

TAROMICK

POCKET

EMERALD

HUSTLER

BEAR TRACK

RANGE

RUBY

LYNX

LITTLE SHELL

DOGFISH

HERITAGE

GUN

EUGENE

NORTH

SOUTH

STEEP

FAT

SHELL

SLIM

LOON LAKE

DEVIL'S CASCADE

UPPER PAULNESS

LOWER PAULNESS

LITTLE INDIAN SIOUX RIVER

THOMPSON

CHAPTER ELEVEN
Lac La Croix

NORTHWEST OF ELY lies a large border lake, Lac La Croix. The border canoe route and Hunter's Island route converge there. Lac La Croix's entire U.S. shoreline is protected by the Boundary Waters Canoe Area Wilderness. However, only the eastern corner of the northern shore is protected in Canada's Quetico Provincial Park. On the north side is an Indian reservation with a village situated at the mouth of the Namakan River. The northwestern part of the lake is unprotected and has two fly-in resorts. Two truck portage routes lead to the resorts — one is the Dawson truck portage from Sand Point Lake, and the other follows the international boundary along the Loon River and Beatty portage from Loon Lake to Lac La Croix. There are several virgin stands of Norway and white pines along the U.S. shore. Near the eastern end, on Irving Island, is a high rock cliff that has excellent Indian pictographs. On the north end of Irving Island is a Canadian ranger cabin among beautiful pines, with a sand beach landing. Lac La Croix is a multiple-use lake, with motorboats, seaplanes, and wilderness canoeists all vying for its recreational treasures.

I once entered the Quetico via the Lac La Croix ranger cabin. I was guiding a family for about five days. We portaged via Brewer Lake to McAree Lake, another of the Quetico's beautiful lakes, with high hills, tall pines, and good but not spectacular fishing for walleyes, northern, and smallmouth bass. We camped at a narrows about two miles straight across the lake from the last portage. We built a small table on our campsite near the route to Wickstead, cutting up a dead jack pine for the base and seat logs and using birch and aspen for a log top.

The route to Wickstead is over a short portage to Pond Lake and two-thirds of a mile to an unnamed lake before Wickstead. I fished Pond Lake for trout but had no luck. Wickstead has many islands and has excellent northern fishing. I also tried Gratton Lake, a small lake just south of the unnamed lake before Wickstead. I walked through the woods to a long, flat rock. Many lily pads floated on the dark water, which appeared to be perfect habitat for largemouth bass. I pushed the canoe off and paddled out 30 to 40 yards to be able to cast toward shore. I had a strike on the very first cast! After a half dozen more, I finally completed a cast without catching a 2- to 3-pound fighter. I caught twelve bass in a matter of minutes and was very impressed. But then my rod broke and my reel became hopelessly snarled in a backlash, with loops of line everywhere. I paddled back to the rock ledge, where I straightened out my reel. By then it was so late in the day that the long portage back to McAree required me to leave my newly discovered fishing hole.

Another day, I paddled down to the southwest corner of McAree and portaged up a hill into Pulling Lake. I was anxious to explore two nearby lakes. I paddled across and pulled over a beaver dam into Dahlin Lake. I explored Dahlin but caught no bass, so I paddled back to Pulling. I caught a few bass in Pulling and continued on back to the north end of McAree. Paddling down the waters in the heat of the sun was a pleasure.

Another interesting bushwhack is through a series of lakes west of McAree. I took a 12-year-old boy over to Brewer Lake, paddled to the far end, and carried over a hill to a long, narrow, clear-water lake. We thought that it might have lake trout so tried deep trolling, but caught nothing. We then bushwhacked through the forest to an unnamed lake just off Lac La Croix. From there, we had a short portage to an L-shaped lake. There was no established route back to McAree, so we paddled to the far end and pulled over several beaver dams to a swampy pond, crossing it with hopes that we'd find a trail or draw back to McAree. But in front of us was nothing but a treeless muskeg, walled by a sheer rock cliff. It certainly looked rough. I decided to force the canoe through the muskeg, and fortunately found a break in the cliff. From the top I could see the dips in the horizon that could be distant McAree. The top of the ridge was like a thicket, with dense aspens and bushes. The trees were only two to three inches in diameter but grew so close together that I couldn't push the canoe through, so I flipped it off and dragged it through the thickts. It remained about five feet in the air and never touched ground. Finally, we reached the shore of McAree, where we took off our wool shirts to enjoy the refreshing breeze. We then paddled back to our camp, catching four walleyes in the narrows in front of our campsite. My young companion had an exciting story to tell his father. Perhaps someday he'll remember that rugged day in the wilderness.

To the north of McAree is Minn Lake. The portage is more like a logging road than a path because Minn Lake was heavily logged. Minn has good fishing for walleyes. Across Minn is the Darky River coming from Darky Lake. There are four portages along the river to Darky Lake, which has several good campsites as well as good lake-trout fishing. There are some Indian pictographs against a cliff on the southeastern end of the lake. A short portage leads to Ballard Lake on the west. From Darky there is a one-third mile portage into Argo, which is another large trout lake, and a series of four portages through Roland, Middle Roland, and Little Roland back to the border route and Crooked Lake.

Crooked Lake empties over mighty Curtain Falls into Iron Lake along the international border. Curtain Falls gets its name from a sheet of water being sucked downward in a broad swath resembling a smooth lace curtain, to be dashed about by large broken rocks below. It produces a deafening roar and is the uncontested king of waterfalls in the Quetico-Superior, dropping straight down about 30 feet. In the early 1960s, two brothers were swept over the falls in their canoe but miraculously survived; their canoe of course was demolished.

When I first portaged around the roaring tumble of Curtain Falls in the 1950s, several dozen city slickers stepped out of a series of giant boats to walk over to a private fishing lodge on the American shore. All of their luggage was placed in a small railroad car and hoisted up the hillside. Speedboats plied the waters of Crooked to bring them to the best fish haunts. Part of the battle for wilderness raged over the purchase of this resort and the return of Curtain Falls to its wilderness state.

Crooked Lake has a series of deep bays on the U.S. side, Sunday Bay, Friday Bay, Thursday Bay, and Wednesday Bay. There was a fly-in resort on Friday Bay, but all signs of civilization are gone from there too. From Friday Bay eastward, Crooked is a maze of turns,

Indian picture rocks on Crooked Lake. Credit: Bill Rom, Sr.

Curtain Falls at the end of Crooked Lake.

islands, and peninsulas, so that it is easy to get turned around. A favorite stopping place past Wednesday Bay is Table Rock, a wide, flat, sloping rock ledge. Table Rock itself is twenty feet across and three feet above the ground, making it a perfect dinner site, lacking only chairs.

Crooked Lake has a quiet current in its narrow channels and actually drops several feet from one end to the other. Walleyes, northerns, and bass haunt its waters.

West of Crooked Lake is Iron Lake, leading to a narrows into Bottle Lake and down another rapids into Lac La Croix. The Bottle portage, which skirts this rapids, is a wide path with logs piled like corduroy over the muddy spots enroute to Lac La Croix. North out of Iron Lake is a 23-foot drop into McAree Lake, Rebecca Falls. A cliff lines the falls' southern side and a 45° rock slope the opposite side. If Crooked is the king of Quetico-Superior waterfalls, then Rebecca is the queen.

The most popular canoe route to Lac La Croix is from the Echo Trail down the Moose River to Nina-Moose Lake and Lake Agnes, and on to Lac La Croix. A half-mile portage leads from the parking lot along the Echo Trail to the Moose River and there are two more portages along the Moose River to Nina-Moose Lake. Nina-Moose has many tall aspens and a few pines. Another river, the Portage River, enters from the east. This route is wilder, with fewer people and good duck hunting, but has many more portages than the Moose River. There are two more portages from Nina-Moose into Lake Agnes. American Agnes is especially popular with local fishermen because it is a good walleye lake. A short portage leads from Agnes into the Boulder River, which leads into Boulder Bay of Lac La Croix.

Another route from Lake Agnes is to Stuart Lake via the Boulder River. There is a one-third mile portage into the Dahlgren River and another portage of the same length into Stuart. Stuart is a pretty lake, has few visitors, and offers excellent fishing for northerns and bass. The four-mile Lac La Croix trail from the Echo Trail skirts Stuart Lake. I've hiked this trail as far as Stuart, a pleasant day trip.

Ramshead Lake is just west of the Moose River before it empties into American Agnes. It once had tall pines surrounding its shores, but has been burned over by a runaway control burn. Lamb Lake west of Nina-Moose has been desecrated by recent logging. When I portaged this route, the trail had been demolished with logs, brush, and skid roads.

My favorite route south of Lac La Croix is from the Pauness Lakes to Gun Lake and Lac La Croix, back to Gebeonequet, and through Oyster to Shell. To get to the Pauness Lakes, one continues on the Echo Trail six miles beyond the Moose River to the Little Indian Sioux River. A short portage from the parking lot leads down to the water. This route is frequented by deer and red-winged blackbirds. After several miles of paddling, one comes to Elm portage. A pretty falls drops down from the Jeannette Creek on the left where one disembarks from the portage landing. A footbridge in disrepair crosses the river several miles downstream. (The bridge was part of the Hustler Trail to a fire lookout near Loon Lake, farther to the north.) The river continues to Upper Pauness.

Two routes go to Lower Pauness: one is a 40-rod portage between the lakes and the other is around a small rapids on the southern end. In the springtime, these rapids are noted for good walleye fishing. From Lower Pauness the river enters a long, deep canyon called Devil's Cascade. From the midpoint of the portage there is a good view of the rapids cascading below. The Sioux Lookout fire tower was located nearby.

Loon Lake below Devil's Cascade is another beautiful border lake on the route to Lac La Croix. I headed my canoe to East Loon Bay and entered the hinterlands beyond, passing a strategically located rock-ledge campsite along the eastern shore. This route goes from Loon up a half-mile hilly portage into Slim Lake, into a pond, to South Lake (a bay of Lac La Croix), and to Steep Lake. Steep is an isolated, clear-water lake, but only rock bass seem to live there. I made a small campsite on its shore and spent the night. From Steep the route goes to Eugene, where I've side-tripped to Bear Track Lake, another isolated gem. Back to Eugene, a beaver pond and a short portage take one to Gun Lake, a deep, cold, spring-fed lake. I caught a nice 4-pound lake trout in the narrows, providing an excellent dinner. From Gun there is a single portage back into Lac La Croix.

About seven miles east on Lac La Croix, there is a route through a series of small lakes back to Pauness. The route enters a river, with portages shortly thereafter. The river soon forks, with one fork going to Pocket Lake and the more easily missed channel, clogged with lily pads, going to Gebeonequet, one more portage leading into the lake. Gebeonequet is a wilderness beauty inhabited by lake trout, northerns, and perch. From Gebeonequet there are portages to Green, Rocky, and Oyster Lakes, all of which are reputed to have small lake trout. A two-thirds mile portage west out of Oyster leads to Hustler Lake, followed by a liftover to Ruby Lake and another long portage into Lynx Lake. There is a channel into Little Shell and a liftover into Shell Lake. North of Lynx Lake is a portage to Heritage.

I've tried following the stream from Heritage northward to Range Line Lake, but the route was unmarked and there were no portages. After bushwhacking one terrible portage along the river, I decided the route wasn't worth it and paddled back to Shell. Shell Lake has many campsites and a number of walleye holes around its islands. South of Shell is a small lake, Dogfish, which I've hiked into. It has excellent fishing for northerns, which can be caught by casting from the shoreline. From Shell back to Pauness is a well-traveled two-thirds-mile portage.

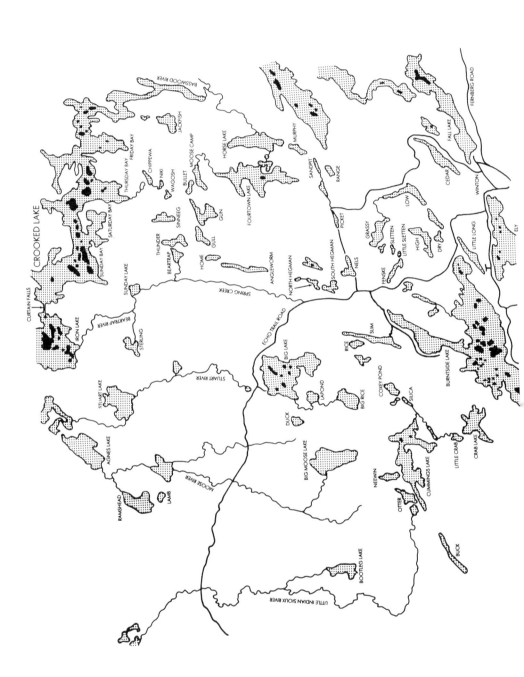

CHAPTER TWELVE
Little Indian Sioux

SOUTH OF THE Echo Trail road lies the Little Indian Sioux canoe country. Cummings, Big Trout, and Big Moose Lakes are the larger lakes in this area, and the major canoe route through this section follows the meandering Little Indian Sioux River to its source at Cummings Lake and on to the west shore of Burntside. Before the construction of the Echo Trail road, which crosses the Stuart, Portage, Nina, Moose, and Little Indian Sioux rivers, this entire area was a wilderness all the way to Lac La Croix.

In the early 1960s, with a canoe party I explored the Little Indian Sioux River upstream, finding it wide and deep for three miles to Sioux Falls, a cascade over several rock ledges. The portage around the falls is only eight rods, and several curious deer onlookers caught our attention. After a later 90-rod portage, we detoured up the Little Pony River to Bootleg Lake. This river is narrow and choked with weeds, and there are two portages, the second leading into Bootleg Lake. The wind was whipping across the lake, and we enjoyed the lake as a respite from river paddling. From the far end of Bootleg, a two-thirds-mile portage goes west back to the Little Indian Sioux. On our route, we had two more short portages along the river, followed by endless sandbars, rocks, logs, and broken beaver dams to pull over, the river narrowing to only ten feet. By nightfall we were exhausted, and we camped on a jack-pine ridge overlooking the river.

The next morning I heard the roar of chain saws in the distance. Multiple use was the U.S. Forest Service policy, but conflicting uses met each other head on here. Wilderness canoe recreation and logging the forest nearby are hardly compatible uses! *Multiple use* can't be defined as all uses on every acre of land; some large areas should be preserved for wilderness and others for forest products management.

We packed our gear, took to the river, and pulled over a beaver dam that raised the water level three feet, providing decent paddling again. There were three more quick, short portages, then two longer ones, and we stopped for lunch. I decided to hike during the lunch hour to see the wilderness destruction firsthand. I walked along ridges of jack and Norway pines, through a swamp of cedar and spruce, and finally reached the portage trail connecting Buck and Cummings Lakes. The logging was occurring at the top of the hill, thirty feet from the portage. I hiked up the hill and was greeted by new stumps, fresh sawdust, and the aroma of oil and newly-cut wood. Two loggers, who were otherwise farmers from southern Minnesota, were cutting. They were working hard and cutting young jack pine into cords. One drove over in a timberjack and skidded out six entire trees. The huge tractor had a winch on the back and a plow on the front and roared through the cutover forest to a logging truck nearby. I felt saddened and demoralized.

I followed my compass back to the Little Indian Sioux and hit the river right at my canoe. There were two more portages to Otter Lake. We pitched camp on the stream connecting Otter and Cummings, where the bass were voracious that evening. A sailor's sunset with a purplish tinge over Otter Lake ended the day. I couldn't forget the loss of the forest as I crawled into my sleeping bag for the night.

The next morning, we began the day by catching a 7-pound northern pike in Otter Lake. Following the victory over the northern, we explored the lake country over to Coxey Pond. We paddled across Cummings and portaged into the Korb River, took the left fork and portaged into Silaca Lake, where we caught several largemouth bass. We then portaged into Coxey Pond, past an old logging road and camp about midway across the portage. Several shacks were still standing, and piles of sawdust from an old sawmill were heaped on the ground. We paddled around Coxey Pond and caught several more smallmouth bass. On the way back, we spotted an otter diving into the river; and as we entered the river's fork, I saw a large cow moose swimming. We paddled hard and came surprisingly close to her, since she was virtually stuck in the mud in the middle of the river. I visualized my chance to actually ride a moose, but she was scared to death. With a mighty effort, she finally made it to shore.

The next day we left Cummings for Burntside Lake. Near the Korb Portage, there was an old but well-built cabin where I remembered staying when I was only seven years old. I still remember sliding down a sloping rock covered with green algae. I slipped in up to my neck and had to dog-paddle and kick until my fingertips reached the rock so that I could pull myself back up.

We paddled across Korb Lake and lifted over an old dam to paddle onward across Little Crab Lake. We pulled over a lift-over into Crab and took the mile-long portage along an old logging road to Burntside. Burntside's western shore is in the wilderness, while the remainder of the lake is largely privately owned and has many summer cabins.

Northeast of the Echo Trail is a series of lakes highlighted by Fourtown and Horse, with interesting canoe routes leading northward to Crooked Lake and the Basswood River. An old logging road provides access to the Fourtown Lake canoe route, but my favorite access is via Jackfish Bay of Basswood Lake. The Range River enters here, and there is a good campsite and fishing hole at the first rapids. From the Range River, one portages into Sandpit Lake. An old railroad trestle, remnant of the logging era a half century ago, passes here and continues onward to Horse Lake. I portaged into Murphy Lake and noticed many logging deadheads en route to the Horse Lake portage.

Horse Lake has several excellent campsites along the eastern shore, my favorite being on a point near the mouth of the Horse River. Fishing for walleyes is excellent, with the best luck trolling with nightcrawlers. The Horse River to Lower Basswood Falls has four small rapids to shoot before the first of three portages. Usually many turtles are sleeping in the sun on rocks or logs along this route. The river is a pleasant paddle with little current, a few double-S turns, and plenty of water.

There are two portages into Fourtown from Horse Lake, bypassing an old logging sluiceway. I saw a vigorous second-growth forest of spruce and aspens. Next I portaged into Boot Lake, which was renowned for its walleyes and had more logging relics. Then I portaged into Fairy Lake and crossed a trail that led to the Crooked Lake cabin near Lower Basswood Falls. Next came Gun Lake, where three private cabins on the left shore were still standing. These

Small waterfalls on the Little Indian Sioux River. Credit: Becky Rom

were once accessible via an old logging road that has now been dynamited and closed by the U.S. Forest Service. On the well-marked and easily traveled portage into Gull Lake, I stopped to watch a woodchuck along the trail. Two more portages led to Thunder Lake through a beautiful stand of white pines. There was another lift-over into Beartrap Lake, which was also full of walleyes. I portaged a half mile to the Beartrap River, stopping once to rest on the soft reindeer moss along the trail.

The Beartrap River forms the Spring Creek draw, and at that time a swamp road paralleled the Spring Creek draw to Sunday Lake, from where the resort owners on Crooked had cut a wilderness trail to Crooked's Sunday Bay. During the frozen winter months, the resort owners brought construction materials and supplies over this route. The road and route are now in the process of growing over and returning to the wild state.

Two more portages in rapid succession took me to Sunday Lake. Sunday was another pretty lake, but I became drenched by a rainstorm and hurried on to the portage back to the Beartrap River. My father and I portaged again before hitting a set of rapids. The first was easy, but the second took a little negotiating. We had to bear left, then right, around a boulder, finally making it through without scraping the canoe. One more one-third mile portage led us to Peterson Bay of Iron Lake on the international boundary. A huge greenheaded mallard came so close as we entered Iron that we could almost touch his beautiful colors.

East of Iron is a canoe route through a series of small lakes from Crooked back to Fourtown. We hoped to complete the circle, and headed past the mighty, misty Curtain Falls and the eyesore resort to Friday Bay of Crooked. We portaged at the far end to a stream that was navigable to Papoose Lake. This was beaver country par excellence. Every bay held beaver houses, many with piles of fresh saplings at the base. We crossed Papoose, paddled up a river to Chippewa, lifted over a beaver dam into Niki Lake, and portaged into Wagosh Lake. From Wagosh, a mile portage led over an old logging road to the end of the barrel of Gun Lake. We found a liftover at the end of Gun Lake to Bullet Lake (on a map, it appears to be shot from Gun Lake) and another to Moose Camp Lake. To the left of the river leading to Fourtown, I saw a clearing that may have been a large logging camp years ago. The river was navigable all of the way, except for a couple of beaver dams and a logging sluiceway. Old stumps and logging detritus were scattered along the river. The Moose Camp River was actually hard to navigate because of boom logs scattered throughout. I thought that these boom logs should be sawed free, towed out, and burned so that the river could be returned to its original state.

As the river entered Fourtown Lake, there was a high cliff on the right, with many pines. I saw several ravens' nests perched up high. Here too were the cribs of an old bridge that served the trail to Crooked Lake cabin. We were happy to be back on Fourtown, the end of an arduous circular canoe route.

Several other canoe and foot trail routes are to the east of the Echo Trail road. One is the mile-and-a-half trail to Angleworm Lake. I once hiked this trail with my dad in early December after three inches of snow had fallen. Angleworm was covered with about five inches of ice, and my dad decided to do some ice fishing while I continued to Home Lake to the north. A fire lookout tower (since removed) stood atop a hill on the southwest shore.

I had reached the halfway point when I saw a gray animal running across the ice ahead of me. A timber wolf! I was exalted. I watched him lope along and finally disappear on the distant shore-line. When I reached his tracks, I marveled at his huge paw prints.

I hiked to the far end and crossed the portage into Home Lake, which was completely surrounded by a spruce shoreline. I hiked out about 30 yards, chopped a hole in the ice, set up my line, and shoved the pole into the frozen snow. I just got back to shore to build a fire when suddenly the pole fell. I ran back to the hole and landed a plump 2-pound walleye. I returned to the shore to stoke the fire and my pole fell again, but this time the fish got away. When snow started falling, I abandoned my fishing and hiked back to my dad, who had caught a small northern. He had a pot of hot chocolate brewing, which I savored as I showed him my frozen walleye and told him of the timber wolf I had seen.

South of Angleworm is a canoe route recently included in the Boundary Waters Canoe Area Wilderness. There is a short portage from the Echo Trail to South Hegman Lake, followed by a lift-over into North Hegman. On the route toward the stream to Trease Lake, on a cliff to the north are Indian pictographs, including a human, a moose, canoes, and a bobcat. I caught a few bass in North Hegman but nothing in Trease. A mile-and-a-half trail leads from Trease to Angleworm Lake; I hiked it once to see Angleworm just as a rain-storm arrived.

Another short canoe route off the Echo Trail starts at the Fenske Lake campground. I portaged over well-groomed trails to a series of small lakes (Little Sletten, Sletten, T) and to Grassy Lake. From there I navigated a river to Low Lake and caught several walleyes, bass, and northerns. Between Low and Bass Lakes there was a huge washout caused by a dam bursting during the logging era. The washout now is partially camouflaged with new forest growth, but the contours of the original hill can still be seen. Bass Lake, which dropped 30 feet after the dam broke, was a short paddle to a half-mile portage leading to the Echo Trail, completing another circle.

CHAPTER THIRTEEN
The Grand Portage

ONE CANOE ROUTE that I longed to explore was the border route from Basswood Lake eastward to Lake Superior, a canoe route steeped in history, known as the Voyageur's Highway. The voyageurs plied this route to the fur-bearing regions to the northwest. Most of the route traverses the Boundary Waters Canoe Area Wilderness, but only a small fraction of the Canadian side is protected by the Quetico Provincial Park.

I left Ely with two friends, Jack Jeffrey and Tom Dayton, in mid-July. Jack was a native Elyite whose father had taught him extensively on the lore of the wilderness. Eager as a beaver, he was always bustling about Canoe Country Outfitters as one of the chief routers. He smoked a pipe and appeared to be intellectually absorbing all of the richness that the forest and lakes could offer. Tom, another stalwart north-woods guide, helped his father run a canoeing service from Jasper Lake.

It was 5:30 in the morning, but with only a few days, we made an early start. We took a special lightweight aluminum canoe and loaded all of our gear into two packs. We headed down the Moose Chain, two of us paddling while the third slept in the middle of the canoe. We went up the border chain of lakes and ate lunch in the canoe as we crossed Big Sag. Staying to the left of all of the big islands, we passed the Canadian customs house, a ranger station, and several summer cabins, all new country to us. We continued toward Saganaga Falls and found an easy portage on the right side, then portaged around Horsetail Rapids entering Maraboef Lake. High ridges to the south and granite slabs along the shoreline made Maraboef a pretty lake. We passed three campsites on the Canadian side, and paddled up a swift current at Devil's Elbow to Gneiss Lake. Paddling upstream along the Granite River to Granite Lake, we encountered three short portages on the right around rapids before taking the level and dry Swamp Portage into Granite Lake. Another portage around a rapids led us to Clove Lake. I noted four campsites here and wished we could linger longer at this beautiful lake surrounded by high hills.

We now had to go up the Pine River to Magnetic Lake. We took the Blueberry Portage of 100 rods, portaged again for 42 rods around another rapids, and portaged on the left around Little Rock Falls. A wrecked wooden boat was caught at the bottom of these falls. We had one more rapids before Magnetic Lake but jumped out of the canoe and pulled it upstream, hopping from rock to rock. The current was mild and the river was only a couple of feet deep.

We finally entered Magnetic Lake and saw a small island as we entered the lake. The island was almost devoid of trees and had a large yellow and brown Swiss chalet to one side! In front of it was an immaculate lawn, complete with flowers. On the other side of the isle were two similarly styled boat houses, one resembling a Finnish sauna, with a dock for diving into the lake after taking a steam bath. We later heard that the owner had married a French girl and had spent his summers there for years. We could hardly believe we'd find such an ostentatious sight in the middle of the wilderness!

We had left the sanctuary of the Quetico at Saganaga and now left the Boundary Waters Canoe Area Wilderness at Magnetic Lake. An iron outcropping apparently had given the lake its name. At the narrows from Magnetic into Gunflint Lake, there were remnants of an old railroad trestle and bridge. (We stopped at Gunflint Lodge and saw a photo of the same railroad trestle, which had been built in 1894. I'm sure we three woodsmen swaggering by looked odd to the well-dressed guests!)

To the left of the trestle was a grassy area, perhaps the remains of an old logging camp served by the railroad. We noted several cabins in the woods, with a high, sheer cliff rising beyond. As we headed down the lake, my eyes followed the old railroad trestle along the northern shoreline. The water was clear and cold, as we discovered when the wind increased and splashed spray into our canoe. We passed several white sand beaches and tall stands of timber, and headed upriver between two sand bars at the eastern end of the lake. We next crossed Little Gunflint Lake and negotiated a short pullover into North Lake. There was a cog railway to transport large boats over this portage. The little cart for ferrying canoes and boats was under water on the far side, requiring us to make a short carry.

North Lake is mostly in Canada. We were impressed when we rounded the corner and saw the lofty Height-of-Land ridge along the famous Laurentian Divide. The waters of North Lake flow into Hudson Bay; the waters of South Lake, on the other side of the divide, flow into Lake Superior. A very high cliff stood just east of the Height-of-Land portage.

As we hiked over the Height-of-Land portage, we envisioned the life of the old voyageurs. Here the paddlers from Montreal were christened true voyageurs. A bottle of rum was always opened to baptize and douse the newcomers. The carefree voyageurs added joy to the wilderness as they sang and paddled the border lakes.

The Voyageur Era lasted from the early eighteenth century into the early part of the nineteenth century. It was based on the beaver pelt trade because the beaver hat was popular among the gentlemen of England and France. Great armadas of canoes filled with French Canadians left Montreal every spring to cross the Great Lakes to reach Grand Portage on the northern shore of Lake Superior by mid-July. In their large canoes, they carried all types of supplies for the fur trading posts of the vast Northwest.

These paddlers were derided by the Nor'westers (voyageurs of the Northwest), who called them porkeaters after the pork that was the mainstay of their diet. With the spring break-up, the Nor'westers loaded their smaller north canoes with the year's trade in fur and plied the border waters southeast to Grand Portage. July was the rendezvous, with the exchange of fur for goods, followed by hours of merriment and contests pitting strength and wit in the stockades of Grand Portage. Rum flowed freely.

After the interlude of song and dance, the voyageurs shouldered two 90-pound packs and headed back over the nine-mile Grand Portage. They put their loads down every half mile or so and returned for another load. The voyageurs, who usually were bearded and wore brightly colored sashes, were mostly small, stocky men so that they could carry much but took up little space in the canoe. While paddling, every couple of hours they stopped for a smoke, or "pipe," measuring the distance across the large lakes in how many pipes it would take to reach the far shore. They paddled furiously between

Rocky shoreline of Saganaga Lake. Credit: Roger Rom

pipes. Their strokes were accompanied by northwoods *chansons*, or songs about love for their Indian maidens, love of freedom and the wilds, or a favorite fort many days away.

South Lake was anticlimactic for us after the Divide. The U.S. side was once again under the protection of the Boundary Waters Canoe Area Wilderness. This section of the wilderness is referred to as the Caribou portion, after Caribou Lake. Primary access points are East Bearskin and Clearwater Lakes, just south of the boundary canoe route.

South Lake Portage was 68 rods and level. Rat Lake was clear and only a couple of feet deep, with what appeared to be quicksand on the bottom. A voyageur legend states that there is no bottom to Rat Lake, only endless mud. We lifted over into Rose Lake, which was as beautiful as North Lake. There was a high hill west by Stairway Portage, which leads to Duncan Lake to the south. That hill would undoubtedly be an excellent ski run for telemark turns on cross-country skis. There were cliffs along the northeastern Canadian side. We carried two miles on the Long Portage in the cool evening air. The trail followed an old railroad bed for a mile and a half. The route to Rove Lake, a half mile of muddy walking, was marked with a sign. Rove and Watup Lakes had dark water and low shorelines, so we hurried along the 100-rod portage into Mountain Lake, arriving just before darkness.

We camped at a grassy spot along the northern shore, cooked dinner, and sat around our campfire drinking tea and enjoying the early evening. Mountain Lake was a beautiful lake, with high hills along the southern shore. Because we saw only a few people along the whole border route, we could really enjoy the evening stillness and solitude. Such an evening will never exist there again, for a road has been extended from Arrow Lake to the northern shore of Mountain Lake on the Canadian side. The easy access will allow noise from campers, radios, motorboats, and the varied detritus of civilization to punctuate the evening stillness.

We awoke early and ate a quick breakfast, for we faced a long day if we were to reach Lake Superior. The sky was clear and the water calm. Mountain Lake looked much like the South Arm of Knife with its high, rolling ridges. We passed an old, dilapidated cabin a mile or so from the Lesser Cherry Portage, which was easy but a little muddy. We crossed a small pond and took Vaseux Portage and Greater Cherry Portage, the latter being fairly long. We paddled Moose Lake, which was similar to Mountain, with high, rocky ridges, especially on the Canadian side. We took the half-mile Moose Portage into North Fowl Lake. These lakes showed evidence of heavy logging, with brush along the shores, stumps, and deadheads. Another road reaches the shore of North Fowl on the Canadian side, and we left the Boundary Waters Canoe Area Wilderness behind as we crossed a narrows into South Fowl Lake. We counted thirteen boats, which belonged to a fishing camp, pulled up on a sand bar on South Fowl Lake.

We decided to canoe the Pigeon River instead of taking the Fowl Portage, but spent over an hour "lining" and pulling through rapids. (In lining, ropes on each end of the canoe serve as lines to shore, so the canoe can be pulled along the bank.) The river emptied through a concrete logging dam and sluiceway in need of repair; I saw the date 1934 inscribed. We portaged on the right around the dam and through a rockpile, crossed a pond, and ran into countless small rapids. Tom usually held on to the back end of the canoe or pushed while Jack and I remained in the canoe. We were hoping to keep our feet dry, for we had the nine-mile Grand Portage ahead of us. I lost my paddle once, but Tom grabbed it just before it went over a small falls. We portaged to the left of these falls and ran another mile of rapids. The white water was easy and fun, but our lightweight canoe was paper thin. We put a few scratches and dents on it, but were lucky not to puncture it.

We paddled down the river to Partridge Portage but missed the trail, sending us down more rapids. More logging evidence was along here, including several huge stumps, branches, and treetops (slash) and a bulldozed road to the edge of the river. The river was about thirty feet wide and more than a paddle deep. The water was very dark, making it difficult to see rocks or logging deadheads. We reached Partridge Falls and carried over an 80-rod portage on the right, there being a muddy landing on the far side.

As we drifted rapidly downstream, Jack, who was in the bow, bent over to get out of the wind so he could light his pipe. Just at that moment the canoe hit a deadhead at a peculiar angle, flipping us over into the water. I can still see Jack flying into the air with his pipe and match. Stunned and very wet, we collected our gear and kicked the canoe into shore. We all had a good laugh at ourselves, since we had been trying to keep dry for the long hike ahead of us. Regaining our senses and composure, we paddled onward. I noticed some red gravel and found it to be quite heavy — probably iron-bearing rock. We finally reached the portage and ate the rest of our food, made a pot of sweet drink, and dried our socks.

The nine-mile Grand Portage, longest of all of the portages in the canoe country, bypassed a series of rapids, cascades, and falls on the Pigeon River. We saw a sign that said Fort Charlotte. During the voyageur days, a small fort was built on this end of the Grand Portage. We searched the end of the portage for any relics but couldn't find the foundations. We saw a concrete ring and a concrete pile with small, round rocks back in the bush, but this was too modern to be an eighteenth-century relic.

We started the Grand Portage at 3:20 P.M., just as the heat of the day was declining. We carried the canoe and packs, rotating our loads every half mile when we would stop to catch our breath and relieve our sore shoulders. The canoe was the heaviest part of our load, and the packs the lightest.

The portage was about four feet wide, level, and well maintained. We crossed an old logging road and the old foundation of U.S. Highway 61 at the four-and-one-half-mile point. We continued for three-

and-a-half miles to the new highway over several long, gradual hills. The trail wasn't muddy or rocky, but there were lots of bugs to keep life miserable. When we reached the highway, our ride home was waiting for us. Our shoulders weren't too sore, but our feet ached. For the sake of posterity, we hiked the last mile of the Grand Portage from the new highway to the rebuilt stockade on the shore of Lake Superior.

Grand Portage National Monument includes the stockade and surrounding fixtures and land. We clamored around the stockade and nearby wharf, where launches take visitors to Isle Royale National Park in Lake Superior. We drove past Teal Lake to Mt. Josephine to view the Grand Portage National Monument and its accompanying bay on Lake Superior. The scenery — hills, forest, and lake in the twilight — was spectacular, providing a grand finale for an exciting canoe trip. Gazing into the distance and the twilight, I reminisced on what the sight must have been for the weary voyageurs, ending a 2,000-mile paddle from the Northwest with their loads of fur and congregating here before heading back into the forest for another year.

CHAPTER FOURTEEN

Forty Hours around Hunter's Island

DEEP IN THE center of the Quetico-Superior wilderness straddling the Minnesota-Ontario border is a division in the Hudson Bay watershed at Saganaga Lake, forming an island 200 miles in circumference. Known as Hunter's Island, it is made up of twenty-three lakes and thirty-five portages as long as a mile in length. At no place along this route does one encounter a road or waters unprotected from private seaplanes. This is one of the finest examples of wilderness left in America.

This vast island challenged Jack, Dick, and me to circumnavigate it in twenty-four hours. After our Grand Portage venture, Jack was eager to tackle the Hunter's Island route, which was even more arduous. We took up the challenge; and on a cold, cloudy September evening we set out to achieve our goal. We chose the time of 8:00 P.M. so that we would have daylight for the dangerous Kawnipi and Maligne Rivers. We used an old five-horsepower motor and a Grumman 17-foot square-sterned canoe to carry us along. The motor was in defiance of the wilderness, but we would pay dearly by carrying it, along with twenty gallons of gas. For food we took only sandwiches, sausage, candy, and Zwieback bread. We loaded up the canoe at Moose Lake and put our raincoats on to combat the spray and coolness of the evening. Moose, Newfound, and Sucker Lakes were a bit choppy but were easily managed. The light faded into darkness as we crossed Sucker to Prairie Portage, where we checked in at the Canadian customs and ranger station. The customs officer and ranger weren't too pleased to be working at 9:00 P.M., but they grinned when we told them of our goal. Then we headed out into the darkness up Birch Lake, with our spotlight leading the way.

We had no trouble at all crossing to Carp Portage and Carp Lake, and portaged over the four Knife River portages into beautiful and crystal-clear Knife Lake. By now, it was as black as the ace of spades, as the sky was completely overcast. As we crossed Knife, the plaintive cry of loons added a touch of northland melancholy.

Knife presented our first problem of finding our way, but we managed to find the narrows into Little Knife Lake and the short portage leading to Cypress Lake. Cypress reminded us of the Grand Canyon, with tall cedars along a hilly shoreline. Monument Portage, at the end of Cypress, leads up over a steep hill into Swamp Lake. It is named Monument Portage because several boundary markers of the Canada–United States border mark the path. We crossed Swamp Lake to the short Swamp Portage; we were now so wet and cold that we decided to dry out and warm ourselves by a fire. We took a half hour, eating an early breakfast and drying our socks and boots.

Once again, we marathonists set out — this time crossing huge Saganaga Lake (meaning "Big Chief" in Ojibway). Our light beam revealed the channels to the main part of the lake. Ahead of us we couldn't see the opposite shore; it was like staring off into space. We thought we found Cache Bay and swung to the northwest, but we made a complete circle and found ourselves back in the main part of Saganaga. Disgusted, we found an island and lit a fire to wait for daylight. On this island I found three birchbark baskets made by Indians. At 5:00 A.M., we tried our luck again and found the channel at once.

We portaged around roaring Silver Falls to Saganagons Lake, where we passed a tent and the equipment of some other campers still asleep. We noticed several comfortable campsites on Saganagons, including several with log tables built by Boy Scouts or ambitious campers. We then portaged across a long point to save time.

A mile past this portage, we entered into a heartbreaking part of the Quetico Provincial Park. The past summer had been terribly dry, and a disastrous forest fire had burned off miles of Saganagons and Kawnipi River shoreline. The fire covered six miles in four hours, spreading to islands and leaping a hundred yards across the river. The trees stood like blackened soldiers that had lost the war of survival, and bare rock showed everywhere, the duff being completely gone. A sea gull and a few blades of grass along the shore were the only life to behold. We entered the Kawnipi River and portaged around a previously unnamed beautiful falls. We paddled with the swift current to the next falls, finally leaving the burned area behind. What a welcome sight to see green Norway, jack, and white pine again. We portaged a third falls and then caught our breath while letting the motor do the work. Next came Little Falls, Koko Falls, and Canyon Falls. Canyon Falls was its usual spectacle with a roar of cascading water passing between two high cliffs. Next, Kenny Lake led us to Kennebas Falls and then into huge Kahnipiminanikok Lake, better known as Kawnipi.

At 9:00 A.M., I relinquished my motor duties to Jack and slept for two hours while we crossed this long body of water. We were now about halfway, 50 miles from the Canadian settlement of Atikokan, 60 miles north of Ely, and 100 miles along the way.

We now entered a few lakes that were new to me at the time, so out came the maps. Shelley Lake was first, a lake with a fine walleye reputation. Then came Keats Lake, perhaps, with Shelley, named after famous English poets. Splitrock Falls, a roaring oblivion, was the next portage. Huge boulders marked this portage; I slipped on one with the canoe on my back and injured my leg, but luckily it was only bruised. Chatterton Lake and Falls were before us, and almost as suddenly behind us, after a 90-rod portage into Russell Lake. Russell is a clear-water lake, beautiful beyond belief as the sun glistened on its surface and grey rocky shoreline. We looked back and stared in amazement at Chatterton Falls — so high, huge, powerful. To the front of us was a boiling mass of swift water that carried us quickly into Sturgeon Narrows. Above the trees I saw a small, octagonal lookout tower, which represented a lonely summer post for a Canadian ranger.

We now faced Sturgeon Lake, and the fury of ocean-size whitecaps swept directly toward us. The canoe would bounce high in the air, then come down with a crash. For two and a half hours, we battled the wind and waves until victory was finally ours. We passed numerous sand beaches, rare in the Canadian Shield, and to our surprise passed a Canadian Department of Lands and Forests seaplane that had sought protection behind a point.

We entered the Maligne, or Bad, River and started off with another unwelcome portage. Deep down in Sturgeon's clear water, I noticed a huge boiler, a remnant of the historical Dawson Trail, which for a few years was the main route of the Canadian migrants to the Canadian West. After a short rest we took another portage, and along several subsequent portages I saw what remained of the corduroy road of the Dawson Trail. We shot a small stretch of boiling white water for a few laughs, but then met a rapids that was too treacherous, so portaged once again. We shot Flat Rapids and entered Tanner Lake.

Tanner Lake was named after John Tanner, who was captured by Indians when nine years old and adopted into a tribe with whom he lived for thirty years. In 1823, he was persuaded to return east and to put his daughters in a white man's school at Sault Ste. Marie. He told his Indian wife of his plans, and on his way east his Indian brother-in-law shot him and left him wounded at Tanner Lake. Fortunately for Tanner, a fur brigade picked him up and took him to Dr. John McLaughlin at Lac La Pluie Trading Post (Fort Frances), where he recovered.

We passed the old ranger cabin before a small lift-over around a rapids that led us back into the Maligne. At the lift-over, we picked up the canoe with the gear inside and carried it the few steps across. Nature hit us again, this time with a blinding rainstorm, driven by the wind straight into our faces. I held my cap in front of me as a shield. We shot another set of rapids before coming to Twin Falls, when the rain stopped and the sun peeked out. We pushed along into Lac La Croix, where I once again claimed the center of the canoe and fell fast asleep. An hour later we were at Bottle Portage, a half mile of mud and corduroy. I slipped on the wet corduroy and went down, canoe and all, but got up and continued plodding through the mud. Bottle Lake came into view at last. We hit several rocks in the narrows entering Iron Lake, but didn't damage the motor.

We now were heading east, the final leg of our circle. We were once again back in border waters since leaving the boundary at Saganaga Lake. Ninety uphill rods and we heard Curtain Falls. The mist rose 70 feet and a rainbow decorated it. The roar was most deafening. We checked our lights, and only one flashlight worked. Crooked Lake was thirty miles long, and darkness was rapidly upon us. The clouds blocked the heavens, but even worse was a rapidly gathering dense fog. We were only seven hours from the finish point, and could still make it around Hunter's Island in a total of thirty hours.

Crooked Lake was a real challenge, our sparring partner. We passed Sunday Bay and Saturday Bay. All of a sudden we hit a reef

with the outboard roaring at full speed. Luckily no damage oc-
curred. We continued on to Friday Bay. Then it happened — we hit
a dead end! We finally gave in to the inevitable: we were lost in the
middle of the fog and darkness. A flat rock ledge appeared, and we
decided to land and build a fire until dawn. As I reached for shore,
I stepped an inch away from a rock and sank into a waterhole over
my head. I scrambled out but was completely drenched. Darkness
had won that round. We built a roaring fire, and I dried out in short
order. Balsam boughs made a soft bed, and we catnapped until 5:00
A.M.

After a breakfast of sausage and raisins, we were on our way. The
fog was so thick that bowman Dick practically had to cut our way
through with his hunting knife. We traveled for an hour but made
a complete circle and ended at the same spot where we had spent the
night. Not to be discouraged, we set out again, heading east, and I
finally recognized a series of islands. Thursday Bay lay to our right.
We were once again on the right road. We passed the Big Current
and turned south to the Basswood River. Passing Table Rock, we
finally came to the Painted Rock. Two miles farther and we approached the Basswood River, where a huge rack appeared in the
center of the lake. It was a full-grown white-tailed deer. It saw us
and turned back for shore. I steered the canoe between it and the
shore, where we hit a submerged boulder head on. The canoe was
grounded, and the deer swam nervously past.

We portaged around lovely Lower Basswood Falls. A mile east,
we took the Wheelbarrow Falls Portage; a downy woodpecker was
busy pecking away as we walked by. Two miles and another short
portage readied us for Horse Portage. Horse Portage is a mile and a
half, but I usually take a shortcut instead, taking two shorter portages instead of the long one. At Basswood, we met two sad, stranded
boys who had shot Basswood Falls and had wrecked their canoe. We
agreed to leave word at Moose Lake for their outfitter to bring them
a canoe to paddle back to civilization.

The sun came out to brighten our two-hour ride across Basswood
Lake as we munched on our last food. When we rounded Ottawa Island, I glanced back to view the beauty of the lake and saw a huge
black bear on an island. I made a 180° turn and landed on the island;
the bear was still standing on his hind legs, but he took off into the
woods as we moved closer. We then passed Merriam, Bayley, Wind,

and Rice Bays as we sped on toward the southeast into Inlet Bay and Prairie Portage. We checked in with customs, where the officer was glad to see us, and stumbled across our last portage. I slept some more while Jack took us down Sucker, Newfound, and Moose Lakes to our landing, the point of departure forty hours earlier. We had failed in our objective of circumnavigating Hunter's Island in twenty-four hours, but we had an unforgettable experience meeting the challenges of the canoe country wilderness.

CHAPTER FIFTEEN
Talkeetna

A GUIDE STORY is not complete without the tale of a north-woods dog. Talkeetna was a princely Alaskan malamute born October 1977 and christened after Talkeetna, Alaska, a town on the Alaskan Railroad near Mt. McKinley. *Talkeetna*, an Ojibway word meaning "range of plenty," is the starting point for Mt. McKinley mountaineering expeditions. In 1976 I had become intimately familiar with Talkeetna as I joined a climbing expedition bound for the summit of Mt. McKinley. We reached our goal after nineteen days of climbing. We were snowbound in a blizzard at 17,000 feet for a week, but when the bad weather abated, we reached the summit of 20,300 feet in glorious sunshine.

Talkeetna went to dog training school, grew to young adulthood, and was a very large dog even by malamute standards. We took Talkeetna on his first canoe trip, disembarking at Snowbank Lake. Talkeetna was quite afraid of water and refused to swim or get his paws wet. This stemmed from a pup experience in the Wind River Mountains of Wyoming, where we were crossing a single-log bridge across a swollen river. Talkeetna was unsure of his footing, especially with roaring rapids all about him, and slipped on the wet bark, falling in upstream of the log. He was swept and pinned underneath the log. I saw that he was certain to drown and reached into the boiling water, fortunately grasping his collar and pulling him upward. He was gasping for breath, totally frightened, and from that point on had to be physically carried across each stream.

We paddled across Snowbank with Talkeetna sitting perfectly still in the bottom of the canoe, displeased with all the water about. He stood up once or twice only to receive a whack from the paddle against his behind to learn that standing up in the canoe was forbidden. Whenever we reached shore, he leaped to land, seldom getting his paws wet. From the first portage onward, he was nicknamed "Dainty Paws."

We took the route to Disappointment Lake and north through Ahsub, Jordan, Ima, and Thomas Lakes. We crossed Fraser and portaged into Sagas. The trip so far was uneventful, and we were looking forward to our first campsite. We loaded our canoe, and I asked my wife where the dog had gone. She thought he was with me and I thought he was with her. I yelled a few times, then yelled and yelled, but no dog came. We began to get a little worried, and I hiked back over the portage, yelling his name the entire way. I waited on the far end but no dog came panting out of the woods. I walked back to Sagas, and he wasn't there either. I got into the empty canoe and paddled eastward along the shoreline to Roe Lake to see if I could spot him. I was a bit tired and frustrated with the darn animal, but I could imagine him chasing a rabbit or a bear through the woods, becoming lost in this strange habitat. I paddled back to the portage, but there was still no sign of him.

There was a three-mile sidetrip via a triangular lake to the west back into Fraser where he might be. I paddled to the south end of Sagas, yelling "Talkeetna!" I portaged into the triangular lake and into Fraser. No dog. I paddled around a point and portaged into Sagas again. After three hours searching for him, we gave up and loaded up the canoe. Just then he sauntered out of the bushes and nonchalantly lay down with a smile and a lot of panting. If only animals could talk, what a story he could tell! With some relief, we paddled over to our campsite. The dog was perfectly behaved from then onward.

A year later I ventured out on a solo canoe trip with Talkeetna. I paddled against a stiff breeze down the Moose Chain and crossed Prairie Portage. The wind continued as we crossed Basswood to the North Portage leading to Sunday Lake. By late afternoon, Sunday Lake was calm, and I paddled to the two long portages into Agnes. I portaged across and Talkeetna carried his dog food in his dog pack. I carried the canoe up the steep hill around Louisa Falls and paddled across Louisa to the northern shore for a late camp.

Talkeetna slept next to the door of the tent, controlling his wanderlust and never straying far from camp. The forest was strange country for a mountain dog. Talkeetna proved to be fine company for a solo canoe trip, though he wasn't much help in paddling and all he carried on portages was his pack of dog food.

Our next day was cloudy and cold, with no luck trolling deep for lake trout. The weather finally cleared, and I paddled down Louisa to explore a trout lake to the north. I let Talkeetna jog along the shore, crashing through the brush and barking for a ride. He came to a series of cliffs and climbed straight up the rocky ridges. I finally stopped and offered him a ride. I found the trail to the small lake and enjoyed paddling around the shore, but caught nothing.

The next morning we had a pancake breakfast, Talkeetna's favorite food. He was fond of most human food except vegetables. I waved to the canoeists paddling a pair of canvas canoes on the far side of the lake. I packed our gear and began the journey to Agnes. At the second portage we caught up to the canoeists, who were fascinated by old "Dainty Paws" Talkeetna, but he wasn't too polite to them, growling as we walked by. They were headed south, and we turned north.

Agnes was overcast, with a fine drizzle falling intermittently. I paddled down a quiet expanse of water, enjoying the rocky hills alongside. As I paddled alone, I felt as if I were hearing a stereo of symphonic sound. A mile or two passed. Talkeetna was sound asleep with his muzzle resting on the yoke. The clouds were moving quickly, with large billows of dark cumulus passing overhead. The rain stopped.

I then began searching the shoreline for a blaze or mark of a portage to a trout lake beyond the western shore. I had been there twice, many years before, and had cut a trail into the more northerly of a pair of trout lakes. I searched to the north, then doubled back, unable to find the blaze or any evidence of the trail. I stopped the canoe several times to explore likely possibilities, but still couldn't find the trail. I paddled to the north again and spotted a rise back in the woods. I walked up the ridge, from which I spotted the lake between the trees. Canoe on my shoulders and fishing pole in my hand, I began crashing through the brush. Talkeetna heeled alongside. Nowhere did I find any evidence of the trail that I had blazed over ten years earlier, the wilderness having completely reclaimed it. It was a sweaty bushwhack to the shore of the small, unnamed lake.

I paddled away from shore to relax and take a deep breath while rigging up my fishing line and snapping a Daredevil onto my leader.

Talkeetna carrying his share across Prairie Portage.

Morning mist rising for another sunny day on Sunday Lake.

Pine forest of Ontario's Quetico Park. Credit: Becky Rom

I dropped it in and paddled along the right shoreline for about ten minutes. That seemed like a long time for a lake that I remembered was full of trout, but then something began pulling. The trout seemed like a big one and kept on fighting, swimming back and forth. I brought it into view and landed a fat 3-pounder. It flopped all over the canoe, annoying Talkeetna. I dropped the Daredevil lure back in and caught two more after a few strokes of my paddle. I paddled back to the trail and placed the three trout on a forked stick so that I could carry everything on one trip through the forest of dense aspens to Agnes.

At Agnes I cleaned the trout and packed them into Talkeetna's harness. I paddled to the end of the lake, portaged into Sunday, and pitched camp on a small island for the night.

It was a cool evening, yet there was time to wander to the western shore of the island and silently watch the sunset. A line of clouds crossed the western sky, catching each shade of light. It seemed as if Talkeetna enjoyed the reds and purples of the sky too. It quickly turned cold, and I returned to my sleeping bag and tent and soon was asleep.

The next morning was a misty array of drifting fog and clouds. I paddled into the fog as it diminished and rapidly vanished as the hot sun emerged. I crossed Sunday to the North Portage and retraced the route back to Bayley Bay of Basswood.

Bayley Bay is seldom calm, but I caught it after a rainstorm and the waters were placid. Only a loon swimming in the distance created any waves to mar a perfectly still surface. Talkeetna looked alert, with his ears straight up. I paddled closer to the loon to pique Talkeetna's curiosity, but then the loon would dive. The dog couldn't understand that and was dumbfounded when he stared one way and the loon surfaced on the other side of the canoe.

Talkeetna fell asleep again as I slowly paddled across the tranquil waters of Bayley. In the distance I could see two more canoes paddling northward, with the waters disappearing beyond them. I had tall Norway pines to my left, the calm lake to my right, and blue sky glistening overhead. It was a glorious day to be paddling. I reached Prairie Portage and loaded up Talkeetna with his doggie pack full of trout. He waddled ahead while I carried the pack and canoe. About halfway across, I met the customs agent, who was an old friend and remembered me from many years back. I showed him the fat trout in Talkeetna's pack, and I mentioned to him that I had caught them in only fifteen minutes. He chuckled and shook his head in disbelief, because lake trout were hard to catch in August. I bade him farewell and finished the portage.

I paddled down Sucker and Newfound and passed through the narrows into Moose and the Twin Islands for a stretch break. Talkeetna and I walked around one of the islands looking to the south and the ridges toward Rommie Lake, Jinx Lake, Thermal, and Found. Memories of hikes among those lakes refreshed my mind. Talkeetna got back into the canoe; I shoved off and paddled on.

CHAPTER SIXTEEN

The International Canoe Derby

THE INTERNATIONAL CANOE Derby, a grueling test of physical and mental endurance, covered two hundred miles of wilderness canoe country. The race was a round trip between Fall Lake near Ely and French Lake near Atikokan, Ontario. The distance one way was a hundred miles, crossing the Boundary Waters Canoe Area and the entire Quetico, with twenty-six portages each way. The first prize, donated by the Grumman Canoe Company, was $1,000 – a lot of money in 1963. The first canoe derby, in 1962, began in Ely and was a considerable success. In 1963, the route was reversed, with the journey beginning at Atikokan (French Lake). The canoe derby was so rigorous that it continued only for three or four years before falling into desuetude due to a lack of able contestants.

This is the tale of the Second International Canoe Derby. There were twenty-two teams entered, all with high hopes of winning. My partner, Ropie Mackie, and I had just graduated from high school and were in top physical condition. We practiced every evening for weeks on end. We perfected a racing stroke of six strokes per side, with a quick switch to develop maximum speed with minimum effort and time spent on steering. Ropie was a native Ely Finlander and took to the wilderness lake like a mallard takes to the water. Like a machine, he paddled a vigorous stroke. Portages were hardly a bother to him.

We bought a chestnut-model canvas canoe and applied a new coat of green paint, adding a layer of white paraffin on the bottom for additional speed. We had lightweight beaver-tail spruce paddles with six-inch blades. Our final preparations included a waterproof beam light, precooked steak and various candies, Duxbak waterproof pants, and khaki shirts with "Canoe Country Outfitters" printed on the back.

To complete our training schedule, we paddled from Ely to Atikokan in a respectable time of twenty-two hours, five hours slower than the previous year's record. We left the village of Winton on the shores of Fall Lake, portaged and paddled to Basswood, and studied the portages and route to Kahshahpiwi. We arrived there at midnight and paddled the long series of northern lakes during the night. Morning greeted us at Cairn, and we paddled on to Sturgeon, crossed Dieux Rivieres portage and Pickerel, then paddled up a small river into French Lake. We crossed French to a Quetico Provincial Park beach and campground. After spending the night, we flew back to Ely the next day, leaving our canoe in Atikokan, where it would be ready for the big race.

The race was to start in the late afternoon prior to the Independence Day festivities — our departure time was 4:00 p.m. Two groups would leave from the beach, and we were in the second wave. With our 94-pound canoe, we began the final wait on the beach of French Lake. The crowd waxed, and to my surprise, my parents appeared. Two special, square-tipped, eight-inch-blade racing paddles had just arrived in Ely, and my father had flown north to deliver them. With our chances now greatly enhanced, our tension mounted, and butterflies filled our stomachs.

The wind had increased all day and had reached forty miles per hour by starting time. The waves foamed and dashed against the beach but didn't seem to bother the first ten starters. The gun fired and they were off! In twenty yards, one of the favored teams turned over and was battered by the waves. An official speedboat helped them right their canoe, and, soaking wet, they continued the fight straight into the wind.

We carried our canoe onto the beach and waited for the signal to start the second wave. Paddles ready, we stared into the stiff wind and watched the whitecaps come rolling toward us. The starter raised his gun, and we grabbed our positions and steadied the canoe. The gun sounded and Ropie splashed into the bow, while I shoved and leaped into the stern. Heads down, we began battling the wind. We were blown to the left, and two Indians (Boudreau Friday and Harry Lightfeather) crept by. We fought to an island and decided to empty the canoe of water. In our haste, we dumped over in shallow water near the shore. After righting the canoe, we paddled across French to the floating muskeg at the mouth of the French River and once again emptied the canoe. We were neck and neck with another team going into the river; coming out we were still even, but then we entered vast Pickerel Lake. The bow swung into the fury of the wind and waves. I saw Ropie and the bow rise, then come down the other side of the wave with a resounding crash, cracking some of the planking in the bottom of the canoe.

An island looming a mile ahead was our goal. Most canoes followed the north shore; I decided to island hop across the lake's center in a straight line. We inched ahead, paddling with all our strength. Two islands passed in this manner as darkness approached.

The next island was two miles ahead; after it we could avoid the wind in various channels. We dug in again and paddled and paddled, to little avail. The canoe filled with water, and we switched to our narrower spare paddles. The waves rocked the canoe dangerously, and we slowed down and inched ourselves to land. We were practically beaten mentally, but after emptying the canoe, we continued.

Darkness fell and we became discouraged. We entered the last bay and missed the portage. Another canoe caught up to us as I finally spotted the portage, and the race was on again. In the darkest and most forbidding of nights, we paddled to the famous Dieux Rivieres portage and then across Sturgeon and Russell Lakes. On Russell we switched paddles again and shot ahead of our pursuers. We were alone in the darkness of a starless night. The cold began cutting at our strength; our hands and backs were stiffening from the arduous paddling. Splitrock Falls hummed in our ears as we portaged on by. A fire showed the portage out of Keats Lake — a pair of contestants had given up and were warming themselves. A half hour behind the leading canoes, we surged forward on our second wind. We had lost time by traversing the center of Sturgeon. The northern shore was more roundabout, but the coves had lessened the wind's fury, so that our competitors had gained an edge.

We passed two more canoes in the misty morning and headed down the fault-line lakes of Cairn, Sark, Keefer, and Kahshahpiwi. Thirty miles of hard paddling brought us to the end of canyonlike Kahshahpiwi. Morning's sweetness had arrived, and we stretched our backs and ran the seven portages into Basswood Lake and the

United States. Rain spattered into our faces and the wind renewed its attack, but we were seeking our victory. We headed our canoe across Basswood, Newton, and Fall Lakes towards Ely. My hands were completely bandaged, and my eyes were bloodshot and sore — we were both dead tired.

The water tower of Ely appeared in the distance. We sprinted the last bay and collapsed into the crowd after our canoe touched shore. We were drenched, blistered, tired, and beaten, but we had persevered through one of nature's and man's toughest tests. That was our real victory — a real sense of achievement. Though our time was twenty-four hours, two hours slower than our trial time and about six hours slower than the leader, we were at least in the top ten. The wind's fury had taken its toll, and we still had to go back.

We collapsed into bed and slept soundly until midmorning. The next day was July 3, a day of rest, for on July 4 we were to begin our race north. We all had a chance to see and partake of the Fourth of July parade and celebration, but our minds were concentrating on the race. Early on the Fourth, Ropie and I were ready to go again. The sun shined brightly and the lakes were as flat as glass — fantastic conditions!

Waiting for the starting gun, we were once again in our roles. The trip reeled backward as we were again underway. Now the weather was on our side, and nature was smiling at us. We crossed Basswood in a clear evening and met the seven portages with full strength. After having been over this route so many times in guiding days, I could pinpoint every portage in the darkness. I wallowed at times through knee-deep mud with the canoe on my shoulder, climbed practically vertical cliffs, and pulled and pushed our canoe over beaver dams. Running across the portages, Ropie and I feasted on our steak while the mosquitoes feasted on us. We navigated around the rocks, stumps, and logs in the shallow beaver pond before the Kahshahpiwi portage with meticulous care. What a glorious, star-filled night greeted us as we paddled down Kahshahpiwi! The black outline of the shoreline seemed friendly and inviting, but we resisted the temptation to sleep as we were making excellent time. Keefer was next, and the cold summer night greeted our strained eyes with a majestic display of aurora borealis. The northern lights shot upward in the sky, turned to green, and then disappeared to be replaced anew. Our rhythm continued with the playful heavens and their mystifying lights.

We portaged into Sark, and the stillness of the wilderness seemed broken by the graying of morn. Our spirit of reverence from Keefer's rare display of light shifted to a seriousness of purpose, and only speed was in our minds. Portaging and floating the rapids into Cairn brought us into the full beauty of the sunrise.

The sun, in all its red, orange, and yellow glory, began to burn off the morning mist. The mist lifted through the trees, leaving them wet, fresh, and brilliantly verdant. The cool air and the tranquility of the wilderness brought back to our minds the feeling of reverence. We stopped paddling. The sky was several shades of amber; we felt as if we had paddled into a new dimension, a world of peace, or maybe even heaven. We forgot the race for a moment to absorb and appreciate the natural beauty of the trees, cliffs, water, and sky all blended into one.

Then we were off again — six strokes to a side. We roared through Shelley and Keats and past Russell and Sturgeon, and jogged Dieux Rivieres for the last time. Pickerel was our last opponent, and it lay down and gave us an easy crossing. We were in glorious spirits at seeing its mighty spaces, so calm and serene. After Pickerel and the French River, we once again found ourselves on French Lake and the beautiful beach — and once again dead tired.

We finished in ninth place, with lap times of twenty-four and nineteen hours, respectively. The winning team had set a new record of sixteen hours on the return. They won with a total lapsed time of thirty-four hours compared to our forty-three. We were exhausted but happy and proud, and considered ourselves to be real voyageurs. We had conquered two hundred miles of rugged wilderness and at the same time had enjoyed its supreme beauty. Now, two decades later, perhaps this test of physical endurance through the wilderness could be revived for a new young generation to test its strength and resolve.

CHAPTER SEVENTEEN

The Battle for the BWCA Wilderness

THE BOUNDARY WATERS Canoe Area Wilderness has been preserved because of the persistence and dedication of a small group of conservationists. The visitor is often unaware of the battles fought to keep wild the lakes, portages, and forests of the canoe country. Preservation of wilderness requires the conservationist's eternal vigilance, for these battles are won with difficulty against the insidious encroachments of civilization. To think that we have gone from one hundred percent to two percent wilderness in the United States makes one realize that the crusade for wilderness protection has been waged none too soon and against overwhelming odds.

The battles of the canoe country have been fought over dams, roads, motors, snowmobiles, airplanes, resorts, development, logging, and, finally, overuse by humans. The most recent arguments concern making access available to practically everyone. The definitions, however, differ. To some, the canoe country should be accessible by motorboat, motor-propelled canoes, houseboats, and snowmobiles, as well as traditional canoes. This premise defeats the whole purpose of wilderness preservation. Stillness and escape from the noises of humans are its essence. In regard to the BWCA Wilderness: motor contrivances may be used on the remaining two-thirds of the Superior National Forest, or two million acres. The cause of motorized travel has its vocal supporters, but the need for wilderness enjoyment is a higher need and right because, as Thoreau remarked, in wilderness we preserve the sanity and future of civilization. The Boundary Waters should be forever wilderness, with humans allowed entry only for the wilderness experience. To preserve that end, all other uses must be excluded, and even the numbers and places where people may visit kept within limits so that our hordes do not destroy that which we all seek.

The battle for the Quetico-Superior canoe country wilderness has been a long, interesting, and hard-fought one. It all began in 1909, when President Theodore Roosevelt established the Superior National Forest. An Ontario Forest Reserve was created in the same year, and in 1913 the Quetico Provincial Park was established across the border from the Superior National Forest. After the defeat of a road-building plan and Backus's plan to build a series of boundary waters dams, the Superior Roadless Primitive Area was established by the U.S. Forest Service in 1939. The boundaries were similar to those of the current Boundary Waters Canoe Area.

Establishment of the Superior Roadless Primitive Area was under the direction of Robert Marshall, who was in charge of recreation for the Forest Service. Bob Marshall was the founder of the Wilderness Society and an ardent explorer of the Brooks Range of Alaska. He was a national leader in the effort to preserve wilderness and chief architect of the U.S. Forest Service's efforts at preservation. He canoed the boundary waters canoe country with Sigurd Olson, exploring the wilderness lakes from Ely to Lake Superior. A rugged New Yorker, Marshall exalted in the challenges and the serenity of wilderness. The huge Bob Marshall Wilderness in Montana was named in his memory.

During the 1930s and 1940s, the U.S. Forest Service acquired many acres within the canoe country through the purchase of tax-forfeited lands; however, mineral rights were often overlooked. In 1948, the Thye-Blatnik Act was passed by Congress, providing for acquisition of more private inholdings, including resorts and cabins. During 1949 to 1951, attention focused on President Truman's executive order creating an airspace reservation over the canoe country, followed by commercial interests' appeal to the Supreme Court to overturn the air ban. In 1956, Public Law 607 extended the area within which inholdings could be purchased and provided more funds. In 1958, the U.S. Forest Service officially changed the name of the Superior Roadless Areas to the Boundary Waters Canoe Area.

During the 1950s, 1960s, and 1970s, controversy raged in the canoe country in three areas: (1) logging and its attendant road building, (2) mechanized travel, including motorboats and snowmobiles, and (3) mining. Logging boomed in the mid-1940s. A railroad spur and highway were built to Isabella Lake, and the community of Forest Center was established at the edge of the BWCA. From there, Tomahawk and other timber companies built gravel roads to clear-cut pulp from the southern third of the canoe country. They cut over to Bald Eagle, north to the Kawishiwi, Hope, and Maniwaki, to Insula, Alice, and Fishdance, and over to Polly and Koma Lakes. Public benefits from the timber sales were small; where the U.S. Forest Service made one large sale of $140,000, the estimate to rehabilitate the cutover region was $120,000. Loggers advanced on the Sawbill country almost to Cherokee Lake and swept southward from the Gunflint Trail. Long, narrow Finn Lake was bisected by a gravel road. Logging was commonplace in the Little Indian Sioux area south of Cummings Lake. Logging trucks frequented the Echo Trail, and large clear-cuts began to appear along the road. Logging from the Echo Trail extended southward to Big Moose Lake and northward to Ramshead and Shell Lakes. As clear-cutting became more widespread and the damage more apparent, conservationists began to mobilize to stop logging entirely with the BWCA.

Outboard motors were used throughout the canoe country, and large speedboats plied the boundary waters. Locals and others used their snowmobiles to run to distant lake-trout lakes in hours — trips that in the summer would take days.

The final threat came from mining. Over 300,000 acres of the Boundary Waters Canoe Area had mineral claims primarily by the state of Minnesota. The gabbro copper-nickel ore body extended north of Lake Superior along a line from Hoyt Lakes to the South Kawishiwi through the canoe country to the Gunflint Trail. Ore drilling just outside of the BWCA found low-grade 0.3–0.7% copper sulfide ores. Nickel was also found, and some surface rocks had samples up to 1%. These ores were complexes, with fibrous asbestoslike amphiboles raising the specter of an occupational and environmental health hazard.

In 1964, the Wilderness Act was passed, but it provided a special clause for the BWCA, prescribing no change in current U.S. Forest Service multiple-use management. Complaints of the Forest Service's mismanagement of the wilderness were ubiquitous and vociferous, requiring Agriculture Secretary Orville Freeman to call special public hearings on the BWCA in early 1964. Dr. George

Selke, a former Minnesota conservation commissioner, chaired the hearings and produced the Selke Committee Report.

During the summer of 1964, I had a full guiding schedule, but I planned two days between trips in mid-July to attend the Selke hearings in the Ely Community Center auditorium. I arrived early and was handed a mimeographed list of speakers as I entered. I was surprised to see that a public hearing was preprogrammed. The list included all of the local loggers, resorters, air-ban opponents, and others opposed to any type of regulations supporting wilderness. There was no one listed in favor of the wilderness! The local Chamber of Commerce had done its homework. Fortunately, the committee had also held hearings in Minneapolis and St. Paul, where the preponderance of support was for wilderness preservation.

The morning began with the reading of a statement by the Izaak Walton League in support of restrictions on logging and mechanized travel. This was followed by a bevy of massive loggers calling for increased logging, resorters opposed to motorboat restrictions, and a young boy calling for continued snowmobiling. I was appalled and submitted my name as a speaker. Over lunch I prepared my speech and compared notes with the dean of wilderness preservation in America, Sigurd F. Olson.

Sig Olson had written *The Singing Wilderness* in 1951, *Listening Point* in 1958, and *The Lonely Land* in 1961. He had been one of the founders of the Wilderness Society and a wilderness advocate on the Quetico-Superior Council. He was nationally famous as a wilderness ecologist and essayist for the canoe country. I was elated and honored to be able to plot strategy with him in support of our beloved wilderness canoe country.

We listened to William Trygg, former forest ranger, present his flawed compromise effort; he was willing to give away all of what we believed in to appease the townsfolk clamoring for more intrusions. Finally it was my turn to speak. I related my background as a wilderness guide and my belief that our goal should be to preserve this remarkable heritage at our footsteps. The whole auditorium was silent as every word was noted, especially by the panel. I talked about the enjoyment my parties had from ten days of wilderness camping and solitude. They were different, renewed citizens. I spoke of the uniqueness of the vast million-acre canoe reserve — it had no equal in America, nor was there any comparable wilderness east of the Rockies. I mentioned the necessity of the wilderness for Ely's economy of canoe outfitters and related service establishments. I encouraged the loggers to go elsewhere, to the two million acres outside of the BWCA but still in the Superior National Forest. I suggested that we could live without the outboard motor. I told them of my winter hikes sans snowmobile. What is to be found in wilderness, one need not hurry to in a mechanized contraption, which destroys what one seeks.

I was elated that the committee allowed me to speak, and they responded with a warm reception. I was followed by a local judge and former owner of a fly-in camp, who rambled on and on for more motorboats and such; at the ten-minute limit he was excused. In his powerful deep voice he bellowed at Dr. Selke that I was allowed to go overtime. Dr. Selke said once again that his time was up.

Later, Sigurd Olson gave his presentation. His speech was as melodic as his writings; few people have such tremendous ability to articulate the meaning of wilderness. We were held spellbound, in awe. Despite the hostility of the crowd, Sig received an ovation for his efforts. The hearings ended, and Sig and I were sharing a warm moment when a burly man rudely interrupted us. I recognized him as the town mayor and physician. He scowled at Sig and viciously criticized him for opposing "the community and its people" by advocating a BWCA wilderness. He glared at Sig, audaciously asking, "How dare you even raise your children in this community?" As quickly as he had appeared, he stomped away. Sig was visibly shaken by the verbal assault but stood straight, firm, and resolute in his principles. Despite the odds, we felt we had won. We knew that for the sake of the birds and deer and forests we loved, we were right. That was a day never to be forgotten.

The Selke Committee unanimously recommended that the BWCA be managed as a primitive-type recreation area. In 1965, Secretary of Agriculture Orville Freeman accepted many of the Selke Committee recommendations and promulgated a new set of rules for the BWCA, to apply for a decade. His regulations established a no-cut zone of approximately 600,000 acres, constituting the heart of the canoe country, and a portal zone of about 400,000 acres where logging was permitted but under strict controls. He also restricted the use of motorboats and snowmobiles to designated routes— generally the international boundary and heavily traveled routes adjacent to access points. He also created a free permit system that would generate data on BWCA usage. We felt we had gained with the regulations, but repined over the vast amount of land still available to logging. The Selke compromise did not settle the issues of logging and motorboats; and lawsuits, challenges, and acrimony persisted into the 1970s, showing that only permanent legislation would ever resolve the issues.

The townspeople were piqued by the Selke resolution, and the summers of 1965 and 1966 saw ugly demonstrations. During one of these, several huge logging trucks blockaded my father's Canoe Country Outfitters and picketed our store. Customers were openly intimidated, and placards brazenly stated that we should be run out of town. Fortunately, during those troublesome summers I was pursuing my canoeing challenges in the far north of the Canadian taiga.

By 1970, the environmental movement had gained added strength. April 23, 1970, was the University of Minnesota's first Earth Day, and I had the opportunity to plan the focal point of the session — the BWCA. I invited Dr. Miron "Bud" Heinselman to speak on "Ecology of the BWCA." Bud had worked for the U.S. Forest Service his entire career and knew the BWCA forest history better than anyone. He was followed by Dr. Clayton Rudd on a "Decade of Wilderness Conflict." Dr. Rudd was a Minneapolis dentist, editor of *Naturalist*, and a dedicated leader of the wilderness preservationists. Since copper-nickel drilling in the BWCA had become an issue, the next two speakers were University of Minnesota professors Dr. Paul Sims, on "BWCA Mineral Exploration — Pro," and Dr. Herb Wright, on "BWCA Mineral Exploration — Con." Dr. Wright's comments are as relevant today as they were then:

> The land is so much more valuable as a wilderness than as a source for metals that it must not be sacrificed. A priceless bronze art object is not melted down in time of war because of the need for copper. The country should rather conserve its existing resources by limiting current demand rather than promoting increased demand through wasteful use, injudicious advertising, and non-reclamation after use. . . . Let the mining development be restricted to the areas outside the BWCA — and let the smelting and refining be so managed that neither air nor the water of the BWCA (or of the rest of the area) be polluted by the operation. If these restrictions and safeguards cause an increase in the cost of the products, so be it — this is the price that must be paid to preserve and restore a clean environment. The time to assure these

safeguards is now, before the operation is permitted or planned. The decisions of industry and the economy and politics of the State and the Nation must be adjusted to an approach of true conservation, for the old approach of unlimited exploitation, waste of resources, and uncontrolled growth is no longer relevant. The context is changing, and the rules should change. The BWCA is a test of the new approach.

He was followed by Dr. Frank Kaufert, head of the university's school of forestry, speaking on "Multiple Use." The U.S. Forest Service, he said, pursued a balanced policy for lands management, with timber harvest, wildlife, watershed, and recreation recognized as valid uses of national forest lands. However, he failed to stress two points: (1) that areas of wilderness or de facto wilderness could be destroyed by logging; (2) that the multiple use policy could not allow all uses for each acre, but should spread multiple uses over an entire forest, which means that the specific use of *wilderness*, to the exclusion of other uses, must prevail in certain areas for wilderness to be perpetuated.

Lastly came William "Bill" Magie with "Wilderness Raconteurs: The Life and Times of the BWCA." Bill Magie, the dean of wilderness canoe guides, had roamed the Quetico-Superior during his active lifetime. Bill was the founder of Friends of the Wilderness, which led the bitter fight for the air ban of 1949; he continued to guide and to fight effectively for the wilderness all his life.

One favorite story of Bill's was of moose hunting when he was a young boy. Just as darkness approached, he shot a moose. He skinned the moose, but then realized he was lost. It was winter and freezing cold. He decided to crawl into the still-warm carcass and spend the night. By morning, rigor mortis had developed in the moose, and Bill was trapped. By firing his rifle, which he had dragged in with him, he attracted the attention of his searchers. Bill decided he didn't want to walk back to camp, so he kept mum while his compatriots dragged the moose back to camp. When Pierre and Gaston, the cooks, commenced to dress the moose, he let out a moan and scared the wits out of them!

During the 1970s, the issues of the wilderness came into sharper focus. Bud Heinselman calculated that 540,000 acres, or 52%, of the BWCA was virgin forest. Ten thousand acres were within six active federal timber sales that were contested in court. There were 160,000 acres of virgin forest in the so-called portal zone of the

BWCA that were available for logging. The U.S. Forest Service had allowed logging on 212,000 acres in the portal zone region since 1940. It was obvious that logging would destroy the wilderness aspect of much of the BWCA.

The second issue pitted wilderness-seeking paddle canoeists, skiers, snowshoers, and hikers on one hand, and motorboaters and snowmobilers on the other. The Selke rules resulted in twenty-one designated motorboat routes that encompassed over 60% of the water area in the BWCA. Snowmobiles were defined as winterized motorboats; a ban on them in 1975 and 1976 was overruled by local pressures. At this time, three-fourths of the use was by wilderness canoeing, and practically all canoeists stated that their wilderness experience was impaired by encounters with motors.

The third issue was prospecting and mining. A prospecting crew in 1969 was ready to begin drilling on the shores of Gabimichigami, claiming more than 100,000 acres of mineral rights for a distant New York businessman. The Izaak Walton League sued successfully, arguing that because the BWCA was zoned as wilderness, private mineral holders could not exercise their rights to their minerals.

Conservationists rallied to form a new group called the Friends of the Boundary Waters Wilderness, chaired by Bud Heinselman, who had since retired from the U.S. Forest Service. They assisted Congressmen Donald Fraser and Bruce Vento in drafting a comprehensive wilderness bill, while Congressman James Oberstar, of northeastern Minnesota, drafted a bill preserving half of the BWCA as a wilderness and making the remainder a national recreation area.

During the development of both bills, I had the opportunity of discussing the BWCA wilderness with Congressman Oberstar, who listened attentively but ignored my suggestions. In order to placate many vociferous locals, he proposed halving the BWCA, making half a recreation area for the boaters and snowmobilers and half a wilderness canoe area. I also had the exciting opportunity to meet with the chief of the U.S. Forest Service, John McGuire, and his recreation staff. I discussed the adverse effects of winter snowmobiling on the BWCA ecology and wilderness in general and what the prospects of copper-nickel mining and exploratory drilling would mean.

The mid-1970s saw extensive posturing, and both bills were introduced in the 1976 and 1977 congressional sessions. In the summer of 1977, field hearings were held on both bills. The Friends of the BWCA and Bud Heinselman coordinated an extensive conservationist effort to oppose the Oberstar bill and support the Fraser-Vento bill. Letters were written, money was contributed, and newsletters kept conservationists abreast of developments. The field hearings resulted in pages and pages of testimony in support of a BWCA wilderness banning logging, mining, and mechanized vehicles.

I was fortunate to testify at the field hearings in St. Paul, Minnesota, during the summer of 1977. My role was to testify on a panel providing data on the positive economic impact of the wilderness area. The wilderness tourism industry was impressive—about twenty-five canoe outfitters employed almost 100 people full time and 350 seasonally, with a gross annual income of almost $5 million. More than one hundred resorts on the periphery of the BWCA employed an additional 2,000 workers, with a $25 million gross income. These outfitters and resorts were successful because of their proximity to the attractive wilderness canoe area. My sister testified further on the positive impacts of the BWCA on the community of Ely.

Next came the formal lobbying effort. Bud Heinselman admirably coordinated the task from a Washington, D.C., apartment with the assistance of Congressman Fraser's staff. My sister and I learned our way through the halls of the Congressional office buildings. We learned a quick sales pitch, with map in hand, that could convince a congressional staffperson to understand that a BWCA wilderness was the next best thing to apple pie and motherhood.

The two bills had many supporters, with lobbyists from the Ely-Winton Boundary Waters Conservation Alliance leading support for the Oberstar bill. Finally, during the waning hours of the congressional session, Charles Dayton, an attorney for the Sierra Club and the Friends of the Boundary Waters Wilderness, met with the Alliance attorney to produce a compromise bill that resulted in the Boundary Waters Canoe Area Wilderness Act, which passed the Senate in the eleventh hour of Congress in 1978. There were many who contributed to this effort: Congressmen Don Fraser and Bruce Vento, Bud Heinselman of the Friends of the Boundary Waters Wilderness, and attorney Charles Dayton of the Sierra Club were especially instrumental in the development and passage of this historic law.

The Boundary Waters Canoe Area Wilderness Act of 1978 (Public

Law 95–495) established a BWCA Wilderness of 1,075,500 acres, adding 45,000 acres in twenty small areas. It repealed the ambiguous exemption in the 1964 Wilderness Act, which had allowed logging and motorboats in the BWCA. Key additions to the BWCA included areas about Moose and Fowl Lakes, South Lake, parts of Brule Lake, the North Kawishiwi River, Fourtown, the Hegman Lakes, and others. It restricted mining, authorized acquisition of mineral rights, and prohibited logging in the wilderness. Motorboats were restricted further, from the previous 60% of the area to 33%, to be reduced to 24% after 1999. Trucks were to be removed from the Four-Mile and Prairie Portages after 1984. Snowmobile traffic was essentially banned except for the Moose-Ensign-Knife-Saganaga route and two smaller routes, where snowmobile use would be discontinued in 1984. The law also permanently allowed motors on a few key lakes, but limited the horsepower to 25 on Big Sag and Basswood and to 10 on Knife and Crooked Lakes. In 1984, motors would be removed from the Basswood River and Crooked, Carp, and Knife Lakes, and horsepower reductions would occur on Basswood and Birch Lakes. It also gave resort owners on peripheral lakes affected by the new BWCA law the option to require purchase of their resorts by the U.S. Forest Service at a value no less than their fair market value as of July 1978.

The law has already withstood legal challenges by the Boundary Waters Conservation Alliance and the State of Minnesota. Implementation of the law's provisions is being undertaken by the U.S. Forest Service. The law is a compromise, but wilderness status, prohibition of logging, further restrictions on motorboats, and the ban on snowmobiles were all victories. However, wilderness gains are hollow without eternal vigilance, and we can hope that those opposed to the wild lands will in time learn to love, support, and appreciate their qualities. Wilderness is a valuable and essential ingredient, much needed to enhance the life of modern man. To paraphrase author Edward Abbey, a dean of wilderness protagonists, "Wilderness needs no defense, only defenders."

CHAPTER EIGHTEEN

The Albany River
to Hudson Bay

UNFOLDING A MAP encompassing the northern half of North America, one can observe a system of lakes and rivers extending from the U.S.–Canada border toward the drainage of Hudson Bay and northwest along the Rockies to the Arctic Ocean. Appearing as the tip of this vast triangle is the crown jewel of the canoe country—the Quetico-Superior. Here countless lakes are so close together that one can paddle for days without crossing one's trail. Practically all of this water drains into the vast Hudson Bay watershed. What is it like to explore those routes to the bay and the vast Northwest traveled by the early voyageurs? After the small BWCA and Quetico lakes, what is it like to paddle across a lake whose distant shores disappear into the horizon? Are the mighty rapids of the northern rivers negotiable by a tiny canoe? What challenges lie beyond Ely? The vastness of what remained of that giant triangle-shaped map of lakes and dashing rivers beckoned.

The ultimate canoe trip is to paddle the *Pays d'en haut*, or vast Canadian northlands, to Hudson Bay. The giant rivers draining the Hudson Bay watershed provide myriad challenges, with rapids, portages, and large lakes, including some that are practically unknown and seldom visited by humans. The Quetico-Superior canoe country was only a prelude.

There are many routes and rivers to the north. I pondered the charts piling up in my home; there were the Abitibi, Albany, Attawapiskat, Winisk, Severn, God's, Hayes, Nelson, Churchill, Seal, Kazan, Thelon, and many others. The choices were practically overwhelming. There are few settlements on the bay, but most river deltas have a Hudson Bay Post with a means to communicate to the outside world. Two railroads have a terminus on the bay. One is at

Moosonee at the mouth of the Moose River on James Bay, and the other leads from the prairie heartlands around Winnipeg northward to Churchill at the mouth of the Churchill River. Thus my choices were narrowed; the railroads provided a safe and economical means of return for both me and my canoe. Since the railroad to James Bay paralleled the Moose River, I chose the next river north, the Albany, which was deeper in the wilderness.

During the summer of 1964, I guided a party in the Quetico-Superior that pondered the challenge of a Hudson Bay journey. One was an employee of the Internal Revenue Service and a rugged individual, while the other was a tall, thin librarian who surprised me by his desire to travel north. In early 1965, they wrote that they wished to join a canoe expedition down the Albany the following July. I updated my maps and plotted our course. I called on Gus Walske, an older Ely guide who had canoed the Albany, for his advice on the rapids. He talked about Tom Flett Rapids and Kagiami Falls, new names to me, but his tales were harrowing. He had missed the portage around Tom Flett Rapids and had been swept down the current. All he remembered were boils, backwashes, rocks, and big drops. This was one I immediately knew I had to respect.

July rapidly came, and my two companions, Rudy and John, arrived. A canoe guide apprentice, Bruce, was anxious to make the journey, so we had a foursome. Two canoes would be safer because we could all escape the wilds in one if the other happened to be lost in a rapids. Bruce would be the sternman in the other canoe and would follow mine. We had canoed together before, and he was expert in canoeing and camping. I packed a month's supply of food, with each package a full meal for four. We had five large Duluth packs, three for food and two for camping gear. We packed special tape and liquid aluminum for canoe repairs, spare paddles, and only extra socks for personal gear.

Our route started with a drive leading across the border into Canada, along the highway to Lake Nipigon, and north to Beardmore, Ontario. The scenery was breathtaking along Lake Nipigon, with high bluffs and sheer cliffs, fjord-like arms of the many lakes, and beautiful forests. Beyond Beardmore we drove north on dusty gravel logging roads, with the countryside bearing the scars of logging. We reached the few shacks of Auden and the tracks of the Canadian National Railroad. The local Hudson Bay Post officer issued us a dominion travel permit for the far North. We could drive another dozen miles, and continued onward to the Ombabika River. Our canoe route was northward on the Opichuan (pronounced with a hard "k") River to the Albany, with a stop at Fort Hope on Ea-bamet Lake, then down the Albany about 500 miles to Hudson Bay. We spent our first night sleeping under the stars and watching a colorful display of the northern lights.

We woke early to begin our canoe journey where the Ombabika River entered Toronto Lake. Leaving the logging evidence behind, we entered the land of black spruce and aspen forests just south of the Canadian taiga. We paddled five miles up the meandering Ombabika River, passing bogs full of cranberries and rice. There was a channel in the river's growth for a canoe's passage; at several Indian encampments, canoes were readying for the season's ricing. We stopped for a snack before paddling Summit Lake, which was shallow — not a paddle deep. This unusual lake straddles the Laurentian Divide, with the waters flowing southward down the Ombabika to Lake Superior and northward down the Powitik River to Hudson Bay. The lake had to be spring fed to serve two watersheds.

We shot a small rapids on the Powitik and passed a trapper's cabin in the woods. Around a corner was an immense muskeg bog with a large cow moose at the far end. She'd raise a root in her mouth and chomp contentedly as we paddled frantically toward her to get a closer look. She caught our scent and disappeared into the forest before we even narrowed the distance between us to a stone's throw.

We encountered two portages on the right around several rapids and fished below the second, where I caught a 3-pound northern. Next we paddled onward to the merger with the Kapikotongwa River and reached our first campsite. There was evidence of campers here previously, including broken balsam fir boughs spread out for a bough bed, and duck feathers. We pitched the tent and built a fireplace with two big logs to balance our pots. Our supper included northern pike, soup, macaroni, chili, corn on the cob (first night only), and pudding.

The next morning we faced the Kapikotongwa rapids — first a series of three dropping 10 feet, then another series dropping 35 feet in two miles. The wind was with us as we paddled northward, passing the small Phillips Creek. The first two-foot rapids was practice, but the following canoe hit a rock that swept it dangerously broadside. They quickly straightened the canoe and safely negotiated the remainder of the rapids. We then encountered the 35-foot series and missed the portage on the first one. We paddled to shore, reconnoitered the river ahead of us, finding a roaring rapids, and waded and pulled the canoe back up to the portage trail. The portage was used only by trappers and Indians and was full of deep mudholes. With the weight of a pack and canoe on my shoulders, I sank into the mud up to my thighs at one spot and fell backward. Finally we came to a thicket of trees and were below the rapids.

We rounded a few more bends before reaching a 3-foot rapids, which we cautiously entered. We hit a rock hidden by the waves, but the high water and current carried us over. The next rapids were around the corner, and I spotted a portage on the right. These rapids looked easy for lining or wading with the canoe; since I was already wet, I decided to wade these holding onto the back of the canoe. I waded to the last 100 feet, where the river turned and ran toward a rock in the center of the current. I tried to cross the river to the left bank but it was too deep, causing me to lose my footing. I grabbed onto the stern of the canoe and floated down the river. The bow struck a log to the right of the rock that swung the canoe broadside. I leaped into the stern seat. John, my bowman, turned to the left to watch me get in and tipped the gunwale of the canoe into the swift current. The current caught the canoe, and water rushed in as I jumped onto the log. My left leg slipped off the log and the canoe flipped, pinning my leg against the log. I yelled to John to grab the floating pack, which he pulled up onto the rock. My leg was being squeezed by the full force of the current. It was solidly wedged, and I hollered for my partner to jump on the canoe to bounce it and free my leg. The log moved a hair and I was able to pull my leg out of the water. The stern of the canoe was swept under the log, but the bow remained fast on a rock.

We managed to put on our life jackets and grab one paddle, but my only shirt and my partner's jacket were swept downstream. I felt under the canoe and found our second pack wedged between two thwarts. Our partners were portaging nearby and saw our predicament. We shivered as we waited for them. They tied two ropes onto the bow and chopped the log in half, freeing our canoe. I portaged the canoe past the remaining rapids, thanking God for life and limb. We built a fire and surveyed our soaked bread, wet flour, ruined camera and film, and wet gear. For the remainder of the day, we dried out, camping at the end of the portage trail.

In the morning we cooked the soggy bread soaked in egg batter for French toast. We continued down the Kapikotongwa much wiser because of our experience. We passed another trapper's cabin, saw an otter, and paddled to the Makoki Creek. Here we headed cross-country toward the Opichuan River. By midday we stopped for lunch, only to be dive-bombed by two angry herons for being too close to their young.

We crossed a small unnamed lake and took a bushy portage to a beaver pond. It had been a long paddle that day, and we camped on a rocky point. No-see-ums discovered our camp and holed up in our tent. These bugs are smaller than a mosquito, but leave a giant swollen welt where they bite.

After another breakfast of soggy French toast, we entered a small stream called Frog Creek. We poled, pushed, paddled, and cursed for about three miles. It was only six feet wide, full of brush, and twisted 90° every twenty feet. We finally reached the Ottertail River and paddled with ease on down to the Ogoki River. The Ogoki was famous in the north, and I was surprised to see the river was like a swampy, meandering lake.

It was time for a respite, to drift slowly and relax in the sun. Bruce, the sternman in the other canoe, stood up to relieve himself. His canoe drifted broadside ahead of ours, so I whispered to my partner to take a couple of swift strokes with his paddle. We rammed them in the middle of their canoe, and Bruce flipped over backwards, with one hand trying to hold his pants up! The joke wasn't a bit funny to him, but we got him ashore, built a fire, and dried him out, which improved his humor.

We continued down the Ogoki to the creek from French Lake and paddled upstream to French. Paddling into a headwind to the far end, we entered a shallow bay, with water only six inches deep covering three feet of mud. We pushed and poled across. When the water became too shallow, I wallowed through the muck, pulling the canoes to high ground. I found the portage to Mahamo Lake on a series of flat rock ridges. A bevy of partridges flew off as I searched for the portage trail. The portage was three-fourths of a mile, mostly wet bog where my boots sank in just over the tops on each step. When the bog was too deep, there were a few wet logs strewn about to balance atop when carrying the canoe. On the far end of the portage, I found a toboggan and half-eaten snowshoes along the trail. Perhaps porcupines ate the rawhide on the snowshoes.

We paddled halfway down Mahamo to camp on a breezy island away from the bugs. After dinner I caught several walleyes to eat for breakfast – along with the soggy French toast.

The next day we paddled into the wind to a river flowing into Kagianagami Lake. The river was monotonous, but a few ducks swimming ahead of us provided excitement. I took out the slingshot and aimed my rocks at them, but missed every time. We entered Kagianagami and enjoyed the open expanse of water after all of the claustrophobic river running. We paddled a mile and stopped at a cabin on a windy point. Fishing nets were drying on racks around the cabin. No one was there except three friendly dogs, who jumped all over us no matter where we explored. After lunch we paddled northward across the lake. The waves were stiff but not rolling, and we were able to reach the mouth of the Opichuan River by evening.

At daybreak we consumed our last two loaves of soggy bread in a French toast feast. The map showed Kagianagami Lake at 1010 feet above sea level, Opichuan Lake at 881 feet, and the point at which the Opichuan met the Albany at 853 feet. It looked like we would be in for one hell of a ride down the Opichuan. We paddled to the river and came to the first portage, which was a half mile long. Next came another portage that was even longer and full of bushes – but it was nice to know that we were bypassing many dangerous rapids. The next portage was well-trodden, perhaps by fly-in fishermen pursuing rainbow trout. We now honed our inchoate whitewater skills and shot the next rapids on the right, coming to the brink of a falls before portaging at a grassy spot on the left side. The carry was above a cliff, with the roar of the falls in our ears. We shot another rapids, pulled through the rocks on the right of another, and shot a third, riding out huge rooster tails of white water at the bottom. Both canoes took in an inch or two of water from the waves splashing over the gunwales. We ran one more, and the white-water tension eased. At Opichuan Lake there was a nice campsite, and we caught three walleyes below the last rapids for dinner. A full moon was out, its shimmering light reflecting across the waters.

The next day we began our venture to Fort Hope on Eabamet Lake. We portaged into Abazotikichuan Lake on the Albany River, leaving the Opichuan behind. We now had to paddle upstream, discovering that the current of the Albany was respectable and a lot of sweaty, hard work. As I glanced up from my deep paddle digs, I noticed a strange animal atop a rock on shore. I paddled closer, and to my surprise saw a half-dozen mink playing. They stuck their heads up and curiously checked us out. We seemed to pass their inspection, for they ignored us and continued their play.

We paddled up the current, against the wind, and into a blinding rainstorm. We pulled up several rapids to Frenchman's Rapids and carried over a long portage in the continuous rain. Our dinner was rain-soaked and cooked over a sputtering fire, using the finest wet wood the forest could offer. At least the cold and rain bothered the mosquitoes as much as us, and they kept away. Just as I finished washing dishes, I saw two Indians below me lining their canoe up Frenchman's Rapids. They had a canvas canoe with a high jutting bow built to withstand the rapids and a small outboard motor. They waved, greeted me in their native Ojibway, and pushed off.

In the morning we paddled Triangular Lake to the entrance of the Eabamet River from Eabamet Lake. The wind, rain, and cold continued. We pulled up one large rapids using ropes on the bow and stern of each canoe. Then we entered huge Eabamet Lake with the lifting clouds revealing the distant horizon and lake blending into one. We had finally reached one of the great northern lakes where one could not see the far shore. We could see part of the Fort Hope Indian settlement on the northern shore of the lake. We sat out a rain squall, then bucked a nasty, biting west wind for several endless hours to reach the trading post on the southern shore. Just as we were within reach of the dock, a seaplane landed next to us, practically swamping us in its wake.

We landed at the post and met the son of Chief Johnny YesNo (a famous Ojibway family), several Indians from Miminiska, and a Scotsman tending the store. The Hudson's Bay Company store was neat, clean, and stocked with practically everything. We all wrote a letter or two, and for twenty dollars bought cookies, candy, five pounds of dry flour, five loaves of bread, twelve oranges, and three cans of Spam. I enjoyed listening to the Indians speaking their native tongue. We left reluctantly and camped on Eabamet Lake enroute back to the Eabamet River.

By morning the weather had cleared, and we celebrated the sunshine with a pancake breakfast. We cruised down the Eabamet River, passing an Indian family, and paddled with the wind down Triangular Lake, portaging around Frenchman's Rapids again. Below that portage was a rapids that dropped six feet, with no portage to be found; the Indians apparently run them. I decided to shoot them by paddling past the huge waves to smoother water on the far shore, but the current caught us and carried us right into the main torrent. We hit a gigantic wave straight on and took in two inches of water. I headed hard right and hoped we could make it, but then the canoe was amidst the waves and I lost sight of my bowman in a mass of white water. When we emerged, the canoe was full of water. John fell out of the canoe to the right, losing his paddle in the melee. The water became calmer, and with my paddling from the half-floating canoe and John's kicking, we were able to beach the canoe and empty out the water. I turned around and saw Bruce and Rudy hit the big wave broadside. I thought it was all over for them, but with sheer luck they straightened the canoe and emerged with only two inches of water in the bottom. We continued through four more rapids, letting ourselves dry out in the wind and sun between thundershowers. We reached Abazotikichuan Lake by evening and pitched camp on an island. The evening was clear and warm as we wrung out our wet sleeping bags and dried everything reasonably well by nightfall.

We had been on the trail for ten days and were becoming seasoned by the river, weather, and our mishaps in whitewater. The rapids were exciting, and we were learning, albeit the hard way, how to negotiate them. John and Rudy were becoming hardened canoeists, and we were a smooth foursome cooperating well in all of the camping chores.

We encountered four easy, wide rapids before entering Makokibatan Lake, and rounded a point to see the whole lake appear before us. The far end was so distant that the earth's curvature cut off the view of it. The wind was with us, and it soon rolled up big swells to scurry us on. We stopped at a sandy cove at the first northern promontory for a little beachcombing and noticed several cabins at a fishing camp. A couple miles farther was an adequate campsite for us on a flat rock with lots of brush and, unfortunately, bugs. Rainbow trout were jumping and rising in the evening, tempting me to cast all of the various lures in my tackle box, but none worked.

The river divided into two channels for the next forty miles. We took the northerly route via Washi Lake because we could count fewer rapids on the map than on the narrower southerly route. We entered the river at the end of Makokibatan Lake and headed for a sandbar on the left, where there was a portage bypassing more rapids. After the portage there were three rapids that we easily handled. The next rapids had no portage, and I tried the left side. We made it through the slick current, around a rock, and into the huge white waves below. We were swept into the high white waves, and the canoe flipped over as fast as lightning. Again we were drenched and humiliated. We kicked our canoe quickly toward shore while the second canoe swamped in the same place. Rudy grabbed a floating pack and John grabbed his paddle. Another camera was ruined and the food was wet again. On closer inspection, the map showed a "P" for portage on the right side of the fifth rapids, the ones we had just come through. We shot the last small rapids into Washi Lake and paddled across, making camp at an abandoned Indian encampment on the north shore. The late afternoon sun was hot, enabling us to dry everything before nightfall.

In the morning we studied the maps carefully, for we had the mighty Kagiami Falls ahead of us. We portaged around a pair of rapids just below Washi Lake and portaged again ahead of the confluence with the southern fork. We entered the full force of the river and decided to be as cautious as possible. The portages often begin right at the brink of a rapids or falls because the Indians who use the river despise portaging their heavy Hudson Bay canvas canoes. They prefer to line their canoes along the shore through the rapids. There were three rapids skirting an island for three miles, and we ran the first and portaged around the next two after seeing a ten-foot falls where the river dove over a ledge.

We then entered the complex of rapids and falls leading to Kagiami Falls. The altitude dropped 80 feet through this section, with the falls marked 22½ feet. After entering the rapids, we lined around several boils, took a channel along the right side, lined through two more, and portaged around the right side of a falls over a ledge. We took a lunch break, cussing the endless peanut-butter-and-soggy-bread sandwiches.

Next the main current went to the left around a banana-shaped island. I decided to paddle to a series of small islands to the right and avoid careening over an unmarked falls. We went to the extreme right and made two easy lift-overs on the flat rocks. There were cliffs on the right shore further ahead, and we crossed the river paddling hard to reach the left shore landing at a steep, grassy portage. Hiking across to the far side, we had our first glimpse of Kagiami Falls. They were a stupendous sight and demanded a canoer's respect.

We paddled another half mile and portaged on the left around an even higher falls of the Kagiami complex. Then we paddled around a tricky rock bank to get to the portage, again right at the brink of the falls. These falls were incredible — much larger than the first. A sheer wall of water came roaring over the cliff, smashing onto the rocks below with spray inundating everything. The mist descended upon us. We shot several currents and lifted-over an island with a steep, slippery landing on the far side. Another mile and we came to an island with eight-foot falls on both sides, and we portaged over the island. Half a mile downstream we reached a tent camp probably used by the Indians and decided to camp nearby.

A beautiful brown mongrel dog, who was very wary and untrusting, was at the camp. He appeared half-starved, with all his ribs showing. With the smell of dinner cooking, the dog became much more friendly. I tossed him a piece of bread and he caught it in midair, clashing his teeth as he swallowed it whole. What a voracious animal! I gave him some more food and leftovers from dinner to assuage his hunger. I named him Kagiami after the falls we had passed. If Kagiami wanted to come with us, we decided we'd take him along.

Breakfast consisted of soggy-bread French toast for the last time. However, I couldn't find our three pounds of Crisco anywhere, having left it on top of the overturned canoe in the evening. Kagiami looked strangely content for a starving animal that morning. Could he have made off with our Crisco shortening? I searched the brush and couldn't find any trace of it, so we packed and loaded the canoes. I motioned to the dog, who surprised me when he hopped into the center of the canoe. He was at least canoe-trained.

We pulled and lined through a rapids, negotiated a wide, shallow one, and heard the roar of a major one — Tom Flett Rapids. We easily found the portage on the right and avoided the disaster Gus

Walske had related to us. The portage began on a beach and headed up a hill, where I found a stone with three names and the date August 1, 1961. Perhaps this was a gravestone for three drowned canoeing adventurers. The portage wasn't long and was followed by another portage on the right around Martin Falls, where I noted an old campsite. We came to another rapids requiring another portage, but were able to shoot the lower part safely.

The river now took on a different character, with a solid current of brute force, high clay banks, no more rocks or rapids, and fewer trees. We had made the last of the portages! Barren Nottik Island with its high-water banks was passed as the current swept us along. The map listed about twenty rapids near the Wabassi River, but the Albany merely became shallower and much swifter. Perhaps at low water the shallows took on the characteristics of rapids. Our aching and well-used paddling muscles appreciated the ride! We passed the Wabassi and camped on the north shore on a gravel bank, with the tent back in the woods. After supper I gave Kagiami some sauerkraut and was chagrined at the strange face he gave me after tasting it. What a fussy starved animal! It was a calm, pretty evening for reflection as the river swept by. We had now conquered the worst of the rapids and falls but still had a long distance to travel before reaching Hudson Bay.

By noon of the next day, we reached Ogoki Post at the confluence of the Albany and Ogoki Rivers. A typical well-kept Hudson's Bay Trading Post was situated on the south shore and a small Indian village on the north. The clerk at the post, a Polish émigré, invited us in for lunch. We ate over two pounds of his frankfurters and heard our first music in days from his radio. Our conversation turned to world events, and we were surprised to hear that Adlai Stevenson had died.

Peter suggested that we visit the Indian village with him, and took us across the river in his wood-and-canvas Hudson Bay canoe. He introduced us to each of the Ojibway families. Here was George Baxter of Washi Lake, with his father (in his 80s) and his wife Josephine. All of the father's teeth were rotted stumps, perhaps from too much white man's sugar. They lived mainly in canvas tents spread across poles, their summer lodgings; cabins on distant traplines were used during the winter. They had gill nets set for fish in the Albany and Ogoki Rivers to supplement their summer diet. Nearby were two wooden houses built by the Canadian government and sold to the Indians for a $50 down payment. We stopped at a one-room white clapboard church to talk to the Catholic missionary, whose diocese had developed a phonetic alphabet providing a written language to the Indians. The strange symbols were fascinating. They gave me several of their booklets with news, stories, and their teachings. We chatted with several Indian families, and one gave me a deer antler with velvet still on it. Another presented me with the skull of a caribou. George Baxter showed us the six-block road they were cutting, which would link the villagers; this was followed by a libation consisting of a glass of sherry. I was fascinated with the Indian language and learned how to count and a few words for the animals of the forest.

We were ready to leave, but Kagiami had disappeared. George said his father had him; we hiked to his distant tent and found Kagiami at the end of a wire trap with the steel end tethered to a stake. He was excited to see us. George told us that Kagiami belonged to one of his far-flung sons. I offered to buy him, but George effusively gave me the dog with a big toothless smile. He saw that I was happy and said that the dog's name was *Ooshi*; Peter interpreted this to mean "yellow." I told him that we had named him Kagiami after the falls and that he had eaten all of our Crisco, which caused the old Indian to burst into laughter.

We went back to the post and I cleaned a 10-pound sturgeon for Peter to cook for dinner. Kagiami devoured the scraps, including a two-foot-long piece of skin from the fillet. The poor dog got half of the skin down but then choked with ten inches still sticking out. I didn't know whether to pull it out or leave it in, but he took a few more chomps and the whole skin disappeared. We enjoyed our sturgeon fillets and spent a pleasant evening listening to the radio and enjoying company in the North.

We left early in the morning, noting that we had been on the trail for more than two weeks. We soon reached Stonebasket Island and continued with a swift current. We were now in the land of the Canada goose and passed several families with goslings. We passed a few gravel bars as the river widened. Kagiami began to get restless with disdain for sitting in the canoe and jogged along the shoreline. He bolted around tree trunks, over rocks, and through bullrushes, and swam the small, frequent tributaries. There were high clay cliffs along much of the shore, and spruces often were toppled into the river. The mouth of the Muswabik River passed by as we headed toward Albany Forks, where the Kenogami and Little Current Rivers entered. Kagiami was running dozens of miles per day. He was certainly getting his exercise now that he was well fed. The river was growing more monotonous, and we enjoyed watching the dog run along the shoreline. He sure was loyal, but perhaps he had enough of being left alone in the wilderness. I think food added to his fealty.

The shoreline became more bushy as we headed east, and the mosquitoes increased severalfold because the muskeg and swampland were perfect for breeding. We passed Albany Forks and several named islands: Oldman, Comb, and Snake. It was overcast and misty, creating a dreamy effect as we paddled and drifted onward. When we stopped for lunch, two herons lifted off. Kagiami ran after them and found a third, who screeched and held the dog at bay. The heron was as terrified as could be, and I ran to grab Kagiami. I was lucky to nab him before the heron had pecked him.

A little farther, a young calf moose was walking along the shoreline. Kagiami was ready to leap out of the canoe, but the moose trotted off. The dog had whined but strangely wouldn't bark; perhaps he was part wolf and didn't know how to bark. We landed the canoe farther on for the dog to run, but he took off in the direction of the moose. I ran after him, yelling his name, but hordes of mosquitoes descended on me. They were thicker than jam and worse than I'd ever seen in my life. I jumped back into the canoe and paddled into the river breeze that afforded a little relief. I thought that the dog was gone for good, but he soon came as we were on our way again, swatting bugs right and left. The weather cleared as we reached Hat Island, where we pitched camp and devoured some morsels before making a beeline for the tent to escape the bugs.

We paddled on to the Ghost River Camp and explored an abandoned Hudson's Bay Company store. The whole camp was grown over with shoulder-high weeds, and the buildings were empty. We passed Norran and headed to Blackbear Island. After a smorgasbord lunch, I wandered along the bank, finding a beautiful orange flower with six petals forming a tulip, with a purple conglomeration at the end of a stalk. That evening I baked a cake for dessert, but the heavy sweet was relished only by Kagiami.

After dinner we decided to travel during the night because we were becoming anxious to reach Hudson Bay. The wind was from the west and added to the speed of the current. A thunderhead loomed behind us, accompanied by lightning. Perhaps it would be our bad luck to be caught by a cold front the one night we chose to travel. As soon as we reached the end of Blackbear Island we bivouacked under the canoes for an hour to let a rain squall pass by. Then we ventured out with our bowmen catnapping. I noticed that Bruce and Rudy were drifting along far behind us. John couldn't fall asleep and continued to paddle. At Fishing Creek Island, Kagiami was sore from sitting and stood up as we entered a converging current; just then we squarely hit a rock that almost turned the canoe over into the deep river. This made us stop and reconsider night travel, since the pitch black darkness obscured the rocks hidden in the river current. Pulling into a sandy cove, I went over my boot tops as I stepped out of the canoe. It was 3 A.M. and completely overcast.

We slept until dawn, taking turns looking for the second canoe. Since they might have passed us, we paddled until 10 A.M. We had last seen them behind us and had not spotted them ahead despite our constant lookout, we figured they must still be behind us. After building a hot fire, we cooked several dinner items in their tins, because the other canoe had all of the breakfast food and cooking utensils. We napped until 2 P.M., but there was still no sign of the other canoe. We worried — had something happened to them, or were they ahead of us? The weather changed to low-lying cumulus clouds. Later, as I walked along the sand and rock shore, I heard John yelling that he had spotted the other canoe coming downriver. They had just been slow and had stopped to sleep also. We all relaxed during the afternoon and ate that longed-for breakfast of pancakes for dinner. I baked another unmentionable cake and the dog again fared well. We brewed a pot of tea and sat around sipping it while swatting Albany River mosquitoes.

The next morning we paddled into the vast delta of the Albany River where it enters James Bay. There were countless islands, and we had presumed there would be no difficulty in finding Fort Albany. Our charts listed a trading post and Fort Albany on Albany Island. We passed Big Island to the left and paddled down a couple of rapids. We reached Sinclair Island, where we had planned to take the right channel to the mission on the south bank; but the channel was dry, forcing us to take the north channel. We passed Sinclair Island and a small island hiding the channel southward to the mission and the entire settlement. The town was on high ground where it could not be seen from the river.

We passed between two grassy islands, rounding a bend to see for the first time — Hudson Bay! We all stopped paddling and spent a pensive moment staring out at the ocean, then I yelled and yodeled to celebrate the end of our journey. But we still needed to find Fort Albany. We reached Albany Island and the site of the trading post, but all that was there was an old dilapidated building. I thought the new one would be further down the island and paddled closer to the ocean. It was getting dark when I noticed a rack on shore. Several cabins back in the trees were part of a goose-hunting camp. We camped nearby; fortunately, the water had no salty taste, and we cooked a scrumptious final dinner to celebrate our arrival at the bay.

We had been traveling for three weeks and had finally reached Hudson Bay. We had conquered the Albany! But we were unexpectedly frustrated because we couldn't find the fort. Retracing our route westward along Albany Island the next morning against the wind and a cold horizontal drizzle, we entered another maze of islands and dried-up channels. We reached another large island and split up to explore each side. Our channel rapidly became too shallow to paddle, requiring pulling and dragging the canoe the whole distance through the shallows and over the rocks. Meanwhile, Kagiami ran and waited for us on the shore. I saw two cabins on the north shore in the Indian reservation and paddled across, finding no one there. Kagiami pursued us and swam the entire width of the north channel in the treacherous current. We paddled upstream against a stiff current to meet our other canoe, then lined the canoes up the shore for a mile to Big Island and several more channels, where we hoped to see the flying Canadian maple leaf. But there was no flag, only the desolation and whispers of more wilderness.

It was 7 P.M. and time to pitch camp again, but then we heard a motor and saw an Indian canoe. We flagged it down and they agreed to take Bruce and me to the fort. The Indians, who were Cree, jovially talked in their incredibly beautiful musical language. We roared off and wandered through the maze to a hidden channel by Sinclair Island. Their motor hit a rock but was not damaged — they just laughed and kept going at full speed. What wonderful, carefree people! We finally reached Fort Albany and walked up a stairway on the south shore and up a high bluff. We were amazed — there were two stores, a mission, two churches, a large settlement, and four microwave towers. There were eight vehicles and several miles of road. We paid the Indians five dollars to ferry our two companions and gear to the fort as well.

We had originally planned to paddle south along the shore of James Bay to Moosonee and return by rail, but we were greeted with a big smile by my father, who had flown his seaplane to Fort Albany. He planned to fly Bruce and me back to Ely for a faster return. He had followed the river for 300 miles to the bay and was quite concerned when he hadn't spotted our two canoes, not knowing that we had overshot Fort Albany.

We met the fur trader and also the owner of the goose camp, who put us all up for the night and who would arrange to ferry the canoes, John, and Rudy to Moosonee for return by rail. Bruce, Kagiami, and I would have the luxury of a flight back to the Quetico-Superior guiding trails.

After a good night's rest, we flew south along the tidal flats to Moose Factory and Moosonee to refuel the plane. The weather turned cloudy and misty as we flew southwest along the Abitibi River, where we landed to wait for the clouds to lift. We continued our flight over endless muskeg, Lake Nipigon, and the rugged Lake Superior northland, finally landing back in the United States. We had paddled over 500 miles in three weeks and covered most of the Albany River on a challenging first trip to Hudson Bay.

CHAPTER NINETEEN

From the Rockies to the Bay

AFTER SAVORING THE adventures of the Albany River to Hudson Bay, I longed for an even greater challenge. To the far north was a mighty river, the Churchill, that was appealing; it had rapids and chutes, and was far enough away from civilization to present a wilderness challenge. But the Churchill did not span Canada, so I ordered and reviewed the Canadian geological survey maps westward to the Rockies. To the northwest was the famous Fort Chipewyan on Lake Athabasca. What a venture it would be to canoe there! I noted that the Peace River flowed from the Rockies past the town of Peace River and on to the headwaters of Athabasca and Great Slave Lakes. From Athabasca I could trace a route over the Arctic Divide to Reindeer Lake and the Reindeer River to the Churchill River. Sigurd Olson, in *The Lonely Land*, had described a canoeing venture along the headwaters of the Churchill to Southern Indian Lake; even that partial journey had given the Churchill the reputation of being the king of the northern rivers.

During the winter of 1966–1967, I planned a canoe trip for the following summer — a college graduation celebration, and also a short reprieve before the hard work of medical school. I charted the route and marked off two-inch segments (about 35 miles) for each day's paddle. I calculated that it would take thirty-three days to complete, and planned for thirty-five days' food. I corresponded with a guiding compatriot, Tom Dayton, and our plans began to crystallize. I painted an 18-foot standard aluminum canoe fire-engine red and christened it "Lara" after the movie *Dr. Zhivago*. I padded the seats with sponge and bolted a new carrying yoke to the center. Packing the food was almost a science — I placed each breakfast in a separate plastic bag (oatmeal, pancake flour, or dried eggs) and did the same

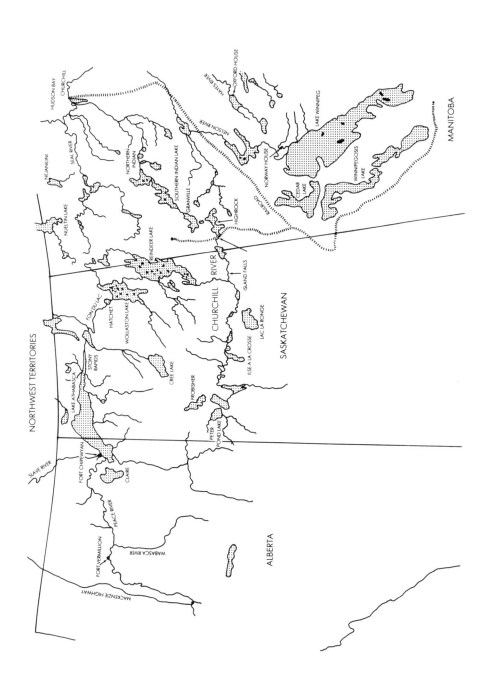

for the dinners (main course, vegetable, soup, pudding). For the lunches I asked the bakery to bake a hard French bread and packed peanut butter, jam, sausage, cheese, and dehydrated juices.

Tom, who had guided many summers and had done the Grand Portage trip with me, was excited and ready. We had the gear and canoe ready but lacked a third companion. A third canoeist was a virtual necessity for a canoe trip spanning 1500 miles of Canadian taiga wilderness. My colleague, Bruce, who had been on the Albany, was unable to guide in the North that summer. I called on a high school friend who was unemployed; he was a stalwart Finnish woodsman. Jack Niemi was enthralled with the idea, and his parents' hesitation soon turned to encouragement. A threesome at last, we studied the route on the maps for a final review. The local grocer's son volunteered to drive with us to Peace River, Alberta, and return the vehicle.

Within a day we were driving across the Manitoba heartland, surrounded by wheat fields and prairie. We crossed into Saskatchewan and passed many ponds with families of ducks. At last we reached the town of Peace River, Alberta, high on the hillsides overlooking the river. In the waning light, we drove onto the bridge spanning the half-mile-wide Peace River. Below us was the silt-laden power of a mighty current. As young canoeists, we were impressed and a little apprehensive of the unknown ahead of us.

The next morning we visited the local gasoline station, where an Indian agent in a mud-splattered car drove up. He had just come from Fort Vermilion and said it was very muddy on the Mackenzie Highway to Hay River, Northwest Territories. He stated that it was an eight-day paddle on the Peace River to Fort Vermilion; thus, we decided to drive 230 miles north on the Mackenzie Highway to Fort Vermilion in order to save a week's paddle. The Mackenzie Highway was generally flat, traversing tall black spruce and thick poplar forests. The farmers were clearing the forest for their precious wheat, and grain elevators had marched this far northward. In the distance were the Birch Mountains, the last remnants of the Rockies as we headed east to begin our trek to Hudson Bay.

We drove to High Level, a booming oil town with a half-dozen new stores and several more under construction amidst pools of mud and rutted roads. Mud was piled car-high near their gas station. We turned and drove the last 80 miles to the Peace River, ending at a

149

ferry dock. We loaded our four packs into the canoe and bade Greg Hutar, our driver, farewell.

The current of about five knots quickly carried us past high sandy bluffs along an otherwise flat, sandy shoreline. We passed several houses at North Vermilion and Boyer Settlement. The wind increased for a short while and gave us a push, but then we turned and it gave us a broadside fusillade. We passed several winter roads, and finally at about 8:00 P.M. saw two cabin sites past Adams Landing. We stopped and pitched our first camp near one of the cabins. Our clothes were clean and untorn, and our tent was fresh. The canoe was unscratched. What a difference two months of canoeing would make!

The cabins were filthy, old, and full of mosquitoes. I cooked a dinner of chicken stew, biscuits, dehydrated fruit, and soup. The water was laden with glacial silt that was so fine that it even passed through the undershirt I used as a filter. It gave each drink a crunchiness, but we didn't notice the silt in our dinner. After dinner, we planned for future stops: we would organize ourselves into an efficient brigade of one person building the fire and cooking dinner while the other two found a flat tent site and pitched the tent. Following that, the two would cut firewood for dinner and breakfast. After dinner, we would all sip our tea and relax among the mosquitoes before nightfall.

We awoke at 7:30 A.M. on our first morning; after that we were always on the water by 7:30 and would break about 1:00 P.M. for a half-hour lunch period. We then continued until 10:00 P.M. every night as our conditioning improved and muscles hardened.

As we emerged from the tent that morning, we donned our headnets to protect whatever the evening mosquitoes had missed. The Vermilion Rapids and Falls were ahead of us. We negotiated the canoe through a sandbar maze that I thought could be the rapids. Tom saw white splashing ahead that I dismissed as the reflection of the sun on small waves, and we continued to paddle nonchalantly down the middle of the river. Then we all saw spray rising above the waves — we were entering Vermilion Rapids! I saw an island on the left and aimed for it, but rapids were breaking above it, requiring a sharp left to make the left shore. The current caught us, and we began to lose ground despite paddling like drowning dogs. Tom saw a sandbar that we could make, where we could stop and observe the breaking fury 50 yards below us.

We portaged to the bushes and forest, following an old trail for a third of a mile. The rapids roared around our island and extended almost a mile to the far shoreline. Paddling onward, we saw more white "dogs" leaping above the water, indicating more rapids ahead. There was a rock ledge on the left side, and we snuggled up against it. We hiked along the ledge, lining the canoe with our ropes for a third of a mile, and lined past the ledge to a series of channels. At one place the canoe went over a curl diagonally, and I let out more rope to keep the stern from tipping or taking in any water. The canoe began to drift broadside; I yelled to Tom, who quickly pulled on the bow rope, bringing the canoe out of danger. There was a drop-off ahead of us, and we beached the canoe in a cove to reconnoiter.

We were hiking on a sandstone ledge about 25 feet above the river. Cliff swallows were everywhere, with each pocket in the ledge providing a perfect location for one of their nests. When we reached the edge, we realized we finally were at Vermilion Falls. The brown torrent dropped 20 feet across the entire mile-wide river. This side was the most dangerous, since ocean-sized waves foamed along the ledge. We portaged around the raging mud torrent to a place below the waves, at a gully interrupting the ledge. We ate lunch, trying the package of sugar-oatmeal bread that the Ely baker had given us as a gift. His concoction tasted much better in the woods than it had back in civilization.

We passed Little Red River and saw a windsock and bush airfield nearby. We were averaging 5 to 6 miles per hour on the river and had covered 57 miles on our second day. Where two red-and-white steel triangles marked the fifth meridian, we stopped at the abandoned Hudson's Bay Company post, but the mosquitoes wouldn't let us stand still. We paddled to a nearby island, hoping for a stiff evening breeze. We unloaded our canoe onto a flat sandbar where we would be past the 12-foot sandy cliffs along the banks of the river and its islands. Jack and Tom pitched the tent while I fought mosquitoes and built a fire in the fine sand. There were two species of mosquitoes here, the regulars and the yellow giants. The latter breed had banded legs, were as large as a thumbnail, and persisted in their merciless pursuit of blood through all swats.

That evening I began reading a book, *The Honourable Company*, that I had found at the abandoned Hudson's Bay post. Founded in 1670, the Hudson's Bay Company established trading posts throughout the vast canoe country to obtain furs and sell groceries and retail goods. The ventures of Samuel Hearne, who traversed the Northwest Territories by foot, and Sir George Simpson, who ruled these vast lands two centuries ago, were most fascinating.

We awoke on schedule the next morning and hurriedly ate our pancake breakfast, eager to leave land and the mosquitoes behind for the breezes along the river. We now developed a system for paddling — we would switch every two hours, with me taking stern duties except for a shift in the center. We passed Garden Creek, ate our lunch, and saw the Caribou Mountains to the north. They were a blue backdrop to the forest along the Peace but only rose to about 3000 feet in elevation. As we passed each mud-bar, a covey of ducks would be awakened by our giant canoe and take flight. Before Big Slough, we ran aground among the sandbars and had to slosh through the mud to get moving again. A short walk into the sandbars made us feel as if we were in a desert rather than the far North.

We passed giant driftwood and several sawed timbers stuck in the sandbars. We camped near Jackfish River and took a quick dip in the warm evening sun. Little can compare to the ooze of the mud as one wades into the miserably cold water, only to be welcomed by the mosquitoes and hordes of no-see-ums as one re-emerges. We washed in our underwear and felt clean again, but it would be more than a month until the next bath.

Early morning sleepiness began to become routine. As we neared Boyer Rapids, the banks of the river were over 80 feet high. The cliffs, which appeared to be limestone or white sandstone, took on a palisade appearance resembling Bryce Canyon, Utah. The overhangs of these bluffs were occupied by hundreds of cliff swallows, who took wary flight as we approached.

We lunched on our half-loaf of bread, further divided into thirds and smothered with peanut butter and jelly. We passed Peace Point warden station, which appeared occupied although we saw no one. We paddled around a horseshoe in the river, and twelve Cree in a bateaux (a boat 25 feet long, with a flat bottom and straight 4-foot sides) motored by. After they passed, we heard shotgun blasts and wondered if they had shot several ducks for dinner. We passed an

Indian sawmill and camped in a cutover area a little further downriver.

We were in Wood Buffalo National Park and kept a constant lookout for wildlife, but were disappointed at never seeing any. Wood buffalo were reported to frequent the Basil Lake ranger cabin, but we saw none as we passed. We did spot the ranger in the nearby lookout tower. We passed the Chenal des Quatre Fourches and entered the Revillion Coupe. This channel connects the Peace River to Lake Athabasca, while the main current of the Peace turns north to Great Slave Lake. The current slowed, and we drifted only a few feet during lunch. Jack spotted our first rock ledges, a familiar Minnesota sight after miles of sandbanks and sandbars.

We entered the Riviere des Rochers and were dismayed to find the current against us. The trees on the shore were flooded, and with the lack of any hills, we appeared to be traveling through the bayous. There were three channels; we chose the center one and had our first glimpse of distant Lake Athabasca. The left shore had barren, rocky hills, and I noticed a radio tower atop one, probably servicing Fort Chipewyan. We paddled across a shallow bay full of weeds and reeds to a rocky island about four miles from Fort Chipewyan. We pitched the tent on top of a high hill and cooked dinner near the shore. We slept expectantly, for tomorrow would bring us to Fort Chipewyan, the destination of the voyageurs two centuries ago.

Rain and drizzle greeted us in the morning, but we devoured Jack's rubbery pancakes and launched our canoe. We had only a short paddle around a point and past several channels to reach Fort Chipewyan. We passed a red brick school and church run by three French Canadian priests. After beaching near the main dock, we walked up to the Athabasca Cafe and the Hudson's Bay Company store.

About fourteen hundred people lived in Fort Chipewyan, most being Cree Indians. Donald Voyageur, a Cree boy of about 13, showed us the Alexander Mackenzie monument, dedicated to the early explorer who was here in 1792 on his journey up the Peace River to the Pacific Ocean. Rodney Mackenzie built the original fort on Old Fort Point in 1730 and moved it to the current site about forty years later.

We bought a hamburger in the cafe and listened to a song on the juke box with the Indians. Tom enjoyed seeing the Indian children and listening to their native tongue. We bade Fort Chipewyan fare-well and headed back out into the wind.

Lake Athabasca is a clear-water lake with a rugged north shore like Lake Superior. The lake is shaped like a 200-mile-long banana, and we elected to follow the southern shore. We crossed to Mouse Is-land, where we stopped for an hour to allow the 30-mile-per-hour wind to abate. Late in the afternoon, the wind shifted to the west, allowing us to venture out in a tailwind. We had to cross the Athabasca River delta to Old Fort Point. Tom built a sail with our poncho and two poles. We launched the Lara and stared back at the humped islands of Athabasca.

The wind began filling our sail as we pushed on to 6, 7 then 8 miles per hour. The waves kept growing as we left our spit of land and quickly became rather fearful. One wave caught us in its grip, and we surfed ahead out of control. I jammed the paddle in to steer and gave the canoe a hard left rudder to keep us level; my rear was hang-ing over the side as if we were in a sailboat, but water still poured in over the gunwale. Fortunately, that wave wasn't followed by more. We paddled to the reeds near Goose Island and followed the delta shoreline. At 9:30 P.M. we saw a light pass by — in the darkness we could make out a tug and barge plying the navigable channel of the Athabasca River. It was bringing supplies to the community out-posts on the north shore of Athabasca. We couldn't get through the channel, so paddled parallel to it until we could paddle to the point opposite Old Fort Point for a late camp and dinner.

The next day, July 5, was nearly our termination. Athabasca is a huge lake, and we were learning to respect the forces of Nature. Nary a week earlier had the ice left Athabasca's freezing clutches. We reconstructed our sail, since the calmness of early morning was broken by a brisk breeze by 8:00 A.M. But there was too much wind for the sail, so we rolled it up in the canoe and headed across a deep bay to Old Fort Point. Rolling with the waves, we were making good time since we were headed almost with the wind. But as we ventured farther from shore, the waves kept growing larger and larger. They began to swell and gently break as they reached their summit. I decided to head for the island in the bay, but the canoe began to take in water as we reached the top of each wave. We had passed the safety point and were in the critical range. I headed for the shore that we had left and quartered the waves to the right. It seemed like an ocean now — we took in water over port; Tom was bailing with his boot; water roared in over starboard and all I could see of Jack was his head. We were sunk. The pack by my feet wasn't strapped in, and I yelled to Tom to do that; meanwhile, I grabbed three paddles. One life belt drifted away; mine was on, and Tom had the orange life jacket. The sail drifted away, and I decided not to leave the canoe in the big waves to grab it. Shore was over a mile away — our situation looked desperate. But since we were sitting upright in the canoe and barely moving, I yelled, "Paddle!"

Our canoe started moving toward shore, and our blood started moving in our freezing bodies. We built up our confidence that we might make it. Every breaker would dunk us; it seemed to take eternity to reach shore. (It turned out to be forty minutes.) Finally, we could see the shore logs with the breakers smashing against them. Tom and I jumped out as the canoe neared the logs, and we all pulled at the wet packs to get them ashore. We beached the canoe and placed it high above the waterline.

We had to build a fire to warm and dry ourselves. We kept moving to keep warm, and Tom hit two dry match heads together and set an old, dry jack pine afire. Our long ordeal of drying our equipment began. We first dried ourselves, then put up clotheslines for our personal gear and sleeping bags. Either in the lake or in the brush as we had unloaded the canoe, I had lost my glasses, which had been in my shirt pocket. All of our cameras were ruined. Fortunately, the food packs were reasonably dry.

We napped in the afternoon, regaining our senses and composure. I hiked back to the groaning logs and whistling wind to stare out across the lake and thank God that our misfortune had not been more severe.

We decided to travel at night and sleep by day while crossing mighty Lake Athabasca. The wind was finally dying as we ate dinner. The cool breeze was actually refreshing by nightfall. By 10:00 P.M. the wind had died and we were relatively dry, packed, and ready to venture out.

We launched our canoe and paddled along the shoreline. The poncho-sail and lifebelt were nowhere to be found. I noticed a cross made of wood along the shore not too far from where we swamped. I beached the canoe and walked up to the cross. The grave was for a 36-year-old man, A. C. Tolatron, drowned September 15, 1954. Rather fateful.

We reached Old Fort Point as the glowing orange sun dipped behind the northwestern horizon. The glow would stay with us all night, moving around the lake's horizon from west via north to the east. There were about ten houses silhouetted black against the light sky at Old Fort Point. As we passed, my watch passed midnight, and we came upon July 6, my 22nd birthday. We paddled deep into Old Fort Bay, mistaking Moose Point for a series of islands. On realizing we were too far south, we headed north to the point with a little trepidation, leaving the shoreline behind. A warm south wind with gentle waves scurried us along. The shore was solid sand when we reached the point, and we stopped to stretch our legs.

I curled up in the center of the canoe and tried to keep warm as my partners paddled on. The coldness of Athabasca came through the aluminum, penetrating my wool jacket and long underwear. The sun rose shortly after 3:00 A.M., but it wasn't warm until three hours later. We passed a few rocky points, and they eventually disappeared into a continuous fine-sand shoreline. High sandbanks guarded the beaches a few yards back from the shore. At noon we stopped for breakfast and a nap in the sand. A blackfly buzzed me in my sleep and stung my left eye, putting me into a fit of misery. It seemed as if my eye was on fire. I taped a gauze pad over my eye to rest it. We left our sandy respite and bucked the wind for two more hours before giving up and pitching camp. My partners did all the work while I nursed a painful eye; we all slept soundly to the rhythm of the rain.

In the morning, we slept in, and then paddled against a northeast wind all day. To break the monotony of paddling, we occasionally lined the canoe along the beaches. We made almost as good time walking as we did paddling against the wind. At the mouth of the William River, the water turned a deep, dark red for several hundred yards, but it cleared again as we rounded William Point.

The next day we continued paddling along the sandy shore against a brisk east-northeast headwind. The wind increased by midmorning, requiring us to beach the canoe and await calmer weather. Landing the canoe was often difficult in the dense willows along the shore. Also, the sand, sticks, bark, and flotsam along the shore made it difficult to procure clean drinking water.

While windbound, I hiked past the sand dunes into the stunted taiga forest. There were birches, jack pine, and spruce, none larger in diameter than a human arm. The forest floor was covered with spongy reindeer moss. I returned to our makeshift camp and read prodigiously about the famed Hudson's Bay Company.

It grew colder, and a thundershower descended on us. I put Jack's rain pants upside down over my head and stood under a few small trees. We decided that we would eat supper and travel at night once again.

We paddled out at 10:00 P.M. and crept onward in the continuing wind and waves. At 1:00 A.M., I took my turn in the center of the canoe and slept a fitful hour or two. Tom and I were wet, cold, and miserable, but Jack was snug as a bug in his rain pants. The wind and waves persisted, and we made very slow headway. We decided this had to be crazy, beached, pitched our tent, and slept until morning, hoping for dead calm.

The next morning was windy again. We were south of Uranium City, and had actually considered crossing the lake to follow the northern shore. However, with our experience on Athabasca so far, the mere thought of venturing very far from shore was repugnant. We dug hard with our paddles to Turner Point, where we saw surf-sized rollers breaking off the end of the point. We decided not to risk paddling out into the rollers, and portaged across the point. We carried two midweight packs, one on the back and one on the front; a very heavy pack that we called the "beast pack," primarily filled with food; and a light pack that was carried by the person carrying the canoe. We rotated loads every half mile. On crossing the point, we were buffeted by eastern headwinds, requiring us to continue our carry. The waves were curling from their wind-born weight 20 yards from shore, causing a constant gurgling noise. I saw numerous fresh caribou tracks as I hiked down the sand.

As the beach turned to parallel the wind and the waves diminished, we unloaded our packs from our aching shoulders. I noticed a clearing back in the forest, with a small cabin. I hiked back into the jack pine forest, to find a log cabin that was home only to a rabbit, which scurried away. A partridge family took flight also, and Jack and I were in hot pursuit. With our portable .22 rifle, we shot several for a scrumptious partridge stew.

After dinner, we headed out again for another night of travel. We passed Turner Point and saw a fishing boat about two miles away. It had an inboard engine and a small cabin. We paddled toward it, half seeking some human companionship and half wondering if they might be headed eastward down the lake. They were two fishermen from Gunnar on the far northern shore (but not on our route). The man on the high stern was very interesting; he was dressed in a black rubber suit and rolled his cigarette around the outside of his gaping mouth as he was all arms, unscrambling the kinks in his net as it played out. They were commercial lake trout fishermen setting their nets. I'm sure they could not fathom the idea of a canoe being paddled to Hudson Bay.

We turned away from the two frigid fishermen and paddled on to Wolverine Point. From 3:00 to 7:00 A.M. we experienced a light, cold drizzle that was driven into our faces by the incessant northeast wind. The sand along the shoreline looked desolate and forbidding. One sand cliff right along the shoreline rose to 200 feet above the lake; others stood further back from the shore.

At 7:00 A.M. we had lunch on a sand dune, with a hot cherry drink. We rested an hour and pushed onward. We bucked the wind for an hour to Dead Cree Point, but as we rounded the corner, there were huge breakers coming at us again. We found a rocky grove of trees and pitched the tent for nine hours of uninterrupted rest.

By 6:00 P.M. I was busy cooking pancakes and rice for a breakfast-dinner. (Our circadian rhythms should have been quite confused by now.) The wind had finally calmed down. We rounded Poplar Point, to witness a beautiful orange sunset over the tumbling mountains along the northern shoreline. The north shore was a steady black, with the heavens a bright twilight. The sand dunes gave way to a rocky shoreline as we rounded the point. Clouds from the passing front cast a magenta hue to contrast with the orange to the north. We made excellent time in the calm and bewitching night. Then the sky seemed to be showering down on us; a brilliant display of aurora borealis shot up in front of us, only to blend in again with the blue-grey of the night. A variety of colors blazed: first orange, then green, red, or blue. The lights would glow, then shimmer and fade. They would shine like tall organ pipes across the sky, at times spanning the heavens from horizon to horizon. The display would last for several minutes before fading. A pair of loons echoed in the distance.

We passed Beaver Point and saw the beginnings of the village

Fond du Lac. The northern shore was rugged, broken, and rocky. We found a smooth rocky spit and stopped for a breakfast of hot porridge and cocoa. Then we continued on in the early morning calms to Fond du Lac. A white clapboard church with a cross perched atop the steeple dominated the simple, small Indian homes. We docked at 6:00 A.M. and walked to the Hudson's Bay factor's home, passing several early-riser Indians peeking at us. A generator was pounding away as we passed the day school between the store and the mission. I knocked on the front door of the factor's home, but there was no answer; I walked around to the back door and, as I passed a window, saw him sitting up in bed reading. He was a bit startled when he answered the door and saw a bristly voyageur, perhaps not too far removed from his voyageur predecessors a century and a half earlier. I explained that I was a canoeist bound for Hudson Bay, which hardly reassured him, since he probably had never encountered anyone on such a route. I said I wanted to mail my camera to Minnesota and buy a raincoat, rope, and a headnet. The gent, who was from Edmonton, invited me in for coffee. He had mail service only once a week and did not have any of the needed gear for sale in his store. I purchased some candy and shared it with Jack and Tom, who had paddled the canoe around to the Hudson's Bay Company dock. We consumed our treats and paddled on to the village at Stoney Rapids.

We continued in a beautiful calm with the morning sun to Pine Channel for lunch, then paddled down the narrowing Lake Athabasca to an old Indian winter camp on the south shore for an early dinner. There were high slate hills beyond the northern shore and an abundance of spruce trees. We slept soundly for nine hours.

We awoke to another sunny day and paddled four hours to Stoney Rapids village on the eastern end of Athabasca. We passed a Model A Ford rusting among the trees, which meant we had reached civilization of sorts. I wondered how such an ancient automobile could find its way so far north beyond any road. At Stoney Rapids there was another Hudson's Bay store, but this one was very disorganized. I mailed my camera and purchased rope and candy, but they had no headnets to fend off mosquitoes and their raincoats were too expensive. We sent a brief note to our parents, telling them about our crossing of Lake Athabasca and assuring them that we were all right.

The Fond du Lac River entered Lake Athabasca at this point, and was a series of rapids from Black Lake. A dirt road connected the village to a fishing camp (Camp Grayling) on Black Lake. We talked to the factor about a ride, and soon found ourselves bouncing on a 16-mile dirt road at breakneck speed to Black Lake for a meager six dollars. We were behind on our schedule and not at all too proud to accept a short lift. The blackflies were unusually furious at Black Lake — we disembarked as soon as possible. Black Lake had a desolate south shoreline; there was a sandy bottom that stretched almost a mile out into the lake near Burr Island. We camped at a creek's mouth at the far side of a deep bay.

We had another sunny morning as we left Black Lake to enter the wild Fond du Lac River enroute to Wollaston Lake. We had a copy of the journal of David Thompson, who paddled this route in the late eighteenth century. I wondered how many humans have retraced his footsteps over the subsequent two centuries. We entered the river at the north channel around Burr Island, passing an old square-timbered cabin on the left. The current was swift and powerful, and we stayed along the shore to take advantage of the back eddies. Burr Falls was a series of roaring rapids, with a steep rock hill along the shore. We portaged from a grassy landing past the remnants of a moose kill. The trail was distinct, with three canoe rests. It seemed like a half mile, but our heavy burdens necessitated frequent stops.

We paddled for the next several hours past numerous blind channels before doubling back in the huge S formed by the Fond du Lac. We found a rare beach where we could have lunch before more rapids. We spent the afternoon lining the canoe up six rapids (two were merely slick currents that were too swift to paddle up). Our progress was dishearteningly slow. Several of the rapids were up to a mile long, and often we were wading in water up to our waists. There was not even a pretense of keeping dry. We would hang on to shore bushes to maintain our balance, and kept the stern rope tied around the waist of the sternman as a safety measure. We saw no more portage trails.

We found an esker with a flat top for our tent that evening. I cast from our shore for grayling, but caught only a northern pike. I kept him anyway but kept casting the Daredevil spoon for a tasty grayling. The sun had passed behind the trees, turning the sky pink, then red. Another northern struck. I gave up on grayling and filleted the two northerns for a fresh fish dinner.

We awoke late and began our day's journey by entering another turn of the S of the Fond du Lac. We paddled up two slicks and faced a rapids lined by high cliffs. We decided to line the canoe upstream by walking atop the cliff and pulling the canoe with our ropes. Our plan worked well until we reached a place where several birch trees were growing out of cracks in the rocks, obstructing our ropes. With a little finesse and considerable luck, we were able to flip the ropes around the trees and continue upward. The vantage point of the high ground allowed us to view the broad rapids gurgling around rocks and continuing ahead around the next turn. We pulled up the next rapids as a downpour completed the soaking of our clothing. I kept my wool jacket dry in the pack, but my cold, wet wool shirt made me feel rather miserable. I kept warm by scouting the next rapids, and heard a shot back near the canoe. When I emerged from the bushes, deadeye Jack was all smiles, with a ruffed grouse for dinner. We ate a meager lunch in the rain and pulled up three more rapids toward Brassy Rapids.

There were many dead jack pines along here, and we saw several bald eagle nests. That evening when I read David Thompson's journal from 1796, I noted that he was swept over the falls above Manilo, gashing his foot and losing practically all of his gear. He, his Indian guide Kosdaw, and their third companion scaled a pine and fought two young "fishing eagles (the bald-headed ones)," obtaining them for supper to fend off starvation. Kosdaw was the only one not to eat the fat, while the other two did and acquired dysentery in the process. We fared better; we camped on a flat site amidst mosquitoes and ate two grouse (the second was shot near our camp), along with applesauce, peas, and potatoes.

We hit Brassy Rapids in the early morning and found an old portage trail. A forest fire had burned this area years earlier, and the burned dead trees had been blown every which way, obliterating most of the portage trail. We carried for a third of a mile before giving up, clambered over more tree trunks, and headed back to the river. We spent two hours portaging and exerted ourselves to the maximum from our heavy loads. We waded a mile up these rapids, only to hit Brink Rapids after a short paddle. We devoured an early lunch and spent the next two hours wading, lining, and portaging for two miles. Exhausted, we paddled in the setting sun along limestone cliffs before lining again atop a series of cliffs. We pulled up a small rapids, then another mile of torrent. Finally, we made camp, wrung out our wet clothes, and bathed, since we were already cold and wet.

That evening, we began to ponder our predicament: we were seven days behind schedule and many hundreds of miles away from Churchill. Would we ever make it? Did we have enough food? We were already pushing ourselves to exhaustion; was it worth it? What about fishing and enjoying ourselves a bit? Tom was really questioning whether these superhuman efforts were realistic, but Jack seemed not to care one way or the other. After a sometimes pitched discussion, we resolved that since we had come this far, we were going to make Hudson Bay.

We awoke to another day of backbreaking work. We bucked the stiff current all day, waded and lined sixteen rapids, and portaged three times. I noted numerous geese with their goslings, and Jack spotted a black bear. The bear was along the river bank, standing on his hind legs looking at us, and disappeared into the brush. We ate lunch before Redbank Falls, where I noted many reddish sandstone rocks. Jack found a 1924 survey marker here. I slept across Kosdaw Lake as Tom and Jack paddled. We passed the burned-over region and entered the dark black spruce forest again. We passed two log cabins en route. We negotiated Flett Rapids to a hilly, verdant section of the river to Demicharge Rapids. Jack cast in the pools below the rapids while Tom reconnoitered up ahead. Jack began screaming on his first cast, and I ran to the shore to help him land a 10-pound northern. He caught another on the next cast! Tom returned with the news that the rapids were too deep to wade and line. We loaded up our gear and portaged. We ate fish for dinner, breakfast, and the next two meals, and were beginning to save enough food to extend our supply another week if we were unable to make up the lost seven days, or approximately 200 miles of distance.

On Tuesday, July 18, we began our twentieth day. We were still in the Arctic watershed and less than halfway to Hudson Bay. (Little did we know that we would reach Churchill in twenty more days.) The rain began early, continuing the rest of the day. As we paddled across Waterfound Bay, a cow moose stared at us as we approached her island. She swam for the far shore, providing us with a racing partner. We easily caught up to her and paddled alongside to the opposite shore. We quickly left her and pulled up Poplar Rapids and

162

two others into Crooked Lake. At Cascade Rapids, we took a long portage on the right around two sets of rapids. The portage traversed deep, spongy reindeer moss. We paused for a respite in the comfortable, moist moss, considering the many caribou who once wintered in this northern forest. We reached Hatchet Lake and paddled across its placid waters. The clouds lifted to reveal the sun and dry our wet clothes. The breaking clouds above us reflected reds, oranges, and pinks before dimming to the light and then deepening purple of twilight. We were exhausted, and slept soundly at a campsite surrounded by the rich aroma of Labrador tea.

I lost a contact lens the next morning. I had lost my glasses on Athabasca, and now I was down to one contact lens. I quickly learned to squint and utilize my one contact to the utmost.

We continued upstream to our next giant lake, Wollaston. The river was bounded by muskeg, but it quickly became swifter as we rounded a bend to Red Willow Rapids. We lined these, which were finally the last; I counted a total of fifty-two rapids, portages, and cliffs that we lined up on the Fond du Lac River. We drifted as we ate lunch, and paddled into Cunning Bay to face the "big opens" of Wollaston Lake. Since our fishing rod was handy, we spent forty minutes trolling and caught four lake trout averaging 7 pounds apiece. We paddled to Blue Island to clean and cook our trout for dinner. The lake was calm and perfect for paddling. The distant horizon blended into the twilight sky. We had had enough of rough seas on such large lakes.

Along with dinner, we also cooked the next day's lunch, and then pushed off. We paddled past Sandy Island and George Island to Morin Island, five miles from Wollaston Post. The canoe glided through the water, the bow rising with each stroke of the paddle. The sun dipped below the horizon concomitant with the rising of a bright orange full moon that appeared to hover above the horizon as clouds drifted in front of it. The horizon turned to a fuzzy black, but I guessed Morin Island correctly, and we pitched the tent after 1:00 A.M.

The next morning we paddled among a series of islands, passing several trout nets as we headed for Wollaston Post. The post was a village of Indian homes built like log cabins, with narrow logs. They looked snug. A fisheries building was along the shore, indicating that the local Cree Indians support themselves in part by commercial fishing for lake trout. There was a co-op store, where the postmaster had heard some strangers were coming; perhaps the Indians had passed the word ahead. As we looked at the shacks about, the dozens of Indian dogs chained to dog houses, bushes, and trees barked and yelped. We paddled until lunch time and pulled out the next map. As the afternoon waned, we paddled on to Compulsion Bay.

A winter tractor road connected Wollaston to Reindeer Lake, leading from the far end of Compulsion Bay. The route passed via a series of ponds over the Arctic Divide. Wollaston flowed north, whereas the waters of Reindeer flowed south, leading to Hudson Bay. We found the tractor trail and portaged a quarter mile to a swampy pond. We crossed this and portaged a mile through flat muskeg to a dry field on the next lake. Much of this area had been burned, and sprouts were appearing everywhere. We camped on the shore of the lake and savored our Wollaston trout.

We left at 7:30 A.M. the next morning to slog through a mile and a half of muskeg. This was the divide portage and a real cuss, with the various loads of front and back packs, pack plus canoe, or the heaviest pack of all, nicknamed the "beast pack" and even worse names. At one place we came across a field, but it turned out to be a bog where we all sank up to our waists at least once. The route was a bulldozer track that thaws in the summer to an impassable morass (impassable except for us!). When we would stop to rest, the mosquitoes would thicken. Our only immediate reward was the many beautiful white flowers.

We paddled the next swamp pond and found a creek on the far end that was navigable between beaver ponds. We loosened a few sticks, mud, and rocks from each dam to keep the water and us afloat and moving. We entered and paddled Middle Lake to the Blondeau River, which flows to Swan Lake near Reindeer. We were now going to go downriver!

On the far end of Middle Lake, among large boulders we found a trickle that gathered force to become a full-fledged rapids. We began on the left side but encountered deep water, requiring a wade across the rapids to the right shore, where there was a washboard of boulders. There was no other way than to drag the canoe through. I remembered that Wollaston was 200 feet higher than Reindeer Lake. We reached a pond and rested for a minute. An esker paralleled the river along the left. We lined another rapids to a falls, requiring a short portage. We paddled farther down the narrow, swift river, rounding a bend, reaching another eight-foot falls. The rapids followed each other in succession; we were in and out of the canoe, wading and lining. Once Tom and Jack were both swept off their feet, and I had to pull like the devil on the back rope. Another time we all went over our heads, with the canoe sweeping broadside, but we reached some rocks to stop our ominous progress. We paddled until 10:00 P.M., when we reached Swan Lake and bade a cursed farewell to the Blondeau.

In the morning we awoke all squished together against Jack, since the tent was pitched on a slant. We fought over pancake rations for breakfast, leaving camp at a late 9:00 A.M. to paddle across Swan Lake to the Swan River. A brisk east breeze hampered us. The lake was dark and shallow, but obviously a loon haunt, for their yodels echoed across the waters.

We entered the Swan River and lined, bushed, or shot eight rapids. Our technique of "bushing" rapids was a new style of hanging on to shoreline bushes to slow our progress as we were swept down the current. Some were quite dangerous and left us with our hearts in our throats as we reached the bottom. At the end of one rapids, there were two trees lying across the river. We squeezed under the first, but the second squeezed us into the peaks and troughs of the white water. The current caught the back end of the canoe and swept us under the log, simultaneously flipping us over. In a few minutes, we had the packs out and canoe emptied with nothing seriously wet. We hit a narrow chute after this, with a rapids V followed by four-foot waves and a washboard of rough water. The canoe took in water again, necessitating another bailing stop. We finally paddled into Reindeer Lake and stopped to rest and study the map.

Reindeer was another northern giant, with the lake disappearing into the horizon. We had 70 miles to cross, but fortunately, there were many islands to shelter our canoe from the high winds. We stopped for lunch and considered another night crossing to gain time on our tardy schedule and escape the wind. At its outlet on the Reindeer River, Reindeer Lake has a dam built with supplies from Lynn Lake. There was a railroad to Lynn Lake and a road spur from there to Reindeer Lake. Several fishing camps were on the lake, as well as four native settlements (Brochet, Sawbill, Kinoosao, and Southend).

I looked around the bay and noted many dead shoreline trees, due, I surmised, to the fluctuating water level caused by the dam at Southend. Where the railroad to Lynn Lake crossed the Churchill, there was another dam, with a hydroelectric power station sending electricity 60 miles south to Flin Flon on the Saskatchewan/ Manitoba border. Pukatawagan would be the only place on our route where we would have the option of returning to civilization.

We paddled past Bedford Island and down the west shore of the lake to Burton Island, stopping at 11:00 P.M. The twilight enabled us to cook dinner and pitch camp. We were exhausted after our day of rapids and paddling. A night of travel on Reindeer did not entice us at the moment; we decided to paddle the morrow and consider crossing the remainder of Reindeer the next evening.

The next day was clear, hot, and breezy, with a favorable north wind. We paddled for five hours until our course reached the edge of one map and onto a new one. To celebrate such an occasion, we stopped for lunch. The lake was empty, with no one to be seen. We reached Milton Island, cooked dinner, and left, paddling into the evening. We headed southwest all night. At midnight, the aurora borealis came out to dazzle us as we continued our paddling. The beauty of the lights forced us to pause to strain our necks and relish nature.

The map was hard to read, even though Tom outlined islands, peninsulas, and the shoreline in heavy pencil. I slept in the center of the canoe from 2:00 to 4:00 A.M. and practically froze. By 4:00, we were quite disoriented as to where we were, but kept heading southwest, the correct direction. Finally, by 5:00 A.M. we were able to spot several islands and place them on the map. We paddled on to Deep Bay before stopping to cook hot cereal for breakfast. The south end of Reindeer had higher hills, larger trees, and a rocky shoreline, and was prettier than the flatter north end. We all took turns sleeping in the center of the canoe as we proceeded to Southend.

The wind circled to the south, gathering force as we closed the distance to Southend. We reached an island in sight of the post and stopped for lunch. A pack of hungry Indian dogs were tied to a number of trees there. I wandered over to one, only to see him cower in fear. I tossed him a piece of my moldy bread and he relished it.

At Southend we checked in at the Hudson's Bay post and, surprisingly, had some mail. Jack received a parcel of baked chocolate goodies that became a priceless gourmet treat over the next several days. We wrote to our parents, telling them all was well. We listened to Flin Flon's radio station for a few minutes, hearing our first man-made music in weeks. Nearby, a small mission and church had large piles of neatly stacked wood accumulating for winter.

We bucked a very strong wind south to Whitesand Dam. The shoreline south to Royal Lake had been burned by a recent fire. However, we had little time to observe the shore, as we had to grit our teeth and dig with our paddles against a 40-mile-per-hour gusting wind. We followed the left shore, searching for lees behind every rock and peninsula.

We finally reached the poured concrete structure of Whitesand Dam. The lake had been raised almost 15 feet by human intrusion. The clear water of Reindeer Lake was gushing out of the spillway on the far side. There was a log pullover, recently built by the Indians, on the right, and we grunted and pulled our canoe over it. We paddled to Devil Rapids, which was only a slick, but with dangerous undercurrents and boils. We camped on the right, on a hilly site shrouded with thick poplar trees higher up the hill. We took baths and washed our underwear while the bugs munched on us. We spent the evening pondering our schedule, the vast lakes, rapids, and distances ahead, and our limited food supply. We were 50 miles from Pukatawagan and 550 miles from Churchill. We had almost two weeks' supply of food, since we had saved seven or eight dinners by eating off the land. We could make Churchill, or we could give up at Pukatawagan. We weren't on a pleasure journey, with our paddling at all hours at breakneck speed. We were now hardened voyageurs of the North. And we weren't going to stop at Pukatawagan!

We had improved our Churchill organization. We rotated breakfast, with the first man up lighting the fire and cooking the meal. The other two struck camp; we were always paddling by 7:30 A.M. We stopped for a half-hour lunch break at 12:30 P.M., and at 5:00 P.M. we stopped for a candy break and rest. We continued until 10:00 P.M., when we would stop for the night. It was an arduous routine, but our 25-to-35-mile days became 55-to-65-mile days. We were beginning to surprise ourselves with our speed and distance. All we wanted was to make the Bay and escape the bush.

Our twenty-seventh day started cold, windy, and overcast, with the wind in our faces. The wind shifted several times, actually giving us a push once. We entered Steep Hill Lake, quite pretty with spruce islands and lighter green rolling hills of poplar beyond the shore. The trees had become noticeably larger as we had moved southward. The wind was now from the west, creating three-foot waves that crashed broadside against us. I zigzagged the canoe along the shore, hitting the waves at a 45° angle that prevented water from coming over the side gunnels of the canoe. We paddled to a beach landing and portaged over a hill, bypassing the 12-foot drop of Steephill Rapids and Falls. We paddled on to Two Rivers and camped three miles farther south.

The morning of our twenty-eighth day began clear and calm. We paddled to Atik Falls (more of a rapids) and pulled over a log ramp. We reached the confluence of the Reindeer River and the mighty king river of the North, the Churchill. We had little time to observe the occasion because the water quickened almost immediately. We lined a rapids along the left shore and shot the lower half; these rapids were extremely powerful, with many boils from the rising undercurrents.

We crossed Iskwatam Lake and followed the southern channel of the river. We lined and portaged the next rapids and searched the shore for a portage into Wapuman Lake. Finding none, we decided to negotiate the next four rapids. We followed a big current into a cove, around a boulder, and spotted the trail Indian-style right at the brink of the rapids. We portaged three-fourths of a mile to Wapuman, and floated three slicks to Wintego Lake. We negotiated Wintego Rapids by lining on the right, portaged the next one, ran a slick by an island, and turned northward for a final line on the right shore to Pita Lake. We took the major channel flowing north and lined a rapids into Pikoo Lake. It was refreshing to be among lakes, rapids, tall black spruces, poplars, and rocky ledges similar to the Quetico-Superior. That evening I found Pikoo Lake on the map next to an elevation mark of 1000 feet above sea level. There had to be many rapids ahead.

We passed a boatload of Indians the next morning as we crossed Sokatisewin Lake in the warming sun. We reached Island Falls and the power dam, man's intrusionary blight on the wilderness of the Churchill. We left our canoe and walked up onto the concrete structure; below us was a half mile of bare rock, stagnant pools, and rivulets. A beaver swam in a pool below. The dam was 63 feet high, and we were wondering how we'd get around it when a friendly Canadian came by in his pickup truck and offered to show us the power plant. After we saw the six spotless generators whirring away, he offered us a ride to the end of the road, saving us a mile portage.

About six hundred Indians lived at Sandy Bay across the river. We paddled down Wasawakasin Lake to the accompaniment of five young Crees in a rickety boat. Their campsite looked like a carnival, with gas-station flags hanging from the trees. While two golden eagles observed us from their perches high on the rocks, we passed by a cliff that had several Indian pictographs. We portaged to Sisipuk Lake, saving 11 miles of paddling by hiking a mile-long trail. The portage was muddy in a few places, with several confusing forks, most ending in a huge bog. We paralleled the bog until we reached navigable water. We crossed half of Sisipuk as the sun set brilliantly in a glowing red. It turned cold quickly as we finished our last hour of work and ate another dinner of dried starchy foods.

Sisipuk Lake was aglow in the morning. A few cumulus clouds marred an otherwise clear sky. A friendly breeze blew our way. Our transistor radio could pick up the latest music from Flin Flon to the south. We were in happy spirits.

We reached the end of Sisipuk Lake and portaged on the right around Bloodstone Falls into Bonald Lake. We lined the next rapids on the left into Pukatawagan Lake. An Indian dog spotted us from the other shore and swam toward us, but we were on our way when he reached the base of the rapids. His forlorn barks carried across the water as we paddled away, but we had no room for him. The wind continued with us as we rounded a point and saw Pukatawagan townsite. About twelve hundred Indians lived there. We stopped at the Bay store to check for mail, and this time Tom received a box of sweets. We purchased dried milk, salt, sugar, soap, oatmeal, and pilot bread to replace our last few pieces of very moldy French bread. The factor also gave us two large boxes to place inside the Duluth packs to organize our foodstuffs and carry better on the portage. The replenishment of these food stocks, especially in giving us decent lunches, elevated our spirits immeasurably.

We returned to our canoe and paddled around the next bend, leaving the village behind. We came across a toothless old Indian, in torn clothes, in the bow of a Hudson Bay canvas canoe. He was pulling on the starter rope of a three-horsepower outboard motor that was half dismantled. We tried to see what was the matter, but the age of the engine bespoke the hopelessness of the situation.

Next we entered a maze of channels that led us to the railroad trestle over Pukatawagan Falls. The railroad went a few miles farther north to the mining camp at Lynn Lake. An Indian in a boat came up the channel and told us where the log pullover ramp was located. As we lost sight of the trestle, we knew we had left the last vestiges of civilization. We had paddled 1000 miles and had 500 more to go. (My calculations at the time of the journey were that we had only 350 miles to go. We planned for 10 more days at 35 miles per day, but we actually made 50 miles per day.) By the time we had reached Pukatawagan, our decision had been fixed; it was to be the Bay!

We passed an Indian fishing camp, and a canoeful of giggling kids paddled out to us. We enjoyed their mixture of Cree and English. We paddled another dozen miles down the south channel to Highrock Lake. A rock ledge farther down the lake looked like a perfect campsite, and there we had rice, beef (freeze-dried), and pudding for dinner.

A world of white, drifting mist greeted me as I rolled out of my sleeping bag the next morning to light the fire. The day passed quickly as we dipped our paddles in the waters of Highrock Lake. As we passed a lookout tower, I wondered if the attendant could see us. A seaplane took off nearby, the pilot tipping his wings to us. We spent the afternoon bucking a headwind to the two falls and portages leading to Granville Lake. We camped on a small beach in a cove between two rock ledges about a mile onto the next map.

The next morning we tried panukah with raspberry jam to accompany our boring dried eggs. Panukah, a fried flour biscuit, was delicious! Devil Rapids was next, and we shot those easily. We wondered how the rapids got that name — we expected something much more threatening. Granville Falls followed soon, and we found an easy portage on the left side. We ate lunch, finally reverting to our oatmeal sugar bread, which was delectable. We relished each crumb! The pilot bread was also a welcome addition in place of the stale, moldy French bread.

We spent the rest of the day paddling against a stiff east breeze in the hot sun on Granville Lake. We began to run out of tall tales, travel experiences, college time, and such stories that we could tell each other to pass the time. Shore breaks to stretch our legs, relax all of our muscles, and leave a cramped canoe were special treats. We camped at a crossroads in the river about four miles above Leaf Rapids and devoured a smorgasbord dinner.

Shortly after breakfast, we portaged on the right shore around Leaf Rapids. Then we paddled down the wide Churchill River to Opachuanan Lake, to join a southeast wind that blew us into Southern Indian Lake. The rest of the day we were hampered by rollers hitting our canoe broadside. Southern Indian Lake was the last of the huge northern lakes that we had to cross, and we planned another night crossing. When we stopped at 8:00 P.M. to cook dinner, clouds were covering the darkening sky, lending the oncoming night an ominous aura. We penciled the outlines of shore on our map and kept a candle burning in the bottom of the canoe to help us navigate. We paddled till midnight, changed shifts, and kept heading east-northeast to a channel 12 miles north of the South Indian Lake village. Clouds had now filled the sky, turning our world to a murky black. By 1:00 A.M. we should have been through the channel, but all we saw was shoreline to our right and left. We had gone through a maze of channels and islands too small and intricate for the large-scale map, and I mistakenly thought we were too far north. We turned south and headed in the wrong direction. Fortunately, we were so tired and confused that we decided to stop, climb a hill, and bivouac in our sleeping bags until dawn. In the darkness, we scrambled over rocks and through a tangle of trees to flat ground. I ate most of my chocolate and bedded down. During the night, wandering mosquitoes had a feast on our haggard bodies. At daybreak, around 5:00 A.M., we rubbed our eyes and, as we tried to find our way back down the hill, marveled at how we had climbed up in darkness. I headed in the wrong direction for about twenty more minutes, when we located our position on the map and turned around.

We reached an island near our channel and decided to stop for hot cereal and panukah. We spent the morning paddling with each of us vying for the center position to sleep. A freighter canoe passed us in the distance. By midafternoon it began to drizzle, then to rain constantly. We ate more of our oatmeal sugar bread with peanut butter and jelly. The steady rain seemed to calm the wind down, a trade of one evil for another. We passed four isolated, abandoned cabins, then turned eastward along Long Point. The continuous rain became intermittent, but my shirt and pants were already drenched. We made an early camp and dried our clothes around the fire.

On the morning of our thirty-fifth day of canoe travel, we had but one thought, and that was to leave the canoe and wilds behind us. A constant 35-mile-per-hour headwind blew at us all day, slowing our progress to a snail's pace and making us battle for every inch. The strong wind cost us another half day of time that had to be added to the lost time from our all-night paddle.

With no native outposts between us and the Bay, thoughts of pneumonia (brought on by wet clothes and cold) or appendicitis (with each stomach pain) were not comforting. I had the first rest, and shivered and hung on for two hours. We paddled through a group of islands to a three-mile open stretch just west of Missi Rapids. We reached a long, narrow peninsula where we portaged 20 yards to save ourselves three miles of windy paddling. Near the portage was a clearing about the size of a football field. When I walked around it, I noticed bulldozer tracks and caught a scent of oil, but there was no other physical evidence of people having been here. Months earlier I had heard rumors of plans for a dam at Missi Rapids, and I began to worry what this clearing could portend. Certainly, I thought, such a misguided venture could and would be stopped.

The wind became more ferocious with each paddle stroke toward Missi Rapids. A more southerly channel was closer, and we decided to try it. The channel had three rapids: the first one we shot; the second one was a snorter, requiring lining and wading (I got wet up to my waist); the third one we also shot. We gobbled up the last of our sugar bread after these! We passed the high falls of Missi Rapids on the main channel, and headed into the wind again. We passed through one rapids that was a series of slicks and boils, and lined the next one along the right shore. A goose curiously inspected us as we paddled by. Then we had to break our backs against the wind on Partridge Breast Lake. We shot two more rapids, but then the sides of the river came together on the map. There were no rapids or falls marked. We paddled cautiously; where the map river narrowed, we found a treacherous chute and a dangerous waterfall. The river looked like a tilted carnival ride through a chute with cliffs on both sides and a tearing current underneath. We stopped on the left side of the snorter and found a distinct, well-trodden portage. Halfway across I looked up from the canoe and spotted a canoe rest! We viewed the chasm from below and remarked at such an awesome sight, such power, such innocent beauty. These were the most impressive falls of the journey, yet they were unnamed and not even marked on the official map.

The swells and eddies below the falls lifted us up and dropped us precariously near shore. We paddled hard, and finally the current slowed. Several grayling broke water and one leaped over a foot out of the water. It was a beautiful evening in the fading rays of sunlight. We were being swept down a narrow river of powerful current; the stunted black spruces along the shore were bounded by rock. Whatever memories or ideas others have of the Canadian sunset, this was mine.

We paddled to a calm ledge to reflect on our day's ventures. We pulled the canoe up, turned it over, and converted it to a cooking table. I built the fireplace and fire while the mosquitoes let me know that they were still around. Tom found a mossy flat area for the tent, and by the time we had it pitched, Jack was calling for connoisseurs for his chili, dried beef, fruit, and dates. Dinner was the right size for once, and we retired in satiety.

We breakfasted on Pukatawagan oatmeal and paddled in calm, sunny weather to Northern Indian Lake. We passed a huge island that had the shape of an anchor on the map and headed for more river. There was a small rapids at the lake's outlet that we shot along the right shore. Next came Kirkness Rapids, where we kept to the right shore and negotiated several obstacles without having to get out of the canoe. A goose family was taking refuge in the reeds along shore—we saw two goslings scramble up the bank. The mother flapped her wings and swam ahead of us to draw us away.

We paddled and drifted on to Fiddler Lake, another widening of the river. The map showed five rapids and two falls directly ahead of us. The first obstacle was a huge slick, with the river forced through a narrow opening and tearing loose below. We portaged along the right. Around the corner came a falls with another portage on the right. Below this sheer drop we had to line the canoe through swells of forceful waves that threatened to leave the canoe high and dry atop shoreline rocks. We then shot the lower swirls, dropping into an unseen hole and taking some splash into the canoe.

Intermittent high sand banks punctuated the forest along the river. The sun had set and the light was fading, but we still had a lot of energy and vigor. A small rapids was negotiated on the left; then we portaged over a small falls on the right. Rapids were fast and furious now, with the river turning to the right, and we stopped to reconnoiter. Everything looked easy; in excitement and trepidation, we shot 300 yards of deafening roar. The fading light tended to diminish the size of the waves. We had taken in only a small amount of water. One more before camp, was our thought. We followed the left shore, finding cliffs ahead of us, and turned and paddled back upstream to cross the river safely to try the right shore. We lined the canoe down to the edge, determined we were at the brink of a snorter rapids, and decided to portage through the forest. The trail quickly disappeared in the dim light. We crashed back to the river and found a flat rock ledge below the rapids for camp. We were all exhausted, practically falling asleep on the rocks shy of our tent.

In the morning we continued our portage on the deep, moist moss. Carrying the canoe, I fell into a hole and everything crashed down. While catching my breath, I put my hand into the hole and hit ice. Permafrost country! We were in the taiga subarctic now.

We shot the lower part of the rapids and lined the next one along the right. We grabbed our paddles and dug deeply into the water. The shore along the left looked lower, and we crossed the river, finding a portage on the left past the next falls. The blazed trail disappeared after 20 yards, requiring more bushwhacking, wading a stream, pushing up a densely forested hill, and exerting ourselves to the maximum before we reached a rock ledge below the falls. We all took turns carrying the canoe in a half-stumble, half-crawl position through the forest of windfalls. The waterfall fell over many boulders, shimmering through the primeval forest. We ran the next rapids, being careful of hidden rocks, and lined the last swirl along the left shore. The lining was rocky and slippery from all of the mist, causing Jack to fall precipitously once, but he was all right. We lowered the canoe through several drops, loaded it back up, and rested.

A few Canadian honkers were perturbed by our presence as we paddled by. We ran a rapids dead center into Billard Lake. The wind was on our side again, pushing us along to a sandy beach, where we ate lunch. A rain squall settled in and lasted long enough to drench our clothes, but a brisk wind in the high afternoon dried us. We had a respite from rapids as the river widened and our course crossed onto a new map sectional.

More rapids quickly arrived. We lined again around two rapids and reached a falls where conditions looked more favorable, with a possible portage, on the other side of the river. There we found lining feasible, and we jumped from rock to rock, pulling the canoe along. We reached a beach covered with driftwood that looked ideal for a camp spot. The trees were now too small for our tent ropes, requiring a makeshift tent A-frame made out of driftwood. We sloshed around continually with water in our boots as we performed our camp chores and did not look forward to the cold, wet socks in the morning. At least the lining and wading around rapids saved time and effort.

It was a blustery early morn, but we had a big day ahead of us because of Mountain Rapids. The map showed about four miles of continuous "R" (for rapids)! Mountain Rapids was a continuous series of portages and scary lining maneuvers. We lined past the first set expertly, but the second set was more formidable. Tom slipped on a wet rock throwing a body block into a boulder, sending the canoe broadside over a small falls, but Jack and I pulled at the rope, rescuing the canoe and gear from a frightful fate. Tom was shaken but not hurt. We portaged the canoe and gear from there. We pulled the canoe over makeshift log pullovers past two four-foot drops, then portaged along a dried-up channel. We lined another hundred yards before hopping into the canoe for a fast, free ride. We hoped we had reached the bottom, but a large gravel bank about two football fields across blocked the way and churned the river into huge waves. We stopped and portaged again. As we crashed through the brush, a dozen geese took flight, having a terrible time because their feathers were molting.

We were finished with Mountain Rapids after four hours of hard work. We shot around the corner only to find a large rock garden with a falls going one way and a treacherous rapids the other. We portaged 200 yards over the rocks in the center. Fortunately, the water was calm below the island, affording us an easy paddle to The Fours.

The Fours was the next series of rapids. Our triumph over Mountain Rapids was short-lived, for our skills and endurance were to be tested again. We were swept along quickly to within hearing range of another ominous roar. I reconnoitered ahead, finding the rapids continuous; the far shore looked negotiable, but the near shore was easier to line. We lined the canoe down two rapids before crossing the river to line the canoe down The Fours. It rained miserably, but stopped as we completed the rapids, giving us a moment of peace to chew our pilot biscuits and peanut butter.

We ran all of the rapids down to the confluence with the Little Churchill River, where I noticed a swath through the trees to the right. This was a winter road to Herchmer on the rail line to Churchill, and a way out if we should lose the canoe in a rapids. We paddled all afternoon, relishing our late afternoon snack, and ran the placid Swallow Rapids in the early evening. The evening weather began to clear, with tall, dark clouds moving on. My hands were beginning to numb in the evening cold. We paddled through a rapids, finding a gravel bar for our camp with a flat, mossy tent site on higher ground.

The morning light brought us into our thirty-ninth day of voyageur travel through the northland. We took a last look at our charts and the ominous Portage Chute, a 16-mile stretch of continuous white water. Portage Chute looked — at least on paper — like the ultimate challenge for the northern canoeist.

The sky was clear; our muscles were hardened. We ran four rapids, keeping a watchful eye for hidden rocks. By midmorning we had reached the summit of Portage Chute, and we looked down the chasm. The river was a mile wide, its current creating treacherous waves across its breadth; high cliffs lined the left shore. We paddled through two miles of white water to reach a rocky island in midstream. The channel along the left was nearly dry and the channel on the right caught the full force of the Churchill during high water. We began to line the canoe in and out of the huge boulders. We came to a steep drop, where Tom lost his balance, falling into the water up to his waist. Water poured in over the front of the canoe, but we pushed it off its precarious position before anything serious happened. The many coves in between headlands of huge boulders caused us to portage over the island rather than continue lining. I climbed to the highest point of the island and observed fuming, foaming white water for as far as I could see.

A high sand cliff lined the left shore, and a steep bank the right; the only course was to cross the river to the right. We loaded the canoe and paddled like madmen. The greatest danger was being swept over hidden ledges or hitting a rock, throwing us off balance or broadside to the current. Our luck finally ran out as we hit a ledge and the stern caught long enough for the boiling waves to sweep over the bow. We had slowed just enough to fill the canoe half full of water, but we were moving again. We dug out our pots and pans and bailed out the water. In a few minutes we hit another ledge and had another half-canoeful of freezing, sloshing water. Dangerous rapids lurked ahead, and the canoe half full of water was precariously unstable. By some miracle we made it through, steering, bailing, and hoping. Our canoe was quickly dry once again.

Another ledge and drop confronted us. We veered to the right and stayed close to the shore, avoiding a sure mishap from powerful currents and jagged boulders. We made a short portage and surveyed the route ahead. Our shore was lined by cliffs; there was a steep bank on the opposite shore, requiring another river crossing. We paddled through more white water, reaching the left shore to line the canoe past another series of drop-offs and rapids. We braced ourselves for Bad Cache Rapids.

I noticed unusual gray cliffs along the shore, but on second glance I was astonished to see snow! We stopped and ran up to the eight-foot drifts and scraped away the dirt. It was corn snow — quite hard, but we were able to scrape two pots full for tasty snow cones for lunch. Snowbanks lined both shores for the next mile, reaching heights of ten feet. We ran Bad Cache Rapids for an anticlimax, and I switched to the center of the canoe to prepare lunch. We ate lunch in the canoe to gain time and distance with the current. We drifted, eating pilot biscuits covered with peanut butter, washed down with rapidly melting strawberry snow cones.

I pulled out the last map sectional, marked Churchill. I was deeply relieved to fold up the Herchmer sectional and happy with our good fortune of successfully passing through Portage Chute. We paddled on, passing frequent gravel bars as the river widened even more. By evening, I climbed the riverbank to see if we had left trees behind and had reached the tundra, but was disappointed to see stunted spruce trees extending off into the horizon. We ate our sweet treat and drifted as we rested.

We began to hear an airplane — a seaplane was flying low up the river. As it passed over us and began to circle back, I saw its

Author, Tom Dayton, and Jack Niemi at Hudson Bay, having completed 40-day Churchill River journey.

orange floats and orange-and-black trim. Only one seaplane that I knew of had such distinctive markings—my father's! He circled again and landed upriver from us. We paddled over to him and had a joyous reunion.

My father, a bush pilot in addition to a canoe outfitter, had longed to fly north to Churchill. He had stopped at a goose camp at Billard Lake. He said that after seeing all the rapids he couldn't see how a canoe could ever make it! Tossing us a lot of food, he said he'd see us in Churchill the next day. He roared off and we paddled happily on.

Our spirits had certainly changed—we now knew that we were on the home stretch and would be home soon. We ran Red Head Rapids; they were big and tough, but in our elation we hardly noticed them. We paddled late that night to a point 30 miles short of Churchill. We had covered 83 miles in one day, our record. We pitched our tent for the last time. There were still trees along the river, but we were now at the juncture of the taiga and the beginning of the vast tundra northland.

Our fortieth day began with a light rain, but it abated as we left camp. We passed Morrier and Thibaudeau Islands, encountering cabins and numerous boats as Churchill neared. The Churchill grain elevator loomed in the distance, and we made that our final destination. We noticed tidal flats along the river, but couldn't taste even a trace of salt in the water. The country was now virtually barren.

We reached the grain elevator docks and parked our canoe adjacent to the season's first freighter. We portaged our gear onto a floating dock and up a flight of stairs to the high dock. We were finished at last, Churchill! The trip was formally completed — a distance of 1517 miles in forty days.

It was strange to see automobiles and hear other people speak. Several Canadians drove us to the Centennial Maple Leaf Monument on the shore of Hudson Bay for the inevitable "after" photograph. We spent the afternoon visiting an Eskimo stone carving craft shop, followed by a visit to Fort Prince of Wales. The fort was across the river and was used from 1733 to 1771 to protect the English fur trade. The French briefly had captured it without firing a shot. The stone walls had been fully restored, and forty cannon guarded the battlements. We passed a dozen white beluga whales on their evening swim as we crossed back to Churchill.

The next day we boarded my father's seaplane for the 800-mile flight back to Ely, Minnesota. We had many tall tales to tell; however, this time they were all true.

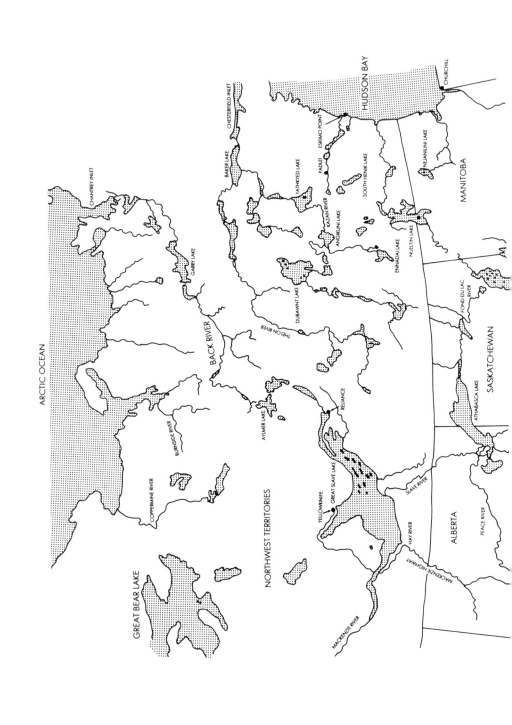

CHAPTER TWENTY

The Back River, Arctic Canada

Sɪɢᴜʀᴅ Oʟsᴏɴ ᴡʀᴏᴛᴇ, "Imagine, the Back River!" as he heard of my plans to fly north to canoe in Arctic Canada. The Back River begins in the far north of Arctic Northwest Territories (NWT) and flows 600 miles to the northeast corner, ending in Chantrey Inlet of the Arctic Ocean. To the northwest are the powerful Mackenzie River and the Coppermine River, famous and frequently canoed rivers to the Arctic Ocean. I chose to paddle the Back River because it was inaccessible, remote, wild, and dangerous. A canoeing article entitled "The Fifth Expedition," about the fifth recorded canoe journey on the river, was written only a year ahead of our planned departure.

Once again I needed two canoeing companions. A medical colleague, Ted Luck, a Minnesotan with extensive canoeing experience, was excited to go; and Dan Luchtel, an ardent mountain climber and a biomedical researcher at the University of Washington, completed our trio. Dan, a rugged giant of a man, was used to devouring a Cascade mountain each weekend. He had also climbed Mt. McKinley, but had never been canoeing. Ted was more diminutive, but a brilliant, hard-working physician who brought his Minnesota work ethic right into his canoeing practice.

We met in Yellowknife, NWT, for our flight to the source of the Back. Dan and I arrived first and camped on the shore of Long Lake near the airport. We strolled the main street of Yellowknife that evening, listening to the Dogrib Indians' language. Ted arrived the next day, and we quickly organized our food and equipment, considering both space and weight. The Back River was entirely above the tree line, with wood or twigs for fires being scarce, thus requiring a portable gas stove for heating the water for our Mountain House cuisine. The freeze-dried food was incredibly improved over the earlier varieties. We had two tents — one a small mountain tent, the other an indescribable contraption that could be thrown into the air and would spring into form. However, we later found that the high winds crossing the tundra plains were very good at collapsing it. My worst mistake was to leave the mountain tent's rainfly behind in order to save weight. The Arctic is considered to be as dry as a desert because of the sparse rainfall and snow; but a cold, constant rain accompanied us throughout much of our journey.

We called Ptarmigan Airways, who met us at the airport and brought us to their dock. We rented an 18-foot aluminum canoe, two large, square-tipped paddles, a carrying yoke, and a rifle in case we had a close encounter with the barren-lands grizzly bear. For a measure of required safety, we registered our route and scheduled pickup point with the Royal Canadian Mounted Police. They gave us two flares for signals, both in case of an emergency and for our pickup plane. Back at Ptarmigan Airways, an incoming party unloaded a fully dressed barren-lands grizzly from which we each took a bear claw for a souvenir.

Yellowknife was on the northern shore of Great Slave Lake, where the taiga with its stunted spruces ended. North of us was the barren-lands tundra. Our plan was to fly almost 300 miles northeast to the source of the Back River, from which we'd paddle 300 miles to be picked up on the shore of vast Pelly Lake, near the coast of the Arctic Ocean. This would allow us to experience all of the challenges of the headwaters of the Back, although we didn't have the time to paddle Pelly and the other huge Arctic Lakes all the way to Chantrey Inlet on the Arctic Ocean. We would be entirely on our own, with no villages or traces of civilization existing en route.

A turbo-engine beaver seaplane was refueled for our journey. We loaded up our gear and began to taxi down the lake. With a roar of the triple-blade propeller, we were off, leaving Yellowknife and its two gold mines in the fading distance. Nothing but vast gray-green tundra stretched ahead. Ponds, lakes, and marshy swamp and connecting streams dotted the landscape. They soon faded into a continuous monotony of barren landscape that passed underneath our float plane hour after hour. Finally we saw a huge frozen lake ahead of us — we had reached the land of ice, and it was mid-July. As the lake neared, we were able to pinpoint its location and identify it as Aylmer Lake on our Canadian geological survey maps. Aylmer was near the source of the Back River and approximately our starting point. Just north of it was ice-free Sussex Lake, which was apparently the Back River's source. We flew low over Sussex and found a huge rock field that looked little like a river. We followed this for a mile to the next lake, unnamed, and circled for a landing. We hoped that the Back River would be navigable from this lake. The plane taxied up to a sandy beach and we unloaded our canoe and gear. Before the pilot left, we studied the maps one last time, identifying our pickup point on Pelly Lake in several weeks. The pilot roared off to return to Yellowknife, leaving us to the silence of the vast northern tundra. All of a sudden we felt incredibly alone.

I walked up the hill behind our beach to scan the tundra. The walking was similar to the English moors, with a firm heather covering the ground. We pitched our two tents atop the hill and staked them down against the evening's chilly Arctic wind. I ran back down to our lake and admired the beautifully clear and deliciously cold water. The evening was warmer in the lee of our cove, but the mosquitoes were abundant. I rigged up my fishing rod and reel and hooked on a Daredevil spoon. This was my first opportunity to fish in the Far North. I cast out and watched the lure fall into the water. A giant fighting lake trout struck immediately. He darted right, then left, until I forced him to the beach, enjoying the scrap. I released him and cast again, only to land another. The next cast brought in a 10-pounder, which was followed by trout after trout. I yelled at the others who came and joined in on the casting. They caught several more, but their luck wasn't as good. It was great to be free of worldly responsibilities and in the free Arctic wilderness at last! We ate a hurried dinner and turned in. In the Arctic twilight through the light-colored tent I sleepily watched the huge, delicate mosquitoes that landed and spread over a full square inch of fabric.

The next morning was our first day on the Back River. We were excited to be in the Barrens at last and paddling our canoe. The sky was overcast and the temperature cold as we paddled across our small lake. The Back River was still a boulder field, requiring a half-mile portage at the end of our lake to open water. The portaging was treacherous because we had to balance on huge angular boulders, about ten feet across, with a pack and canoe. To make matters worse, the wind was continually blowing, destabilizing the perfect balance of the canoe. On top of the rocks was a wet and slippery lichen that would detach from its base and slide with the lightest footsteps. Obviously we couldn't afford a sprained ankle, twisted knee, or broken leg when it would be several weeks before we'd see civilization again.

We paddled a short distance before making another portage, only three times as far. We shortly ran out of river again and portaged a mile and a half to a series of river lakes. We were exhausted and set up camp after this carry.

The next day brought a dreary, dark cold front with a constant freezing rain and whitecaps rolling toward us. We gathered in the oblong contraption of a tent because the mountain tent was leaking profusely without the rainfly. The wind collapsed our oblong tent on us with each gust. We did manage to sleep, read, and cuss the day away. Our tight schedule slipped a day and a half. By midday, I tried fishing, but there were too many rocks and shallows for fish to be caught. We cooked dinner and went back to sleep.

The next morning was overcast and cool, but the wind had died down. We loaded the canoe and began paddling in the icy water. Several small icebergs floated by. Arctic terns occasionally landed on the ice. We passed the Icy River and chuckled, as it was totally frozen — virtually a solid river of ice. Now we knew the source of the icebergs. Next we paddled into Muskox Lake and braved a headwind along the left shore. We stopped for lunch at a jutting peninsula, but the bone-chilling cold required us to eat standing up, continually jumping up and down. I wore a turtleneck with a wool shirt and long underwear, and we all wore life jackets for the warmth as well as safety in canoeing across the icy water.

Muskox Rapids was only a short paddle away. We shot through two rapids and lined along the right shore past the next one. We then portaged past a large rapids. Along the higher ground I saw several scats that appeared to be from a grizzly bear. Along the left shore, we portaged on the tundra for a mile past the next series of treacherous rapids. Above us the sun poked through the clouds to illuminate a gloriously verdant tundra plain. The rapids ceased, and we boarded our canoe to cautiously nudge our way into the swift current. The river banks were steep and the current fast as we began to negotiate one, two, then several rapids. The river grabbed us in its clutches and led us into a larger rapids that we rode out perfectly by staying dead center. Next, a ledge caught the canoe momentarily,

Camp on the Back River, Northwest Territories.

but a quick, hard shove with a paddle got us off and moving fast. We could see the river bottom whipping by in the clear water. Another river entered on our left, adding more water to the next mile of rapids. We relaxed as we easily cleared these and paddled over to the right shore. We were now wet as well as cold, and we hustled to prepare our dinner and pitch camp.

The following day was cold and windy, requiring tactical skill in quartering the waves. A long, jutting peninsula loomed ahead, and we portaged across it rather than battle the waves around it. With no trees, a breeze across the tundra may raise two-to-three-foot waves in seconds. Another small tributary to the south of us was locked in ice. We reached another rapids and welcomed the portage to escape the splash and dangerous rocking of the choppy waves. But the cold and wind did keep the mosquitoes at bay.

The terrain soon became hilly rather than the flat plain, and large boulders were strewn helter-skelter. Dan caught a flicker of movement on the hillside among the boulders — then we all saw a large, brown, shaggy muskox run at full speed across the horizon. It was alone, perhaps a wandering bull. It turned to stare at us and we could see the dark, curved horns. It quickly disappeared, impressing us with its dexterity running across such rugged turf. Then we lined

Portaging around rapids and snowbanks, Back River.

Author with mosquito headnet, Back River.

another rapids along the left before stopping in a cold rain to pitch camp.

In the morning we continued our cold paddle down long river lakes. We spotted six tents in the distance and paddled to a Canadian geological survey party that had been flown in. They were assigned to surface mineralogical exploration, and were looking for gold-bearing strata rather than oil or uranium. We paddled the remainder of the afternoon and spent the evening lining the canoe through a half dozen rapids.

By the next morning, Dan was beginning to think the Arctic winter was close at hand. Our hot cereal warmed us only momentarily. We loaded the canoe and warmed ourselves by paddling. We portaged twice before lunch, reaching a long series of rapids on the map. We climbed the highest hill and saw rapids stretching into the distance. Thus, we had to portage for several miles on the tundra around the raging torrent. Snowbanks lined the river banks below us. The canoe kept drifting in the crosswind, sapping half of my energy.

Following this portage we were able to shoot several rapids before coming to a series of headwalls. We clambered up these to see the river drop into a chasm, but all the rapids looked runnable. We were tired of portaging and headed back to the canoe. I turned the bow into the current and we rode the waves for three exciting miles without incident. That evening we portaged again to a late camp. The sky had cleared, but the midnight sun provided little warmth and only dim light as it skirted around the horizon. With the absence of any wind, the mosquitoes came out and found us at last.

Early the next morning, Ted and I were awakened by incoherent, excited shouts concerning several bloody whales out there. Dan was fishing. He had just landed a fat and handsome lake trout near our camp. He had been casting with a tiny spoon for grayling when the monster trout struck. However, he had more stories to tell. While we were sleeping, he rigged up a float above the Daredevil spoon and filled it with water, enabling the light spoon to sink in the currents. A monster lake trout (a *whale* in his terminology) gobbled his float, breaking his line. Ted and I had a good chuckle as we broke camp.

We paddled for a long morning and afternoon in the current, under a hot Arctic sun, en route to Beechey Lake. We had one series of rapids before Beechey. I climbed a high hill on the right to determine if we could line the canoe or should portage. I glanced off to the tundra on my right as I concentrated on the river, and to my surprise saw an entire herd of muskoxen quietly grazing. I ran back to the canoe for my camera and compatriots, and we stealthily returned across the tundra. There were over two dozen in the herd, including numerous calves. They seemed unperturbed by our presence and continued feeding. Perhaps they had no fear of humans. I walked to within only a few yards of a handsome bull who had massive shoulders, dark brown-black curved horns, dark eyes, a small rump, and a shaggy, knotted mane that hung almost to the ground. The mane appeared to be a heavy fur coat to the beast. As I took another step, the large bull took several wary steps and ran off, stampeding the herd over the crest of a gentle hill. Their agility on their home turf was impressive.

We elatedly returned to the rapids to line the canoe and portage past a small falls. We reached the shore of Beechey Lake for our camp that night. Beechey was long and narrow, requiring a full day's paddle to cross. The next day was clear and sunny for our crossing, but the mosquitoes returned in hordes as we donned our headnets in the middle of the lake. As we paddled, we observed the wide variety of rock formations along the shore. We caught two lake trout that evening for dinner.

The next day, the break in the weather continued as we paddled down the remaining miles of Beechey Lake. There was an abandoned fly-in camp along the north shore, with dozens of bright red 45-gallon fuel drums lying about. Through them a lone caribou ran along the shore and over the horizon. I wondered if the young animal had been separated from a herd and would soon become a wolf's meal. We passed a tributary with high sandbanks and reached the end of Beechey Lake. Rapids began immediately and continued in a broad northern curve. They were nonnegotiable, requiring a two-mile portage in a straight line across the tundra. We noted the remnants of a human camp here, including a stove made out of a metal washtub. At the end of our sweat-generating portage, we stopped at the base of a roaring white-water falls. The power of the river would make any hydroelectric promoter dance with glee. We hoped we were far enough north to prevent that from ever happening.

As we paused for lunch, I absentmindedly bit right through my headnet to get at my sandwich. By now the headnets had become a part of us rather than merely clothing! We floated several long bends of the river, lining the next two rapids and portaging over a gravel bar. As we camped, another cloud front rolled in to end our brief celebration of sunshine.

When we woke the next morning, the north wind was bellowing and the whitecaps on the river looked foreboding. Ahead was the deep canyon of the Back. We encountered three rapids in succession; after reconnoitering each one, we ran them all. The views from the cliffs as we studied the rapids ahead of us were refreshing. We were finally becoming one with the river, the tundra, and the Arctic, with the wilderness our home. Our confidence of canoeing the Back successfully was growing.

Sandbars and shallows became more frequent as the river widened. However, the shallows provided another opportunity for the wind to blow up more whitecaps. Around the next bend, the wind caught us on the windward shore, necessitating a battle with all of us digging our paddles deep into the water to get us behind a northern promontory and away from the treacherous waves. After this struggle we found a flat meadow to camp on amidst the muskox dung.

The next day we hiked along the riverbank and lined our canoe from rapids to rapids. Several more muskoxen observed us. We saw many lemmings scurry into their burrows along the riverbank. Perhaps another one of their peak years was approaching.

After the next rapids, the river widened again, with sandbars frequent in the middle of the river. Dan shouted and pointed with his paddle to the far shore. There was a light yellow animal — a wolf — running along the sandy beach. He stopped and looked at us. What a beautiful animal! He walked, loped, then ran again. We could see his fur playing to the wind, his tongue hanging out as he ran, and admired his coordination and balance with the many forces of nature.

Around the corner we came upon his prey — the caribou. We encountered herd after herd in the next few miles. The great barrenlands caribou were beginning their migration to the taiga forest of the south. Their young walked, ran, and swam to the pace of their parents. Dozens of flashing, jagged-antlered tuktu (Eskimo for *deer*) were swimming and gliding through the icy Back. We enjoyed paddling among them. The young had rather whitish and light tan hides; the older ones were browner-grey, with bellies of white. They often emerged on top of the sandbars to be silhouetted with thin, long antlers against the sky. Another herd of muskoxen walked along the shore. We watched them walk easily along the shoreline rocks. Several flocks of geese swam in and out of the willows along the shoreline, their honks adding to the clicks of the caribou hooves. The shoreline beaches were becoming a melange of animal tracks to and fro.

We neared Hawk Rapids and heard a mighty, low-pitched roar. The banks of the river were like parallel cliffs. We could see the downhill turns of the powerful current. We ran over a dozen rapids through the canyon, crisscrossing the river several times to maintain the safest line. Whenever the rapids were too big, we nestled ourselves among the shoreline rocks and lined our canoe safely down. We ran over 10 miles of rapids in one breathtaking stretch. Our luck held, and we even began to think we were acquiring white-water skills! As we sipped our tea that evening, we talked of our exploits down the rapids. Just then a young caribou walked straight into our camp, gave us a look of alarm, and ran off.

It rained all night, seeping through the seams of the mountain tent onto my once-dry sleeping bag. My partners reminded me who suggested that we leave the rainfly behind to save weight because it never rains in the Arctic. I covered my sleeping bag with three plastic garbage bags, trying to keep it from getting any wetter.

We were now only 50 miles from Pelly Lake, our agreed-on pickup point, but the wind turned against us again. We struggled for 5 to 10 miles and stopped on a beach to wait for the wind to weaken. The wind howled across the tundra as we hiked and explored our beach, finding goose feathers, an old human fireplace, and little else. We battled the wind that afternoon for another 10 miles. We were still 30 miles short of Pelly Lake, and tomorrow was our meeting day. There was a broad, green tundra hill, which appeared to make a fine signal area, with a sandy beach along the northern shore. We paddled to it and beached our canoe to ready our final camp. Pelly Lake lay to the eastward and dominated the remaining portion of the Back River route to Chantrey Inlet on the Arctic Ocean.

In the strong light of the late afternoon, we photographed the pink and purple heather flowers. Our sleeping bags dried in the evening breeze. We all enjoyed hiking across the barren tundra in various directions, relishing our final day.

In the morning the turbo-beaver appeared at practically the appointed hour. He flew past the beach we had lunched on yesterday. We all jumped and waved our hands as he flew straight toward us, banked right, and flew past us to Pelly Lake. He hadn't even seen us. Our bright red sleeping bags were out, and our yellow tents were still up. All of a sudden we realized how small we really were in the world. Later, the pilot told us he landed forty miles away on Pelly Lake near our pickup site and spent two hours refueling the plane with a hand pump. Pelly Lake was at the 500-to-600-mile range of the seaplane; thus the pilot had completely filled the fuselage with barrels of aviation fuel because there were no outposts or gasoline caches along the Back River. After two hours of pumping, the pilot and seaplane took off to begin a methodical search of Pelly Lake for us. There were no signs of human life, and he turned around to head back up the Back River.

Around the distant corner we saw the seaplane again. All of the search lights were on and the red lights were flashing. The plane was only 20 yards above the water and roaring along. I jumped into the canoe, paddled into the middle of the river, and waved my paddle high in the air. Ted and Dan lit our flares and waved them. We saw his wings tip to and fro as the turbo-beaver rolled into a smooth turn, and the giant floats skidded across the water into our cove. We had been found! After initial greetings and talk about rapids, caribou, and muskoxen, the pilot told us that there were two grizzly bears just down river from our camp (and headed our way). We managed to pack up our gear in a very short time and helped the pilot refuel the airplane.

We took off, the turbocharged seaplane quickly reaching 10,000 feet. The barren lands and Back River disappeared below the clouds. We had flown for two and a half hours when our pilot realized we couldn't make Yellowknife. Fortunately, there was a gasoline cache at Fort Reliance along the western shore of Great Slave Lake within our range. We changed course and soon saw the great expanse of Great Slave, its taiga spruce, and the red roofs of the buildings at Fort Reliance. We landed at the small outpost and weather station, but there were no fuel pumps, which meant more hand-pumping to refuel the plane. In the evening we flew at treetop level across the island-studded northern reaches of Great Slave. Speeding by below us were narrow bays, with lakes nestled between rock-ribbed ridges. Yellowknife's lights greeted us from afar. We landed and taxied to the dock at Ptarmigan Airways, completing our Arctic venture.

CHAPTER TWENTY-ONE
Ihalmiut

BETWEEN THE NORTHERN reaches of the Back River and the Reindeer-Churchill country are the vast barren lands of the Dubawnt, Thelon, and Kazan Rivers. This is the land of the inland Eskimo, the Ihalmiut — or the "people of the deer," as Canadian writer Farley Mowat called them.

The inland Eskimos developed a lifestyle and culture that revolved around the caribou. They were dependent on the migrating caribou for food and clothing; their language had more than a dozen words for *caribou*. The press of civilization brought rifles that increased the kill of the caribou, particularly in the caribou's winter range along the more southern taiga forest. The Indians and white fur traders killed caribou by the thousands in the taiga forest, and summer fires raged for weeks, destroying the winter forage of reindeer moss. In his book *The People of the Deer*, Farley Mowat chronicled the final dying days of the Ihalmiut during the late 1940s and early 1950s, concomitant with the decline of the barren-lands caribou herds.

Mowat wintered during 1947–48 at Windy River cabin on the northern shores of Nueltin Lake in Northwest Territories. From there he encountered the Ihalmiut in the land of the Little Hills northeast of Ennadai. He lived among them and learned their tales. In the early 1950s, the Canadian government built a radar station at Ennadai Lake as part of its early-warning system for Soviet attack. The starving Ihalmiut congregated there for gratuities and, subsequently, meager government rations. The life of the Ihalmiut was rapidly disintegrating from disease and starvation. Following a near-tragic government-forced resettlement at Henik Lakes, a few escaped to the Hudson's Bay Company post at Padlei to the northeast. From there, the few surviving Ihalmiut were transported to Eskimo Point, where Mowat last encountered them. He wrote about the denouement of a fascinating tribe on our own continent in our own time.

I longed to go north explicitly to visit the haunts of the Ihalmiut. My father and brother Larry were both seasoned bush pilots and shared the same urge. Our seaplane was ready. In a matter of a day we were flying to the taiga and the town of Churchill.

It had been 15 years since I had last gazed out on the bay at Churchill. There were a few new well-insulated apartments, a modern new community center, but otherwise the bleak town looked much the same. The Eskimo village of Akudlik had been boarded up and abandoned. The town still bustled with its grain-shipping trade, railroad terminus, regional airport, and Arctic soapstone carving shops for the few tourists. However, I had heard rumors that the Churchill River was no more.

I walked over to the edge of the town and shore of the Churchill River. Where once a mighty current met the sea, only a skeleton remained. Bare rocks stretched across to the far shore. In the center there was a remnant of a river. The Churchill River was dead. The dam at Missi Rapids far upstream had finally been built. The waters of Southern Indian Lake were raised over 200 feet to be diverted via the Burntwood River to the Nelson River and its vast hydroelectric scheme. The additional water diverted from the Churchill and added to the Nelson could produce a few more kilowatts. The mighty Churchill River had become a desolate rock garden. I could only imagine what Portage Chute, Mountain Rapids, or Northern Indian Lake would look like. I would truly never see them again.

In the morning we had clear weather and flew off to the vast Northwest Territories. I felt like Farley Mowat flying across the tundra 35 years earlier to distant Nueltin Lake. The tundra was still there, unchanged. We passed a fly-in fishing camp, consisting of three plywood shelters, at Nejanilini Lake. The horizon began to fade into a smoky haze. We heard that vast uncontrolled fires were burning in the Saskatchewan and Manitoba taiga. Now I realized how the forage of reindeer moss necessary for winter survival of the caribou could be so easily lost. We were only a few hundred feet above the ground and found navigation increasingly difficult in the smoke and haze.

We reached the shores of Nueltin and followed our compass reading across the open waters. We spotted barren islands below that we could pinpoint on our maps. When we reached the far shore, we followed the shoreline northward to the Windy River. Before seeing the river, we spotted the square frame of Windy River cabin. The roof had fallen in, but the side logs were still there. A tower for food caches still stood in front of the cabin. I remembered from Mowat's books that the roof had been made of animal skins, which explained why no roof remained. A few trees lined the Windy River nearby, enabling the early trappers to find enough logs to build the cabin. A boat was overturned on a hill behind the cabin. We circled the cabin several times, spotting a moose feeding at the mouth of the river. The river and shoreline were both rocky, which could prove dangerous for a landing on floats. After several circles above the cabin, we decided to fly on to the northwest and Ennadai.

Ennadai was the next large lake and the site of a Canadian radio outpost. We were there in an hour and spotted several cabins along a high sandy esker. We landed our seaplane and tied it down to a log dock that had been partly destroyed by the ice. The post was abandoned. The cabins were locked, and a refuge cabin nearby was open. We carried our food packs and stove to the refuge cabin for our evening's lodging.

That evening and the following day we explored the country around Ennadai. To the north were several coves and rolling hills. I found countless caribou bone splinters; these remnants were telltale signs of hungry Ihalmiut, because the bone's marrow is a delicacy. Rusted tin cans also were strewn everywhere. Refuse had dates up to 1979, when the outpost was ostensibly closed. I hiked to the top of the high esker above Ennadai, noting two ponds in depressions near the top of the esker. The radio towers were still standing.

On the southern side was a flat plain with long sandy beaches. The last great Ihalmiut settlement must have been there, and circles of stones for their tents were numerous. The Eskimos placed large stones about a foot across on the edges of their caribou skin tents. In the center I often found rocks and charcoal from their long-dead fires. The tent circles had diameters of almost 20 feet. The skin tent was held up with a single pole that was carried from camp to camp. A 20-foot tree was a true rarity in the tundra and had to be obtained from a place like the Windy River far to the south. Shards of caribou bones were numerous at the site. There were fewer rusty tin cans, but many were large tea cans. The Eskimos apparently savored their tea, obtained from their fur trade. My brother and I explored several large camps, wondering about their final years; the old ones must have known that with their lives, the tribe was coming to an end. I hiked northward toward the "Little Hills" but found only bog, tundra, and mosquitoes. I wondered how Farley Mowat and the Ihalmiut could ever hike across this country.

That evening, a turbocharged twin otter seaplane landed at Ennadai. A dour inspector was making his appointed rounds at government outposts. He was quite disparaging of the plight of the Eskimo, describing Farley Mowat as "Mr. Hardly Know It!"

After a windy day, the smoke had cleared, and we readied the plane for an air search of the Little Hills country. We were unsure what we were looking for, but surmised that the ruins of an Eskimo camp would do. We flew over the small lakes that were home to the groups Mowat visited. There were several tent rings at the entrance of a river on the shore of one of the lakes, probably Ohoto Lake. We searched the shoreline of each of the succeeding lakes, spotting nothing that appeared out of place with the order of things.

I urged my father and brother onward to the north to the great Angikuni. Angikuni Lake was described by Mowat as the great burial place of the Eskimos. Mowat had described entire villages of the Ihalmiut who had been decimated by disease, while their camps remained virtually intact. It was the lake of the living dead, referred to as the Great Lake in *The People of the Deer*. We flew back toward Ennadai and followed the Kazan River northward. The river widened and deepened as it entered Angikuni, a vast tundra lake scattered with islands. We flew low along the southern shore, looking for tent rings. There was nothing but more of the barrens. Perhaps the northern shore was the base for the camps. We crossed the waters and searched the northern shores. The land appeared empty. No caribou were on the game trails. No white man's intrusions could be seen. We turned to the west to search a river's mouth entering Angikuni from the distant Dubawnt Lake. The river was rocky but wide.

I heard my father shout "Inukok!" and the plane dived into a turn and banked steeply. Inukok? He had spotted a ridge of Inukok near several tent rings at the entrance of the river into Angikuni. We landed the plane to examine his find. The shoreline was rocky, and no sand beaches could be found to pull the plane's thin floats up onto. My father and I put on hip-waders and pulled on ropes attached to the pontoons to bring the seaplane close to shore. The water was incredibly clear and clean. We tied the ropes to handy rocks on the shore.

My father and I clambered up onto the tundra and put on our hiking boots. On top of the hill was a miniature Eskimo Stonehenge. The Eskimos turned rocks up and placed several rocks on top of each other on selected Arctic ridges to warn and befriend the spirits. The rock statues were called *Inukok*. I walked among the overturned rocks and statues of men long gone. It was a strange communication. I hiked to the far edge of the ridge, encountering a striking Inukok. There was a large upturned boulder with a perfectly round white rock about 10 inches in diameter sitting on top of it. This Inukok appeared to lead into all of the others and probably meant something special. I dared not touch it. There were caribou bone splinters everywhere. Nowhere was there a sign of the rusted tin cans that we had seen at Ennadai. The Angikuni Ihalmiut were truly early man, unaffected by white man's coming — or were they? As Farley Mowat observed, the Ihalmiut in the camps at Angikuni were all but eliminated by white man's infections. My father found several bones in a crack between two boulders and thought that they might be human, not caribou.

We wandered back to the seaplane and took off. The route to Padlei passed over the vast Angikuni. We saw no more Eskimo camps. The Henik Lakes were far to the south. Padlei's Hudson's Bay Post was our next destination. Farley Mowat wrote of the final relocation of the Ihalmiut in the Henik Lake region, but caribou migrated far to the west of this area. Thus, the Eskimos suffered further starvation, and several members walked to Padlei Post to find food. We buzzed the old Hudson's Bay Post on a river near the Maguse country west of Eskimo Point. The post appeared deserted, and we landed and secured the plane. The buildings were emptied and abandoned. We hiked upriver to a log building built into the rock ledge. Here we found a series of log cabins built from stunted spruce along the river. These may have been one of the final refuges of the inland Eskimo. The handiwork with the logs was impressive — there were crafted tables, bunkbeds, doors, and windows, but the roof was rotting, and the dwellings had not been inhabited for years. In the opposite direction was a one-room church with a cross atop and what appeared to be graves behind. Padlei was also dead. We walked back to the plane and took off. As we flew southward to Churchill, we saw no caribou and no signs of human civilization; we were welcomed back into Churchill by a school of beluga whales skimming atop Hudson Bay.

An Innuit at the Churchill motel told us that the Ihalmiut had settled among the Innuit at the coast, becoming craftsmen making stone carvings, mining nickel at Rankin Inlet, or working the new gold mine near Henik Lakes. The Ihalmiut had been assimilated.

While we were waiting to return home, there was another plane loading up supplies to deliver to far-flung northern outposts. North of Rankin on the map was the small town of Repulse; I wondered what was there. I thought of the Ihalmiut who could not "repulse" the coming of change. North of Repulse was an Arctic outpost named Resolute — that name seemed to fit their character.

Resolute in character through the battles for the BWCA and canoeing everywhere was Sigurd Olson. He died of a heart attack while snowshoeing through the north woods at the age of 82 during the winter after my last journey to Churchill. In his typewriter his wife found these words: "A new adventure is coming up, and I am sure it will be a good one." His ashes were spread about his famed Listening Point, where they may forever be enraptured by the sounds of the canoe country.

A few weeks later, Bill Magie, the founder of the Friends of the Wilderness, joined Sig. As the Ihalmiut and caribou have gone, these stalwart protectors have, too. But their message has captured the minds and bodies of many more to carry on the struggle and message for the spirit of wilderness. At Bill's funeral, it was announced that the U.S. Supreme Court upheld the law establishing the Boundary Waters Canoe Area Wilderness against a state challenge concerning regulatory authority over the surface waters of the BWCA. The federal government not only could create a national wilderness but had pre-eminent authority to regulate the waters for wilderness canoe travel.

The canoe country wilderness spans the northland from the Quetico-Superior wilderness canoe reserves to the rivers crossing Ontario and spilling into Hudson Bay, to the taiga of stunted spruces, to the vast barren lands of Northwest Territories. Its beauty and challenges of nature provide a change of pace and a respite from the pressures of civilized society. A soothing solace can be found in the wilderness spirit captured in a loon's echo, the aurora borealis, or the rocky, cliff-lined shores of a lake. Unfortunately we have gone from an entire continent of wilderness canoe country to mere pockets like the Quetico-Superior; the wild rivers of the Canadian North are disappearing to hydroelectric developments such as the Churchill, the Nelson, and many others in Quebec. There is one other important need for wilderness — the challenges of rapids, portages, wind, cold, rain, endurance, perseverance, and appreciation of nature's beauty — that create a human's character.

Human intrusion and handiwork have irrevocably changed some of the canoe country wilderness, particularly logging in central and western Ontario and the dam-building and water diversion projects of Manitoba, but most of the northern rivers and lakes remain wild. From the late 1950s into the early 1980s, the BWCA and Quetico have actually become a more pristine wilderness. The pressures of wilderness canoe travel of the 1960s have receded as canoeists have become more dispersed to the Gunflint, Echo Trail road, Brule Lake, and other areas. In August 1962, I counted forty-three canoes passing my remote campsite on Brent Lake, but in 1974 I paddled the entirety of the lake without seeing a single canoe. The resorts that were on Basswood in the 1950s have been purchased, and the large boats gone. With implementation of the BWCA Wilderness Act, mechanized travel will be reduced further. Wilderness canoe travel has found its place, and in the BWCA and Quetico has found a home.

CHAPTER TWENTY-TWO

Epilogue

A Guide's Guide to Safe and Healthful Canoeing

Several "pearls" gleaned from my seven summers of guiding and three canoe expeditions to the Far North might prove useful to the canoeist planning a brief venture into the BWCA Wilderness, Quetico Provincial Park, or Far North. Calvin Rutstrum's *The New Way of the Wilderness* is an excellent compendium of camping and canoeing lore for further reading.

I begin my preparation by obtaining the proper maps and planning the route. Excellent waterproof maps of all segments of the BWCA Wilderness and Quetico, showing portages and campsites, are available from outfitters and camping stores. Maps of the Canadian North may be obtained through the Map Distribution Office, Department of Energy, Mines and Resources, 615 Booth Street, Ottawa, Ontario. These are generally geologic survey maps at a 1:250,000 scale and are highly accurate depictions of coastlines for canoe travel. The route should be chosen with care, considering the amount of time one has and what one's objectives are (for example, a circle route, desire to see rapids, exploring lakes off a main route). One needs to keep the first day easy to allow for conditioning muscles, and to plan a day for bad weather, including high winds. I plan on an average of 30 miles per day on expeditions and chart the route with a string, approximating each night's camp in advance. Every evening I study the maps and plan for the next day's course. A five-to-seven-day canoe trip of approximately 50 miles is perfect for an initial venture into the BWCA Wilderness. Also, as part of the planning process, one needs to obtain required permits (travel permits for certain entry points into the BWCA Wilderness during holidays should be reserved in advance at the Voyageur's Visitor Center in Ely or through the supervisor's office of the Superior National Forest in Duluth). An outfitter can provide excellent assistance in obtaining permits as well as providing one with requisite canoeing and camping gear.

Following route planning, I plan my personal gear. A wool shirt, light canvas pants, a hat (a pointed guide's hat or red beret are my favorites), red handkerchief for tying about the neck, a wool jacket, an extra pair of underwear, wool socks, and an extra pair of socks complete my clothes planning. A light poncho is best for rain gear. For the Far North, I recommend a sturdy jacket-style life jacket to be worn at all times, and a mosquito headnet. In the BWCA Wilderness and Quetico, I prefer well-greased leather boots with the tops reaching above the ankle, but boots with rubber bottoms and leather tops are even more waterproof. Hiking boots are also excellent and are preferable in the tundra, where the corrugated sole provides a good grip on slippery, lichen-covered rocks when portaging. A light pair of moccasins for wear about base camp is comfortable.

I carry a limited number of personal goods. In my right pants pocket I always carry a compass with a protective cover and a waterproof match case full of stick matches. I always have additional stick matches in my food pack. In my left pants pocket I carry a Swiss army knife and a small bottle of mosquito dope. On my belt I carry two items: a good all-around knife or Finnish "pook" knife, and a pair of pliers in a special leather case. The pliers are of inestimable value in removing a fish hook from a fish's mouth and removing hot pots from the fire. In my shirt pocket I carry the day's map. I carry a spare of each map in my personal gear. In my personal bag I carry the following: flashlight, toothbrush, toothpaste, sunglasses, the spare clothes, needle and heavy thread, diary and pen, coil of rope, and fishing gear. I always take a rod and reel, nylon fishing line of 10# weight or greater, and a small 4'' x 8'' x 1'' flat tackle box. In my tackle box are a half-dozen spoons for trout, a couple of jigs, a couple of plastic lures including one that floats, and an assortment of leaders and sinkers.

There are also a limited number of gear items to take. A down sleeping bag (3#) plus a mattress are standard. On short trips I usually prepare a balsam bough bed with 12'' balsam boughs placed upside down, with the springiness downward, instead of carrying a mattress. A three-person tent with a mosquito net and rainfly are necessary. An axe, well-sheathed, and a collapsible saw fit into the side of the Duluth pack, with the axe facing outward to keep it from rubbing against one's back when carrying the pack. I carry a light fire grate wrapped in a gunny sack for Quetico trips; the fire grate is placed in the front of the pack, away from the straps. On top of the gear I place the cook kit: four pots, silverware, plastic cups, candle, spatula, cooking spoon and fork, lid tops, plates, two dish-ups, and a frying pan. The pack is always grabbed by its ears, never by the straps.

The food planning has become much easier with the advent of freeze-dried foods and the BWCA Wilderness regulations banning cans. I plan each day's hearty meal (plus ten percent extra) in advance. For breakfasts I plan on pancakes (which means Bisquick, dried eggs, dried milk, and a syrup mix), oatmeal, or scrambled eggs, and hot cocoa. For lunches, standard fare consists of peanut butter and jelly sandwiches or summer sausage and cheese sandwiches. Dinners consist of chicken noodle soup, main course, and a dessert of pudding, followed by hot tea around the campfire. A fresh meat dinner (steaks) and a head of lettuce and carrots for salad are special treats on the first night out. A reflector oven is a luxury for baking brownies, gingerbread, a velvet crumb cake (from the recipe on the back of Bisquick box), pies, or cornbread. I once tried an angel food cake with a round can in the center to create a hollow space in a three-inch-deep dish-up. The cake rose on only one side, however.

Filleting fish is a necessary skill to enjoy fresh walleye (unsurpassed in the North), bass, or trout. I use my sharp Finnish fillet knife and the blade of a dry paddle, to place the fish on, as my only tools. First, I cut across the fish behind the gill and gill fin. Second, I cut along the belly. Third, I cut parallel to the spine, transecting all the ribs to the tail. Fourth, I flip the fish over and repeat the process. One now has the two sides of the fish separated from the bones and entrails. Fifth, I cut out the rib bones with several careful strokes to preserve as much meat as possible. Sixth, I notch the meat near the tail and cut the fillet away from the skin. The procedure is repeated on the other piece. The fillets are washed in the water and the entrails disposed of properly. I prefer to leave the skin on for trout because they have no scales.

Canoeing is an easy skill to learn, although a little practice helps. The paddles should be light and sturdy and reach up to your chin when standing. Always take one or two spare paddles with you on a canoe trip. The objectives of paddling are to propel the canoe straight, rapidly, and with ease.

The bowperson sets a constant pace, keeping the arms relatively straight (and not bending them when retrieving the paddle, because that consumes energy). The paddle is feathered when brought forward. The sternperson follows pace with a J-stroke on every second or third stroke to keep the canoe going straight. The J-stroke basically is a push outward with the paddle near the end of the stroke. The draw stroke (drawing water toward the canoe) can quickly pull one side of the canoe over to avoid a rock. Paddling is always done on opposite sides and in perfect rhythm. When alone in the canoe, one should sit in the bow seat facing the stern, which puts one closer to the center of gravity, allowing for greater stability while paddling.

There is Styrofoam in the bow and stern of the canoe, enabling it to float when turned over or swamped. Always stay with the canoe in a mishap. Never try to swim for shore. The canoe should be righted, and one can kick it ashore or get back inside and paddle. Once near the shoreline where the bottom can be felt, one turns the canoe over and lifts it out of the water on the yoke and flips it over. The yoke is attached to the center thwart and is perfectly balanced for carrying the canoe upside down on one's shoulders. The canoe should also be pulled up on shore at night and turned over; otherwise, it could drift away in a storm.

Sighting a portage or campsite takes practice; a portage is spotted from afar by looking for a blaze on a tree, a clearing in the underbrush, worn ground or bare rocks, and a dip in the horizon. Campsites are usually on small points and rocky ledges. When portaging, there is a special technique for "throwing" on a canoe. Stand at the canoe's center and roll it on its side with the bottom toward your legs. Next, place one arm between your legs and with the other, grab the opposite gunwale. The canoe is rolled up onto your thighs, and when your arms are in place, push with the legs and arm under the canoe and pull with the arm across the canoe, rolling it up onto your shoulders in a perfect balanced movement. Attached to the center thwart should be a carrying yoke with shoulder pads for resting the canoe on the shoulders. I prefer sticking the two paddles as a "V" between a thwart and the front seat; the handles then make a convenient rest for one arm or the other while carrying the canoe. I prefer to carry one of the lighter packs when carrying the canoe.

On longer portages, there are occasional canoe rests to set the bow of the canoe on for the portager to have a pause and respite. These are opportunities for putting on more mosquito dope. When reaching the far side, flip the canoe off your back onto the thighs and lower gently into the water. The stern may be rested on the ground when doing this, but under no circumstances should the canoe be dropped, because rivets will be popped loose on an aluminum canoe.

I usually carry a tube of liquid aluminum for canoe repairs; after the canoe is dry, I spread the aluminum on the hole and cover it with heavy duct tape. However, with proper handling and respect, canoe repairs should be rare.

Setting up camp has several routine chores. One person searches for a flat spot for the tent, without any uncomfortable rocks or roots, and sets up the tent. One must be sure it is well staked down and that the rainfly is attached. Be sure the mosquito netting is zipped closed to keep the bugs out. If need be, a mosquito aerosol bomb can be sprayed inside the tent about fifteen minutes before retiring. After setting up the tent, the next chore is to gather dead and dry wood for firewood. The other person can prepare the fireplace and cooking area. The canoe can be turned over, propped and leveled with rocks, and used for a cooking table. Several pots are filled with clean, clear water (potable directly from the lake).

Next, the fire is started. I prefer breaking up small twigs, placing them in a crisscross fashion, building up to larger pieces of wood (one inch in diameter) at the top. Birch bark is an excellent aid for starting a fire, but should be gathered from a dead, fallen tree far back in the woods. I light a stick match, holding it near the kindling long enough until the fire is sure to catch. Once the fire is roaring, I add the larger pieces of wood. If the wood is wet, I split it open to obtain the drier center pieces. When chopping wood with an axe, I grab the handle at midshaft and at the end, and never grab the end of the handle with both hands. By holding the axe this way, it is very difficult to chop one's foot. Also, I only chop at wood lightly, just enough to sink in the blade; then I hit the wood against a stump or chopping block to split it.

A layer of soap on the pots will ease the scouring of the pot-black. I try to conserve on how many pots are used for cooking. My father always had the reputation of being a one-pot cook because everything was cooked in one pot. The last pot that I put on the fire is full of water for making after-dinner tea and for washing the dishes. At night, I pull the canoe up and turn it over the unstrapped food packs and place the pots and pans on top of the canoe. The packs are left unstrapped so that if a bear gets them, at least he won't tear the packs open to raid the contents. If there are numerous people camping on the lake, it is wise to hoist the food packs on a rope tossed over a bear pole, about 20 feet off the ground, lashed between two trees. That is an excellent method to keep food safe from nocturnal marauding bears.

Being lost in the wilderness can be rather frightening. The most important thing is to remain calm and sure of yourself. The easiest place to get lost is bushwhacking through the forest between lakes. I always take a compass heading from the map and follow the compass once leaving the lake's shore. Furthermore, one can follow the compass across a large lake or into a bay and use the heading to find a river or portage.

Survival in the wilderness, particularly in the Far North, can be a different matter. The distance to a railhead or roadhead may be too far to walk out; thus, the only hope for rescue is for discovery by a search team. All of my journeys are registered with the Royal Canadian Mounted Police; the route is fully described to the bush pilot and fully known to multiple relatives. I admit that there is a real empty feeling out there 500 miles from the nearest sign of civilization. Even more impressive is how difficult it is to spot a canoe party from the air. I remember how the pilot flew right past us when we were on the Back River only 30 miles upriver of our prescribed pickup point! When survival is at stake — once again — remain calm. Invariably, the best advice is to stay put until a search party comes. Move all of your equipment to a prominent point on a river or lake where a seaplane can safely land on the water. Build a giant "SOS" out of rocks, with an arrow pointing to your camp. Search for twigs, sticks, or wood to light large smoke fires if you hear the noise of an airplane engine. A flare is bright and the red flicker can be spotted for miles. A canoe is much more easily spotted on the water, with the canoeists waving, than pulled up on shore.

In the interim, survival is basically by gathering food: fish from the water, rabbits, partridge, ducks, and other small game from the land, and berries from the bushes. Most of us have adequate fat stores to survive for days without nourishment other than water.

When traveling in the Far North, it is wise to carry in your shirt pocket a spoon (for example, a two-inch Daredevil) wrapped in tape plus fishing line, and eight feet of wire for a rabbit snare. Rabbits travel frequently in swampy areas along game paths termed *runways*. A snare is set up along this path and surrounded by twigs, directing the rabbit to jump through the hole encircled by the snare. The end of the wire needs to be attached to a strong branch, root, or rock.

In the barren lands, I always carry a breakdown .22 or heavier-gauge rifle (last-ditch safety against a barren-lands grizzly). A .22 rifle can be used for hunting rabbits, ptarmigan, ducks in shallow ponds, geese, lemmings, and practically whatever else moves. Berries are very nutritious; a rule of thumb is to eat only a few and wait several hours for any adverse symptoms before eating more. Several roots found in the Arctic are also edible. The inner bark and buds of the poplar are edible, and lichen can be baked and eaten. Shelter can be found in the lee of a rock ledge or under a makeshift lean-to.

Wilderness first aid is important for both the casual and the serious canoeist. I recommend a short first-aid manual for the casual canoeist and a soft-cover book for the expedition (the best is *Medicine for Mountaineering*, edited by James A. Wilkerson, M.D., and published by The Mountaineers, 715 Pike Street, Seattle, WA 98181. 2nd edition, 1975. $8.95). The table at the end of this chapter lists items to include in a first-aid kit and suggestions for canoe expeditions.

Resuscitation is vital for all canoeists to know. Victims of drowning, and more rarely lightning or heart attacks, might be revived by these methods. The comatose victim should be laid flat, a radial or carotid pulse checked for, and artificial respiration begun. If breathing is impaired or absent, the respiratory passages must be cleared of any obstruction. Insert your fingers into the victim's mouth and throat and remove any foreign matter or vomitus. Tilt the head backward by placing one hand on the back of the neck and lifting upward while pushing down with the other hand on the forehead. Give artificial respiration using the mouth-to-mouth technique. The hand behind the neck holds the head forward, while the hand on the forehead pushes downward and the thumb and forefinger pinch shut the nostrils. The rescuer should inhale, place his mouth over the victim's open mouth, and exhale with enough force to cause the victim's chest to rise. The rescuer then removes his mouth and inhales again, while the victim's lungs empty. Artificial respiration should be carried out at a rate of approximately twelve to fourteen breaths per minute. If there is no pulse detected, then cardiac resuscitation must be given also. Cardiac massage can be effectively delivered by pressing the heel of one hand on the lower sternum, the other hand on top of this, and firmly pressing down, moving the sternum one to two inches. This is done rhythmically once every second. Both procedures are delivered until the subject recovers or does not respond. In the latter instance, the pupils will be dilated and will not react to light.

The last resuscitative maneuver is removing a piece of food from a choking victim's larynx. Such a victim cannot speak and cannot cough, or coughs ineffectually. Death ensues within a matter of minutes if the obstruction is not relieved. Rarely, the food can be dislodged by a finger inserted through the mouth. If this is not successful, the victim should be stood up, if possible, grabbed from behind with both arms around the waist and the fists in the upper abdomen just below the sternum, and squeezed suddenly and as vigorously as possible (Heimlich maneuver). The sudden pressure on the chest and abdomen forces air out of the lungs and often pops the obstructing food out of the larynx.

Hypothermia is a decrease in the core body temperature to a level at which normal muscular and cerebral functions are impaired. Hypothermia occurs most rapidly in a cold, wet, windy environment. It's most dangerous immediately after spring breakup or in Arctic canoeing, where the water is frigid and where there is little firewood for a bonfire. At a water temperature of 32° F, death may occur in fifteen minutes. When one emerges from a swamping of the canoe, it is vitally important to get out of the wet clothes and into dry ones, and warm oneself by a crackling fire. In the Arctic, or when a fire cannot be started, place the hypothermic victim in a sleeping bag and crawl in with the victim to provide body heat.

Lacerations and soft-tissue trauma are common injuries. Bleeding must be stopped first. This is done by direct compression with several 4″ x 4″ gauzes for at least five minutes. A lacerated artery will have spurts with the heart beat; pressure may have to be applied multiple times to stop the bleeding, and a compress bandage (gauzes surrounded by an elastic bandage) may be needed. If this is done, circulation to the injured limb must be maintained; this can be ascertained by checking a peripheral pulse (radial at the wrist, posterior tibial just behind the inside ankle bone). Tourniquets are almost never necessary or even justifiable. After the bleeding has been stopped, the wound should be cleaned as thoroughly as possible. The skin right up to the edge of the wound should be washed with soap, and the wound thoroughly rinsed. Use of an antiseptic agent is prudent, and benzalkonium chloride (Zephiran) is recommended. Zephiran is a detergent that kills bacteria without causing damage to the tissues and can be used directly in the wound. Soft-tissue wounds never have to be closed. The wound should be covered with sterile gauze and a gentle compression bandage applied to control bleeding and swelling and to provide immobilization.

Occasionally, fish hook injuries may occur, for example, casting and catching the hook in the back of the neck. Removing the barb is the major difficulty; the fish hook may be advanced out of a new hole and the barb cut with pliers. Pulling the hook backwards may also be done, but the barb catches on the skin and may enlarge the wound. If the skin is thin and resilient, this latter method is preferred to avoid the second puncture site of the former method.

Fractures are an uncommon mishap; they can be recognized by pain and tenderness, swelling and discoloration, and deformity. Fractures may be *simple*, in which there is a single, clean break, or *comminuted*, in which the bone is shattered into numerous fragments. Most fractures are closed, with no break in the overlying skin. If the skin is broken, the fracture is called *open* or *compound*. The treatment for any fracture is immobilization; additional measures are necessary for open fractures and fractures associated with massive blood loss. Immobilization prevents further damage to surrounding tissues by the bone ends, reduces pain, and decreases the risk of shock. For a splint to provide effective immobilization, both the joint above and the joint below the fracture must be immobilized. Materials for immobilization include rope and a light tree, paddle, heavy piece of clothing, or similar object. An expedition should carry several inflatable plastic splints. A deformed, fractured limb should not be set or manipulated in the field, unless it will be many days before help can be obtained or unless the distal extremity is blue, or cyanotic, indicating that a bone end is compressing a vessel. To straighten the extremity, apply strong traction by pulling on the end of the limb while someone holds the body from above.

A forearm sling using a triangular bandage can be used to keep a hand elevated. An upper arm binder in addition to the forearm sling can immobilize fractures of the elbow, upper arm, and shoulder. A sprained ankle should be treated with cold to reduce swelling and hemorrhage, followed by the application of an elastic bandage.

Burns are common injuries in the wilderness, including the nuisance of sunburn and the more serious burns from fire or scalding grease or water. Sunburn is best prevented by using a sunscreen containing para-aminobenzoic acid and wearing sunglasses to protect the eyes. The severity of a burn of the skin depends on the size of the area it covers, the depth to which it extends, and its location on the body. First-degree burns are superficial, do not kill any of the tissue, and only produce redness of the skin. Second-degree burns cause death of the upper portion of the skin, resulting in blisters. Third-degree burns produce death of the full thickness of the skin. A superficial burn can be immersed in cold water to reduce the pain and covered with a bandage. Other burns should be carefully washed with sterile cotton soaked with warm, previously boiled water and liquid soap. The burn should be covered with a layer of sterile dressing made of material that does not stick to the wound (such as prepackaged gauze impregnated with petroleum jelly).

In truly remote areas, appendicitis may be a legitimate concern. Lack of appetite, high fever, right-lower-abdominal pain, nausea, and vomiting are usually present. The best treatment is immediate surgery, but some cases of appendicitis have been cured by antibiotic treatment alone. Tetracycline, in high doses for ten days, or intramuscular ampicillin may be tried; if the patient's fever and all abdominal pain and tenderness completely disappear and the appetite returns, the person may have been lucky. In this and any emergency medical situation, evacuation is the wisest measure.

The water in the Boundary Waters Canoe Area Wilderness, Quetico, and Far North is potable. In other circumstances, the water should be boiled or treated with 15 ml. of saturated solution of potassium iodide per quart of water for fifteen minutes.

In medicine, as well as outdoor exploration, the first and final word is *prevention* for a safe and healthful journey.

FIRST AID KIT SUGGESTIONS

Aspirin 300 mg tablets	20 or more
Meperidine 50 mg tablets	10 or more

A wound antiseptic such as benzalkonium chloride, an appropriate soap, or 70% ethyl alcohol or isopropyl alcohol

Sunburn preventative containing para-aminobenzoic acid

Moleskin or similar material	4–6 four-inch squares
Band-Aids, large	2 dozen
Sterile gauze pads, four-inch square	6 or more
Adhesive tape	1 two-inch roll
Gauze roll or Kling	
Elastic bandage	2 three-inch wide
Triangular bandage	2 or 3
Tweezers	
Manual of medical care	
Tetracycline 250 mg	#80
Ampicillin 250 mg	#80
Neosporin ophthalmic drops	
A local decongestant spray	
Codeine 30 mg tablets	#20
Epinephrine injectable	
Antacids	
Antidiarrheal agent	
Antihistamine	
Sterile absorbent cotton	

Expeditions may also carry more extensive medications, inflatable splints, tracheostomy needle, plastic oral airway, syringes, scalpel, IV fluids, and so forth

About the Author

WILLIAM N. ROM, JR., the descendant of Slovenians who emigrated to Minnesota's Iron Range, was born in San Francisco on July 6, 1945. His parents, Bill Sr. and Barbara, soon returned to Ely, Minnesota, where in 1946 Bill Sr. founded Canoe Country Outfitters.

Bill Jr. attended the Ely public schools, where he won four letters in skiing. He wrote a senior paper on Sigurd Olson and Bob Marshall, defenders of the wilderness; spent one summer working in the Student Conservation Program of Olympic National Park; and spent another summer touring the West, working on a ranch, learning climbing skills from Glen Exum, and practicing those skills in the Grand Teton and the Canadian Rockies.

Throughout his high school and college years, Bill also devoted his summers to guiding in the Boundary Water Canoe Area Wilderness and Quetico and to exploring the canoe trails he describes in this book. While in college, he traveled in Europe and competed in Alpine skiing.

Bill was graduated cum laude from the University of Colorado with a major in political science and went on to the University of Minnesota Medical School. There he inaugurated the Medicos Latinos program to send medical students to Central and South America. Bill traveled to the Yucatán, Peru, Chile, Argentina, and the Amazon.

After graduation from medical school, Bill went on to Harvard School of Public Health, where he earned a master's in public health. During the year at Harvard, he also hiked with his brother Roger across the Brooks Range more than 150 miles to the Arctic plain.

Bill interned at the University of California, Davis—Sacramento Medical Center, finishing his residency in internal medicine there in

1975. He then took a research fellowship in pulmonary and environmental medicine at Mt. Sinai in New York.

In 1976, Bill and a companion climbed Mt. McKinley, reaching the summit on Bill's thirty-first birthday after nineteen days of climbing and fighting blizzards.

Bill was an assistant and associate professor of medicine at the University of Utah from 1977 to 1983. He founded the Rocky Mountain Center for Occupational and Environmental Health to train physicians and do research in occupational medicine in such trades as mining, smelting, and asbestos insulation work.

As an expedition physician, Bill explored Tibet in 1982, adding it to a list of countries traveled that includes the USSR, Iran, Lebanon, Israel, Egypt, India, Nepal, Burma, Australia, and Tahiti. In Tibet, he climbed and explored the western Rongbuk valley, below the north face of Mt. Everest, with a Tibetan colleague.

Since 1983, Bill has been a senior investigator at the Pulmonary Branch, National Heart, Lung, and Blood Institute at the National Institutes of Health in Bethesda, Maryland. His formidable tasks there have been to work out the mechanisms of injury and fibrosis of the lungs due to asbestos or silica, and to purify and identify the gene for the key growth factor causing these diseases. He also led a group to Madras, India, to study acute and chronic tropical pulmonary eosinophilia for the NIH.

Bill has been married since 1973 to Holly Meeker, an artist, who has shared many of his more recent canoeing adventures. They have one daughter, Nicole.

Site Index